ISSUES AND RECOMMENDATIONS OF TWELFTH FINANCE COMMISSION

ISSUES AND RECOMMENDATIONS OF TWELFTH FINANCE COMMISSION

R. Sudarsana Rao
Deptt. of Economics,
Andhra University,
Visakhapatnam (India)

SERIALS PUBLICATIONS
NEW DELHI (INDIA)

First Published - 2008

ISBN : 978-81-8387-190-7

Published by

SERIALS PUBLICATIONS
4830/24, Prahlad Street, Ansari Road
Darya Ganj, New Delhi-110002 (India)
Phone : 23245225. Fax : 91-11-23272135
E-mail: serials@satyam.net.in

Dedicated

to

My Teachers

CONTENTS

डॉ. सी. रगंराजन
Dr. C. RANGARAJAN

अध्यक्ष
प्रधानमत्री की आर्थिक सलाहकार परिषद
विज्ञान भवन सौंध 'ई' हाल
मौलाना आज़ाद रोड
नई दिल्ली–110 011
CHAIRMAN
Economic Advisory Council to the Prime Minister
Vigyan Bhavan Annexe, 'E' Hall
Maulana Azad Road
New Delhi-110 011

FOREWORD

Vertical and horizontal imbalances exist in all federations. This is mainly due to the fact that generally more resources are assigned to the central government, may be on grounds of equity and efficiency, compared to its responsibilities. On the other hand, states– the federating units– are assigned larger responsibilities in comparison to their revenue sources. Moreover, states differ with respect to capacities and needs. Managing these imbalances is a major task in all federations.

Visualising the existence of fiscal imbalances and the need to make appropriate adjustments, several provisions have been made in the Indian Constitution. Under Article 280 of the Constitution, a Finance Commission is appointed once in every five years to review the fiscal situation at the centre and the states and to make appropriate recommendations for correcting vertical and horizontal imbalances. So far twelve Finance Commissions have been constituted and they have made recommendations in accordance with the statutory provisions and the Terms of Reference. Whenever a Finance Commission is appointed, it has to take stock of the existing fiscal arrangements and the contemporary fiscal challenges faced both by the centre and the states before making its recommendations.

The Twelfth Finance Commission under my Chairmanship was constituted at a time when the fiscal situation at the centre as well as at the states was not that happy. The fiscal deterioration was seen in terms of falling tax-GDP ratio, rising revenue and fiscal deficits, rising proportion of revenue deficit to fiscal deficit and a high proportion of outstanding debt to GDP. This Commission was required to make recommendations to restructure public finances both at the centre and the states.

The Terms of Reference also included provision relating to debt. After a careful scrutiny of the finances of two tiers of government and given the constraints, the Commission made recommendations in terms of tax devolution and grants. In making inter se distribution among states, the Commission made its best efforts to strike a balance among different criteria reflecting differences in fiscal capacities, cost disabilities and fiscal efficiency. The grant element as a proportion of total transfers was substantially enhanced. An innovative feature of the recommendations was the application of equalization principle with respect to expenditures on health and education. The Commission made an important departure from its predecessors by recommending a scheme of debt relief that encourages fiscal prudence. One is happy to note that as a result of the recommendations almost all state governments have now passed fiscal responsibility legislations.

The present volume is the outcome of discussions and deliberations on papers presented at a National Seminar on "Recommendations of the Twelfth Finance Commission". These papers cover almost all aspects of fiscal federalism and thus constitute an important contribution in this area. Some of the papers focus on the recommendations as they affect the two states of Andhra Pradesh and Orissa. I congratulate Prof. R. Sudarsana Rao in bringing out this volume with the papers thematically grouped. This volume is coming out at a time when the next Finance Commission is about to be appointed. I am sure that the deliberations presented in this volume would be of immense use to the next Finance Commission. I am confident that scholars, academics and policy makers will welcome this volume.

C. Rangarajan
Economic Advisory Council to the Prime Minter

ACKNOWLEDGEMENTS

The present volume is an outcome of the National Seminar on Twelfth Finance Commission Recommendations held in the Department of Economics, Andhra University, Visakhapatnam in March 2006. The Seminar was sponsored by the University Grants Commission besides several other sponsors. About 40 delegates presented papers and participated in the discussion and deliberations. I express my thanks to all the sponsors for their financial assistance, particularly to the University administration.

I owe my gratitude to a good number of academic and administrative luminaries for their valuable participation in the Seminar as well as for their encouragement in brining this volume.

I am very grateful to Dr. Rangarajan, Chairman of the Twelfth Finance Commission, former Governor of Andhra Pradesh, former Governor, Reserve Bank of India and presently the Chairman, Economic Advisory Council to the Prime Minister for having kindly written the Foreword to this volume sparing his precious time

I express my grateful thanks to Shri T. R. Prasad, IAS, former Union Cabinet Secretary, Govt. of India and Member, Twelfth Finance Commission for his inaugural addressof the seminar. My sincere thanks are due to Dr. D. K. Srivastava, Director, Madras School of Economics and Member of TFC who has kindly delivered a special lecture in the Seminar and to Prof. J.V.M. Sarma, Economic Advisor to the Twelfth Finance Commission and former Head, Department of Economics, University of Hyderabad for sparing his valuable time for preparing and delivering the Keynote address.

I express my thanks to Prof. K.C.Reddy Chairman, APSCHE, Hyderabad, Prof.L.Venugopal Reddy, Vice-Chancellor, Andhra University, for their encouragement for the smooth and successful conduct of the National Seminar.

I express my thanks profusely to all the Paper writers for sparing their valuable time in preparing and revising their Papers. I am thankful to Prof. M.Jagadeswara Rao, Prof. Ch. A. Krishna Rao, Prof. C. Ratnam, and Prof. Ramachandrudu, and other colleagues in the Department.of Economics, Andhra university for their advice and cooperation in this endeavour. My thanks are due to my research scholars and supporting staff for their secretarial support in brining this volume to the present shape.

LIST OF CONTRIBUTORS

D. K. Srivastava, Director, Madras School of Economics, Member, Twelfth Finance Commission, Chennai and an Eminent Fiscal Expert.

Prof. J.V. M. Sarma, Economic Adviser, Twelfth Finance Commission, Professor of Economics snd former Head, Dept.of Economocs University of Hyderabad, Hyderabad and Eminent Fiscal Expert.

N. Sridevi, Associate Fellow, Centre for Economic and Social Studies, Hyderabad.

Jagannath Lenka, Reader in Economics, **Minati Mallick,** Dept. of Economics, North Orissa University, Takatpur, Baripada, orissa

A. C. K. Nambiar, Professor & Head, Dept. of Economics,University of Calicut, Trissur, Kerala.

G. Satyanarayana, Professor, Chairman, Board of Studies, Reddi Ramu,M, Research Scholar, Dept. of Economics & Applied Economics, S. K. University, Anantapur.

Prof. M. Chandraiah, Professor, Dept. of Rural Development, Dr. B. R. Ambedkar P. G. Centre, Etcherla, Srikakulam, A.P.

V. P. Gupta, Director, Planning Commission Chair, Dept. of Economics, University of Rajastan, Jaipur, Rajasthan

Prof. E. Nagabhushana Rao, Professor, Dept. of Applied Economics, Andhra Unuversity, Visakhapatnam

Bagabata Patro, Reader in Economics, Berhampur University, Berhampur, Orissa.

S. S. Rath, Associate Professor, Dept. of Economics, Sambalapur University, Sambalapur, Orissa.

O. P. Bohra, National Institute of Public Finance and Policy, Sadsang Marg, Institutional Area, Near JNU,New Delhi

B. Jhansi Lakshmi, Ex-Chairperson, Vizianagaram Z..P., Vizianagaram District., and presently Member of Parliament, Lok Sabha.

Mr. G. Nanaji Rao, Lecturer in Economics, Dr. V. S. Krishna Govt. Degree College, Visakhapatnam.

M. Nageswara Rao, Assistant Professor in Economics, PG Courses, M. R. College,Vizianagaram,

B. Ratna Kumari, Centre for Women's Studies, Andhra University, Visakhapatnam.

Shamshuddin Shaik, Assistant Professor, CMS, GITAM, Visakhapatnam.

A. Ranga Reddy, Professor, Dept. of Economics,Sri Venkateswara University, Tirupathi, A.P.

M. Prasada Rao, Associate Professor & **Prof. T.koteswara Rao,** Dept. of Economics, Andhra University, Visakhapatnam.

M. L. Kantha Rao, Professor, (Rtd) Dept. of Economics, S. K. University, Anantapur, A. P.

Prof. (Smt) K. Rani Gopal, Professor, Chairperson, Board of Studies (PG), Andhra University, Visakhapatnam.

Prof. P. Tarakumari, Dept. of Economics, Andhra University, Visakhapatnam,

Addai Biddiki, Associate Professor & **Dr.B.Lilly Grace Unice,** Asst Professor, Dept. of Economics, Dr. B.R. Ambedkar P.G. Centre, Etcherla, Srikakulam. A.P.

G. Durga Prasad, Reader & **Dr. Atcyutam,** Lecturer, Dept. of Economics, DNR College, Bhimavaram, A.P.

Prof. N. B. Reddy & D. Pulla Rao, Dept. of Cooperation & Applied Economics, Andhra University, Visakhapatnam.

K. Suryarao, Reader & Head, Dept. of Economics, D.N.R. College, Bhimavaram, A.P.

G. Appala Naidu, N. Satyanarana, M. Sankara Reddi, & M. Ramesh, Dept. of Rural Development, Dr. B. R. Ambedkar P. G. Centre, Etcherla, Srikakulam.

P. Srinivasa Rao, A. Rajini, Research Scholars, **B. Sailaja Kumari,** FIP Scholar, Dept. of Economics, Andhra University, Visakhapatnam.

K. Radha Pushapavathi, S. K. S. D. M. Kalasala,Tanuku, West Godavari District., A. P.

Khadar Baba Shaik, Dept. of Commerce & Management, Andhra University, Visakhapatnam.

P. Krishna Babu, Professor, Dept. of Economics, Dr. B. R. Ambedkar, P. G. Centre, Etcherla, Srikakulam. A. P.

1

INTRODUCTION

R. Sudarsana Rao

A fresh separation of powers and functions between different layers of government is inevitable in any federation. However scientific may be the principles followed for he division of powers and functions between different tiers of government, fiscal imbalances exist in both developed and developing federations. Mrs. U. K. Hicks rightly observes that there is a built in imbalance between resources and needs in all the federations. Persistent and huge amount of fiscal imbalances cannot be left unnoticed and unaddressed as they may pose a threat to the very existence of the federation itself or may distort the healthy relations between the centre and states. But there are no once-for-all solutions to fiscal imbalance problems. R. J. May opines that 'even if there is an initial balance, changes in economic conditions and new demands for public services would be bound to upset the balance. It necessitates the need for more or less a continuous fiscal adjustment through a system of fiscal transfers from the relatively richer layer of the government to the relatively poorer layer of the governments.

In India there exist both vertical and horizontal fiscal imbalances. While the very division of powers and functions between the centre and states is the main reason for the existence of vertical fiscal imbalance, the differences in the endowment of various physical factors and revenue efforts among the states are the main reasons for horizontal fiscal imbalances. Visualizing the existence and the importance of reducing these fiscal imbalances, the constitution makers envisaged a fiscal adjustment mechanism where in they made a provision under Aıticle 280 of the Constitution for setting up of a Finance Commission every five years or even earlier if the need arises. Accordingly the Finance Commission has been entrusted with the onerous task of reducing both vertical and horizontal fiscal imbalances through a scheme of fiscal transfers from the Centre to States. Inspite of the inroads made by a parallel agency like the Planning Commission into the area of fiscal transference right from the beginning the role of the Finance Commission has never been undermined.

In fact it has ever been expanding as successive Commissions have been asked to make their recommendations on several fiscal matters 'in the interest of sound finance' under sub-clause C of Article 280(3). So far twelfth Finance Commission being the latest one, and made attempts to reduce fiscal imbalances of both the types. But to reduce fiscal imbalances of both the types. But no Finance Commission has ever satisfied all the States with its recommendations whatever may be the quantum of resources transferred and however scientific the criterion of inter se distribution is. This is mainly more due to the conflicting interests of the States rather than the lacunae in the criteria adopted by the Commission. Moreover, every state puts forward a criterion that is more suitable to it. Therefore, it is always necessary to critically analyze the recommendations of a Finance Commission with a view to arrive at a better design of the scheme of fiscal transference. It is with this view a modest attempt is made to critically analyze the recommendations of the Twelfth Finance Commission.

The Twelfth Finance Commission was appointed when the fiscal scene in the country was precarious and needs a thorough scanning. In view of the prevailing fiscal environment, it has been asked to make its recommendations on wide-ranging fiscal issues. The Commission made several departures in making its recommendations. Amaresh bagchi, Member of the Eleventh Finance Commission and a renowned fiscal expert rightly observes that the "TFC has broken a new ground in several key areas and the recommendations will have a far reaching impact on the finances and functioning of governments in the country at all levels". As the important recommendations of TFC deserve a critical review and thorough analysis, a modest attempt is made in the present volume by several learned scholars.

D. K. Srivastava a fiscal expert of national repute in his article makes a critical analysis of the Centre and State finances and discuses the issues relating to vertical and horizontal imbalances. The restructuring plan of both Union and State finances in general and that of public debt in particular have been discussed at length. The debt relief package as recommended by the TFC has been summarized before presenting important structural and institutional problems in the system of fiscal transfers. After a careful, precise and a thorough discussion of the above mentioned issues, the Paper concludes that equity and efficiency need to be the main guiding principles in designing a robust system of fiscal transfers. He further concludes that the hidden transfers and transfers by multiple channels made the fiscal transference as proportional rather than progressive which needs correction in future.

J. V. M. Sarma an eminent fiscal expert felt the need to assess the methodology adopted in resolving various issues that emanates from the tasks of the Finance Commission. His paper focuses on important issues like fiscal transfers to reduce vertical and horizontal fiscal imbalances, restructuring of public finances, and fiscal consolidation and fiscal transfers to local bodies in the context of recent decentralization.

He concludes that there is a need to inject objectivity and stability in the Centre-State relations in general and in the system of fiscal transfers in particular. He further opines that the States have to pay more attention to policies aiming to accelerate growth and for reduction of intra-state inequalities. He contends that the TFC is successful in reducing the vertical and horizontal fiscal imbalances, inequalities of service levels besides fiscal consolidation at the Centre and the States.

The Paper of N. Sreedevi makes a critical analysis of the fiscal transfers of the successive Finance Commissions and the reduction of horizontal fiscal imbalances in India. After an elaborate theoretical justification, she examines the approaches of various Finance Commissions for horizontal distribution of fiscal transfers and the link between the approach and the criteria adopted by the Finance Commissions. The comparative analysis of the criteria of the EFC and TFC is very useful. After a thorough discussion of the methodology of the Finance Commissions for fiscal transfers to States, she observes that the TFC should have adopted a comprehensive measure that would reflect the triple criteria of need, a criterion for inter se distribution of shared tax revenue and grants and equity principle. She further feels that the increased central budgetary transfers to reduce horizontal fiscal imbalances enhance the role of the Finance Commission.

Jagannath Lenka and Minati Mallick made an attempt to examine to what extent the transfers recommended by the TFC would reduce the horizontal fiscal imbalance. After making a comparative analysis of the criteria adopted by EFC and TFC, the authors concluded that the TFC paid less attention to the issues relating to equity. They further observe that there is visible discrepancy between what the TFC set out to do and what it actually did.

The Paper authored by ACK Nambiar critically analyses various issues of State finances in India. He attributes the Finance Commission partly responsible for the fiscal deterioration which has been disregarding the efficiency of States in terms of revenue mobilization and its utilization. While appreciating the efforts of the EFC and TFC for injecting fiscal discipline into the criteria of inter se distribution of fiscal transfers, opines a comprehensive composite index is better than a single fiscal parameter. He makes a good attempt to construct a composite index to measure fiscal performance of the States. It is concluded that the composite index is a better measure than that of the Finance Commission's to examine the fiscal performance of the States.

G. Satyanarayana and M. Reddi Ramu in their Paper present a synoptic view of fiscal transfers as recommended by the successive Finance Commissions. After an analysis of the fiscal implications of the TFC and the criteria adopted by the last three Commissions, it has been concluded that the criteria adopted and the weightages given by the TFC are highly improvised compared to its immediate predecessors. They are of the view that the TFC made an attempt to balance the twin considerations of –equity and efficiency.

After a brief explanation of the structure and the functions of the Union Finance Commission under different Articles of the Constitution, the grants-in-aid awarded by the TFC for different purposes have been presented in their Paper by Chandraiah, Appala Naidu and Suryanarayana. They felt that grants-in-aid are necessary to reduce economic disparities among the States in India.

V. P. Gupta in his article makes an attempt to analyze the problem in States' indebtedness in terms of composition, inter-state variations, fiscal and revenue deficits, interest payments etc. Section II of the Paper examines how the issue of states' indebtedness has been viewed and dealt by the successive Finance Commissions including the TFC. The measures recommended for debt relief of states by the TFC have been presented in Section III of the Paper. While largely appreciating the measures recommended by the TFC with regard to States' debt relief, he opines that the delinking of Central government leading to the States may pose problems to the poorer Sates in raising market borrowings.

Nagabhusana Rao, Chandraiah, Sankara Reddi and Ramesh in their Paper makes a detailed presentation of the important recommendations made by the TFC. They opined that there is a need to reconstitute National Development Council as Economic and Development Council and also to implement the recommendations of Sarkaria Commission and Ramanamurty Commission.

Bhagabata Patro in his Paper mainly examines the role of the Finance Commissions in general and the 12th Finance Commission in particular on the public investment situation due to their emphasis on fiscal reform programmes. Explaining the incentive scheme for debt relief as adopted by the 10th, 11th and 12th Finance Commissions with special reference to Orissa, he shows with empirical evidence that such conditionalities would lead to compress the development expenditure and slows down the rate of growth of the economy. He further suggests that backward States like Orissa deserves a more flexible stipulation on debt-revenue receipt condition. He opines that Orissa needs more non-plan revenue grants under the TFC.

S. S. Rath makes an empirical analysis of fiscal transfers, particularly grants-in-aid to Orissa after a brief discussion about the fiscal transference in the context of vertical and horizontal fiscal imbalances in India. The Paper mainly focuses on the fiscal transfers-both for Plan and non-Plan purposes - to Orissa from the Centre particularly the grants-in-aid. Analyzing deficits, debt and debt relief under different Finance Commissions, the empirical analysis justifies the relevance of grants-in-aid for improving the State's effort for debt sustainability. After making a critical analysis of the composition and growth of plan and non-plan expenditure of the State, he observes that with a lower percentage left for capital expenditure, the state government creates less permanent infrastructure and poor capital base leading to less efficiency and productivity of human capital. At the end, he makes several suggestions to improve the fiscal standing and economic growth of Orissa in view of its large potential for growth.

Explaining that decentralized governance through devolution of resources and powers would offer socio-economic benefits, better mobilization of resources and efficient delivery mechanism, O. P. Bohra in his Paper endeavours to analyze the extent of decentralization taken place in India. The Paper makes an analysis of international experience of decentralization by citing the examples of a select countries. Further the Paper makes a critical review of the quantum of grants given to local bodies, the criteria adopted by the respective Union Finance Commissions and provides useful suggestions for a balanced devolution of resources to the third tier of governance. He opines that there is greater need to adopt a more equitable performance based criteria for the justifiable devolution of resources by the future Finance Commission.

Asserting that the 73rd and 74th Constitution Amendment brought a sea change in democratic fiscal federalism in India,

B. Jhansi Lakshmi presents a cross-country comparison. Appreciating the initiative taken by the 10th Finance Commission in awarding grants to local bodies, she makes a detailed analysis of the amount of grants to Panchayati Raj Institutions and the criteria of inter se distribution under the different Finance Commissions. She opines that the conditions prescribed by the Finance Commissions while awarding grants curtail the freedom of the local bodies with regard to their utilization She feels that the utilization of grants should be in accordance with the felt needs of the people.

The Paper written by Nanaji Rao and Srinivasa Rao makes a comparative analysis of the quantum, inter-state distribution and the criteria adopted by the EFC and TFC with regard to grants to local bodies. Appreciating the index of deprivation adopted by the TFC, they opined that it may not be correct to drop the index of decentralization.

Nageswara Rao, Sudarsana Rao and Radha Pushpavathi in their Paper make a detailed review of financing of calamity relief expenditure of the states under the successive Finance Commissions. The paper makes a critical analysis of this aspect with particular reference to Andhra Pradesh. It is suggested that the States may be allowed to spend a fixed percentage (10%) from the unspent balances of CRF towards developing some programmes of preparedness and mitigation of natural calamities in the vulnerable areas. They opined that the National Centre for Calamity Management should take more initiatives with long term objectives in future.

Ratna Kumari and Rajini in their Article emphasized the importance of gender budgeting and discussed how this issue has been given significance in the Five Year Plans. They make an attempt to present gender budgeting component under different programmes at the Center as well as at the State of Andhra Pradesh and suggest that the Finance Commission should give direction and guidance to all the governments to adopt gender budgeting to strengthen empowerment of women in India.

Shamshuddin Shaik and Khadar Baba Shaik make an attempt to explain the amount of grants-in-aid recommended to Panchayats and Municipal bodies, the criteria of inter se distribution, the importance and the functions of the High Level Committee, the mode of release and utilization of grants, auditing issues etc. They opined that the recommendations of the TFC especially with regard to the State Finance Commission should be followed to strengthen the local bodies in India.

A. Ranga Reddy in his Paper presents various issues like tax devolution, central assistance for State Plan Schemes and the formulae of intra-state distribution, the FRBM Act in the context of States finances. While appreciating the efforts of the Commission for the fiscal consolidation measures, important recommendations of the Commission have been presented. He felt that the urge to control fiscal policies in order to please international capita should not undermine economic democracy and social cohesion in India.

Prasada Rao, M and Koteswara Rao, T in their Paper presents the existing Centre-State financial relations in India and opines that the States are placed at disadvantage position with inadequate fiscal resources compared to rising expenditure commitments. After making an analysis of revenue centralization in the Indian federation, they opine that, if necessary, relevant Articles of the Constitution need to be amended to have a stable and rational financial relations between the Center and States in India.

M. L. Kantha Rao in his Paper examines by making a critical empirical analysis whether the share of Andhra Pradesh in the total devolution has been coming down. By making comparative analysis of Per capita Income of Andhra Pradesh and All India as estimated by different agencies, he observes that because of the level of Per capita Income attributed to Andhra Pradesh, the share of A. P. has been adversely affected. He observes further that Per capita figures to be considered by the Finance Commission are crucial variables, there should not be any ambiguity or distortion of any type. It is felt necessary to reexamine whether or not AP's share in the tax devolution got reduced due to the inflated average Per Capita Income attributed to it by the TFC.

An attempt has been made by K. Ranigopal, Sudarsana Rao and Sailaja to examine the grants-in-aid given for upgradation of essential social and administrative services under successive Finance Commissions. After a detailed review of grants for upgradation under different Finance Commissions, the grants for education and health under TFC have been critically analyzed. They made an attempt to justify empirically for grants-in-aid for upgradation of education and health standards in Andhra Pradesh.

P. Tarakumari in her Paper analyses the efforts and performance of the government of Andhra Pradesh in terms of several indicators of education. Explaining several programmes initiated by the government of Andhra Pradesh to promote education at different levels, the author feels that the TFC should have given grants for upgradation of education.

B. Lilly Grace and B. Addai analyse the status of Local bodies-Panchayati Raj Institutions in Andhra Pradesh both pre and post 73rd Constitution Amendment. The analysis centres round both functional and financial devolution which is not satisfactory at the moment. They made several suggestions to strengthen the working of PRIs in Andhra Pradesh, the important being division of State budget into State wide and district wide and to prescribe any conditionalities in accordance with the Union Finance Commission only and to allow the District Planning Boards to utilize funds even after the closure of the financial Year.

G. Durga Prasad in his Paper makes an analysis of finances of Municipalities in Andhra Pradesh in general and that of Bhimavaram Municipality in West Godavari District of Andhra Pradesh in particular. After carefully examining the revenue, expenditure variables of the Municipality and their individual relative growth during the period pre and post 74th Constitution Amendment, he observes under fiscal dependence on outer sources. He explains the award of grants-in-aid to under Local bodies by both EFC and TFC. In order to improve the fiscal performance, the municipality may privatize the basic services and be allowed to access the capital market. He suggests that the municipality should look within but not outward for resources.

N. B. Reddy and D. Pulla Rao have made an analysis of State finances of Andhra Pradesh in terms compound growth rates in the context of Centre Sate financial relations. It is concluded that there is a decreasing trend in the sharing of central revenues, grants-in-aid and also loans from the Centre during the period 1984-85 to 2003-04. They suggest that the expenditure policy of Andhra Pradesh in future should reflect in controlling growth of population, increase in per capita income and to increase Foreign Direct Investment.

D. Atchyutam also makes an analysis of State finances of Andhra Pradesh wherein she discusses the macro economic performance as well as fiscal performance. Appreciating the progress of the State in the reforms path, she is hopeful of successful completion of ambitions programmes initiated by the new government with changed priorities.

K. Surya Rao makes an attempt to examine the state of economy in terms of select macro economic variables and analyses revenue and expenditure policies of the government of Andhra Pradesh. He also explains the measures initiated under fiscal reforms. He opines that change in priorities due to the change in the ruling party may bring some positive impact to the people.

The Paper written by Lilly Grace Unice and Krishna Babu examines the programme of fiscal restructuring in Andhra Pradesh and the fiscal performance of the state in the light of the FRBM Act. After a detailed discussion, they felt that a Composite Index is better than the one adopted by the TFC as a measure of fiscal discipline of the State.

The present volume is an outcome of a National Seminar organized in March 2006 makes a critical analysis on a wide-ranging issues concerning the recommendations of the Twelfth Finance Commission and provides necessary insights. It will be useful to academics and researchers interested in the pursuing issues and analysis of Centre-State financial relations in India in general and the Union Finance Commissions in particular.

2

TWELFTH FINANCE COMMISSION: ISSUES AND RECOMMENDATIONS

D. K. Srivastava

India's public finances, at the time when the TFC studied it, showed symptoms of both chronic and acute problems. The size of government as a proportion of GDP, after steadily rising for a period of four decades showed signs of stalling; public finances after maintaining comfortable surpluses for a long period slid into chronic fiscal imbalance; tax buoyancies had fallen to sub-unity levels and the tax-GDP ratio particularly at the level of the centre fell adversely affecting not only the central but also the state finances because of its impact on transfers. After more than fifty years of fiscal transfers attempted by the Finance Commissions, inequalities not only in growth but in the level of publically provided services continued to be large and rising. Management of public finances with large government dis-savings was not proving to be conducive to growth. Many of the state governments showed signs of getting close to a debt trap.

The central-state financial relations, in terms of mechanisms of fiscal transfers, planning mechanism and related transfer systems including on-lending of borrowing and centrally sponsored schemes had proved to be distortionary and inefficient without having contributed much to equity. A basic restructuring of public finances in the country was called for. The TFC diagnosed these problems as structural and interlinked and suggested an extensive reform program, many components of which now stand implemented. There are clear signs that government finances in India are now in a better shape. The next few years will show whether these changes will have strong enough roots to successfully bring about the desired restructuring as envisaged by the TFC.

Here, in section 1, we look at the ground conditions. Section 2 provides TFC's approach to vertical transfers. Section 3 looks at the main issues in horizontal transfers and TFC's approach and recommendations in this regard. Section 4 provides a discussion of TFC's restructuring plan. Section 5 looks at TFC debt restructuring plan. Section 6 mentions main outstanding problems in India's fiscal transfers. Section 7 provides concluding observations.

SECTION I

GROUND CONDITIONS IN GOVERNMENT FINANCES

The TFC deliberated on fiscal transfer issues in the background of severe fiscal imbalance affecting both central and state finances. The government finances had gone through a particularly difficult phase since 1997-98 for three reasons. First, the sharp increase in burden of salary and pension payments, second, extremely high nominal interest rates in the latter part of the nineties and third, a recession in the first three years of the new decade. The nominal growth rates in respect of GDP at current market prices in the four years during 2000-01 to 2003-04 were 7.9, 9.2, 8.2 and 12.3 per cent. In comparison, the EFC had assumed a trend nominal growth rate of 13 per cent for this period. During this period, state finances deteriorated more sharply than that of the centre. In this period, the debt-GDP ratio increased, both for the centre and the states with consequent rise in interest payments relative to GDP. State finances suffered more because states faced higher interest rates. Fiscal tensions are bound to increase when states witness an increase in the need for fiscal resources precisely when the center experiences a fall in its revenues relative to GDP.

Comparing changes over the period 1987-88 and 2001-02 and looking at three-year averages at both ends, the following main changes characterized the combined account of the centre and the states:

(a) Revenue deficit has increased from 3 per cent of GDP on average during 1987-90 to 6.7 per cent during 1999-2002, showing a deterioration of more than 3 percentage points;

(b) Fiscal deficit, which was 8.8 per cent of GDP on average during 1987-90 rose to 9.5 per cent of GDP during 1999-2002, showing a deterioration of 0.8 percentage points;

(c) The ratio of debt showed the sharpest deterioration rising to about 76 per cent of GDP at the end of 2002-03 and an estimated level of 80 per cent of GDP at the end of 2004-05. Much of this deterioration came since 1995-96 when the debt-GDP ratio was about 56 per cent. Thus within a span of 7 years, the debt-GDP ratio increased by about 20 percentage points. This represents a rate of decline, which is quite unprecedented in the history of accumulation of debt in India. It may be noted that the debt figures referred to here contain external debt evaluated at historical exchange rates. If these are calculated at the current exchange rates, the debt-GDP figures would be higher by about 6 percentage points in recent years.

(d) The ratio of revenue deficit to fiscal deficit, which indicates the quality of deficit, that is the proportion of borrowed resources that are spent on consumption or non-asset forming expenditure also deteriorated significantly over this period.

States finances had deteriorated more sharply. Comparing the averages over 2000-03 and 1993-96, the following features in regard to aggregate state finances are worth highlighting:

(a) Revenue deficit was higher by a margin of 1.9 percentage points, and the fiscal deficit, by a margin of 1.5 percentage points.

(b) The primary deficit relative to GDP had reached a peak in 1999-00, but has since evinced a decline.

(c) In fact, in 1999-00, both revenue deficit and fiscal deficit had reached a peak at 4.64 and 2.82 per cent of GDP.

(d) The outstanding debt to GDP ratio increased from 21 per cent in 1996-97 to 31 per cent in 2002-03. Comparing the average over 2000-03 with that of 1990-93, the increase amounted to about 9.4 percentage points.

In the background of this difficult situation of public finances, the TFC was asked like its predecessor to suggest a plan for restructuring public finances in India apart from the conventional tasks of vertical and horizontal distribution of resources. We first look at the TFC's approach on the conventional tasks.

SECTION II

RESOLVING ISSUES IN VERTICAL IMBALANCE

In practice, resources are generally assigned more to the central government and responsibilities, more to the state governments. This is because in raising revenues, there is need to obtain economies of scale, set uniform laws and in many cases tax rate structures. States are given the larger share of responsibilities because they understand the local needs and conditions better, and can better reflect the preferences of the people living in their jurisdictions. This pattern of allocation of resources between the centre and the states, where the central government has more resources than they need to spend on, and state governments have more responsibilities than they can finance by their own resources, gives rise to vertical imbalance.

Vertical imbalance in resources relative to needs is present in India by design where revenues are more centralized and responsibilities more decentralized. The long term trends show larger share of states in combined revenue receipts after transfers; long term stability of relative share of centre and states in the combined revenues also indicated; more recently, central transfers to the states fell relative to GDP. The role of fiscal transfers is to redistribute resources between the central and the state governments in a manner such that vertical and horizontal imbalances are simultaneously removed with a view to maximizing the welfare of the citizens by promoting equity as well as efficiency.

Determining the aggregate share of states in the central taxes requires a comprehensive view of (i) the expenditure needs of the centre; (ii) the aggregate resources of the centre; (iii) the aggregate requirements of the states; and (iv) the resources of states from own sources. In the context of vertical devolution, the share of states and consequently that of the centre is supposed to be determined in a manner that provides both sides with adequate resources subject to the overall resource constraint.

Table 1
Share of States in Combined Revenues

(Per cent)

Average	*Revenue Receipts*		*Revenue Expenditure*
Finance Commissions	Before Transfer	After Transfer	
Seventh	35.3	61.4	58.0
Eighth	34.6	62.0	55.7
Ninth	37.5	64.7	56.9
Tenth	38.6	63.0	56.8
Eleventh (2 years)	39.0	63.9	57.1

Source (Basic data): Indian Public Finance Statistics.

The TFC took the view that dimensions of vertical imbalance are stable and cannot be disturbed except marginally. Accordingly, it recommended that the benchmark for aggregate transfers kept at 37.5 per cent may be raised to 38 per cent. The share of states in the divisible pool in central taxes may be raised to 30.5 per cent as long as the present scheme of additional excise duties continues. The TFC increased also the overall volume of grants and introduced some new grants.

RESOLVING HORIZONTAL IMBALANCE

Given vertical transfers, the scheme of transfers must tackle the issue of horizontal imbalance. This arises because some states, compared to others, have larger resources because of their higher level of development and natural endowments. It is often the case that a state has larger needs precisely when they have less resources compared to others. This is referred to as horizontal imbalance. The horizontal imbalance can be resolved by transferring relatively more to those states that have less resources and larger needs. The system of fiscal transfer in a federal system must resolve both the vertical and horizontal imbalances in a fair and equitable manner that does not compromise the efficiency of the system. Disparities in size and capacity of states can be addressed through progressive transfers but built-in adverse incentives require to be neutralized.

Resource gaps may arise because states have inadequate capacities as also because the revenue effort is deficient in relative terms. While the former may need to be taken into account for correcting the horizontal imbalance, the latter should not qualify for such correction.

Chart 1 shows the relative position of different states in terms of per capita GSDP. A comparison based on comparable per capita GSDP over 1993-94 to 2001-02 indicates that the ratio of minimum GSDP per capita (that of Bihar) and maximum GSDP per capita (which, after excluding Goa, has pertained to

Chart 1
States Arranged in Ascending Order of Average per capita GSDP(1999-2002)

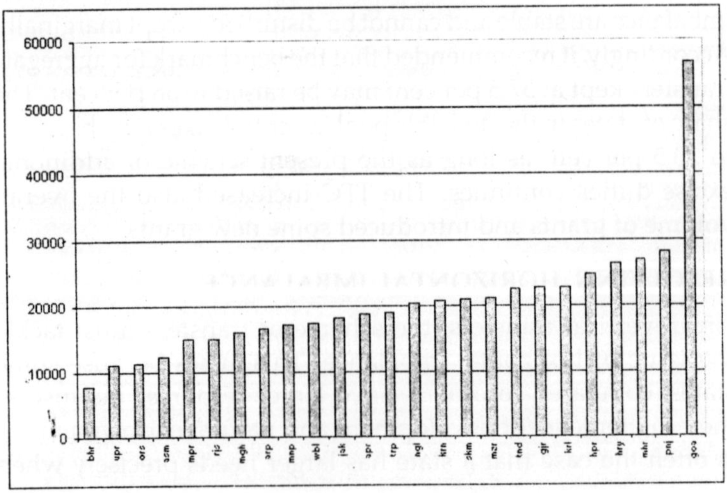

either Maharashtra or Punjab in different years) decreased from 30.5 in 1993-94 to 26.1 in 1995-96, after which the ratio improved until 1998-99. It again declined reaching a level of 26.5 per cent in 2001-02. In the weighted coefficient of variation also there is some reduction witnessed after 1995-96 and again in 2001-02. The absolute levels of disparities are extremely large with the poorest state having per capita GSDP only in the range of 26-30 per cent of the highest but one state. In comparison to the highest, i.e. Goa, the ratio has been less than 15 per cent.

Poverty, both rural and urban is concentrated in a few states. In the case of rural poverty, six states accounted for nearly 74 per cent of the total number of poor. In the case of urban poverty, eight states account for 79 per cent of total number of the urban poor. In this case, the first four states, namely, Orissa, Madhya Pradesh, Bihar, and Uttar Pradesh are the low-income states showing the highest incidence of urban poverty. The other four states are the middle to high-income states like Maharashtra, Tamil Nadu, Karnataka, and Andhra Pradesh.

Equity is as important as efficiency. In considering the issue of equitable growth, the TFC looked at three of its manifestations: (a) disparities in levels and growth of per capita GSDP, (b) disparities in per capita government expenditures, particularly those in priority sectors like education and health, and (c) the inter-state pattern in the index of human development.

The trend growth rates of GSDP at 1993-94 prices (Table 2) show that, in general, the higher income states have grown at higher rates. There are some significant changes between average growth rates in the eighties and the nineties. In the case of Punjab and Haryana, growth has come down although Punjab has the highest per capita GSDP considering the average over 1999-00 to 2001-02. Among the poorer states, cases where the growth rates fell in the nineties as compared to the eighties are Assam, Bihar, Orissa, Uttar Pradesh, and Rajasthan. The ratio of minimum GSDP per capita (that of Bihar) and maximum GSDP per capita (which, after excluding Goa, has pertained to either Maharashtra or Punjab in different years) decreased from 30.5 in 1993-94 to 26.1 in 1995-96, after which the ratio improved until 1998-99. It again declined reaching a level of 26.5 per cent in 2001-02. The absolute levels of disparities are extremely large with the poorest state having per capita GSDP only in the range of 26-30 per cent of the highest but one state. The Gini coefficient also showed progressive increase in income disparity till 1999-00, except in 1996-97. Thereafter, it has shown a decline.

Table 2
Trend Growth Rates of GSDP at (1993-94) Constant Prices: State Series

	1980-81 to 1989-90	*1990-91 to 2001-02*		*1980-81 to 1989-90*	*1990-91 to 2001-02*
Andhra Pradesh	5.35	5.60	Madhya Pradesh.*	4.02	4.81
Arun. Pradesh	8.14	4.68	Maharashtra	5.64	6.27
Assam	3.50	2.53	Manipur	5.12	5.35
Bihar*	4.60	3.79	Meghalaya	4.94	5.81
Goa	4.79	8.40	Orissa	5.01	4.21
Gujarat	5.05	7.20	Punjab	5.44	4.66
Haryana	6.21	4.72	Rajasthan	6.01	5.85
Him. Pradesh	4.70	6.09	Tamil Nadu	5.18	6.26
J & K**	2.80	4.89	Tripura	5.29	8.94
Karnataka	5.36	7.17	Uttar Pradesh*	4.80	3.84
Kerala	3.16	5.51	West Bengal	4.70	6.93

Source(Basic data): CSO

* These states were divided in 2000. Data relates to the combined states.

** Upto 2000-01

Pertains to State GSDP series

The horizontal imbalance has its roots in the differential capacities and needs of the states as also the differences in the costs of providing services. In India, not only the number of states is large, they differ widely in respect of area, size of population, incomes, tax bases, and mineral and forest resources. Resource gaps may arise because States have inadequate capacities as also because the revenue effort is deficient in relative terms. The former should be taken into account for correcting the horizontal imbalance, but the latter should not qualify for such correction. Fiscal equalization is considered to be the response to horizontal fiscal imbalance, which implies that states are unable to provide comparable services to their citizens except by imposing different levels of taxation. Fiscal equalization constitutes a mechanism for ensuring, with the help of inter governmental transfers, that all states can provide comparable services if they also undertook comparable levels of revenue effort.

The instruments of transfers available in a system comprise all instruments whereby redistribution can be affected between states. These means can be both explicit instruments and implicit mechanisms. The main explicit instruments for redistribution are revenue sharing, general-purpose grants, specific purpose grants, conditional grants, and matching grants. The implicit means of redistribution may relate to central policies/rules, and centrally administered prices, which may differentially affect tax rates/bases in the states. The local incidence of central expenditures, especially, central investment would also be a means by which redistribution can be affected.

The sharing of central tax revenues, individually or globally, can be a potent means of redistribution among states. The extent of redistribution that can be affected through this means depends on the vertical shares of the centre and the states, and the horizontal shares pertaining to individual states. The horizontal shares will bring about redistribution depending on the weights attached to such criteria as can give higher shares to low revenue capacity states, and the total amount (vertical share) that is redistributed among states.

Grants, as an instrument of fiscal transfers, provide a range of options. First of all, grants may be conditional or unconditional. The justification of conditional grant is premised on the judgment that local decision making will fail to produce the socially optimum outcome, especially in the presence of inter-jurisdictional spillovers or externalities. Within the category of conditional grants, we may have matching grants where the sub-national governance may be required to contribute matching funds. The matching grants can be open ended or subject to caps. An open ended matching grant will encourage the local governments to internalize identified spillovers and provide the required level of services.

Unconditional grants are general-purpose grants meant to augment the revenues of the low revenue capacity states without attaching any strings that may affect the preference pattern of spending in the concerned state.

The answer to disparity lies in redistributive transfers that are neutralized for adverse incentives. An agreed approach in many countries is equalization. This could be fiscal capacity equalization as in Canada or capacity equalization adjusted for cost disabilities as in Australia. Fiscal equalization constitutes a mechanism for ensuring, with the help of inter governmental transfers, that all states can provide comparable services if they also undertook comparable levels of revenue effort. The overall equalizing impact of transfers should be considered considering all transfers together, that is tax revenue sharing, unconditional grants, and conditional grants.

Table 3
Selected Devolution Criteria and Weights

Criterion	*Relative Weight (Percent)*	
	TFC	*EFC*
1. Population	20.0	10.0
2. Distance	60.0	62.5
3. Area	5.0	7.5
4. Index of Infrastructure	5.0	7.5
5. Tax Effort	10.0	5.0
6. Fiscal Discipline	-	7.5

Fiscal equalization is achieved more easily if the states with low fiscal capacity also have relatively low population, because transfers involving small per capita payments are translated in large per capita grants for the recipient states. Sometimes one has to settle for less than full equalization particularly when federal revenues are limited and the amount of grants, which full equalization requires, is large. The horizontal and vertical dimensions of transfers need to be considered together, particularly where the central government has access to the major sources of revenues.

RESTRUCTURING OF PUBLIC FINANCES

The reference relating to the restructuring of government finances was given to the Finance Commission under the constitution provision relating to "sound finance" mentioned under article 280. The TFC was asked to "...review the state of finances of the Union and the States and suggest a plan by which the Governments, collectively and severally, may bring about a restructuring of the public finances restoring budgetary balance, achieving macroeconomic stability and debt- reduction along with equitable growth."

Public finances have a major role to play in the context of growth and stability. Macroeconomic stability refers to the capacity of the economy to keep close to levels of output consistent with full employment while inflation is also contained within acceptable limits. In practice, there may be structural rigidities that keep the economy below full employment on a long term basis. Issues of stabilization should, therefore, be considered with reference to growth of 'potential' or trend levels of output. In a period of recession, real output may fall below potential output. In a period of expansion, inflation may exceed its long term levels. Both departures constitute a threat to stability. The objective of stabilization is to keep the economy growing close to its long term growth path while also keeping the inflation rate within acceptable limits.

For attaining stability without the need for discretionary intervention, the economy should have a built-in capacity to return to its long term path following any departures from it due to exogenous shocks. Automatic stabilizers can exist if the structure of public finances is such that the responsiveness of taxes is larger than that of expenditures following a change in nominal output. Thus, in an inflationary situation, taxes will withdraw more from the expenditure stream than what increased government expenditures would put in, and there will be a net contraction in aggregate expenditures, thereby dampening the cycle. In a recessionary situation, government expenditures contribute more to the expenditures than taxation withdraws, thereby reducing the impact of recession.

In considering the issue of growth with stabilization, the TFC considered (a) whether potential output along its growth path remains persistently below full employment levels and (b) whether actual output in any given year is above or below the growth path of potential output. When the long run growth path is below full employment levels, it is desirable to design public finances to remove the structural constraints such as supply bottlenecks and bring potential output closer to full employment levels. In this context, the structure of government expenditure, particularly the share of capital expenditure and its allocation becomes important.

For sustaining or augmenting aggregate government demand, particularly in the context of persistent demand deficiency, a major structural feature of India's public finances must be highlighted. What is material in affecting aggregate demand is government's current purchases of goods and services, that is, its primary expenditure. After reaching a peak in the late eighties of about 28 per cent of GDP (Chart1), government expenditure in India declined, considering the combined account of central and state governments. The decline was even sharper for primary expenditure, which fell from a peak of about 25 per cent in the late eighties to less than 20 per cent by the late nineties. The lesson is quite clear: growth in primary expenditures of the government cannot be sustained for long based on the basis of borrowing, if the debt-GDP keeps rising.

The manner of financing government expenditures also affects stabilization and growth. Governments have to resort to borrowing, i.e. fiscal deficit to the extent their expenditures are not covered by the revenue and non-debt capital receipts. Excessive dependence on domestic market borrowing can push the interest rates, while excessive dependence on borrowing from the central bank can unduly accelerate the inflation rate. The use of external borrowing under certain circumstances can put pressure on the exchange rate. Fiscal deficit also needs to be viewed as consisting of two components: a structural or long term component and a cyclical component reflecting deviation from the long run average. The cyclical or the temporary component of fiscal deficit may be used to stabilize fluctuations around the trend growth of output. Many studies have highlighted that fiscal deficits in India are pre-dominantly structural in nature.

Looking at the public sector saving rate, it is clear that it became negative in 1998-99 and the magnitude of negative savings went on increasing until 2001-02. Within it, dis-saving of the government, consisting of administrative and departmental enterprises showed a sharp deterioration from 1.7 per cent of GDP in 1996-97 to 6.2 per cent in 2001-02. The aggregate saving rate had peaked in 1995-96 at 25.2 per cent. In 1998-99, it reached its lowest level in recent years at 21.5 per cent. Correspondingly, the investment rate had peaked in 1995-96 and reached its lowest level in recent years at 22.6 per cent in 1998-99. The three years in the mid-nineties provide some evidence for the kind of saving and investment rates required for a 7 plus growth. The three years covering 1994-95 to 1996-97 had an average investment rate of about 26 per cent and. domestic saving rate of about 24.7 per cent. In contrast during 2000-01 to 2002-03, the investment rate on average was 23.6 per cent and the average saving rate was 23.8 per cent. There has been a persistent fall in public investment in the nineties. The rate of gross domestic capital formation in the public sector fell from an average of 10.1 per cent of GDP during 1985-1990 to 5.7 in 2002-03. Since private investment was increasing up to the mid-nineties, it made up for the fall in the public sector investment. However, after 1995-96, the private corporate sector investment also fell.

There are four main features that can be highlighted in comparing the growth-saving-investment profile of the mid-nineties with that of the first three years of the new decade.

(i) In the mid-nineties, the average growth of GDP at factor cost was 7.5 per cent per annum, which fell to an average of 4.7 per cent during 2000-03;

(ii) The public sector saving rate fell during this period from an average level of 1.8 per cent to -2.3 per cent of GDP, amounting to a fall of 4.1 percentage points;

(iii) The public sector investment fell by 1.9 percentage points from an average level of 7.8 per cent of GDP to 5.9 per cent and the overall investment rate fell by 2.2 percentage points from an average level of 25.8 per cent to 23.6 per cent. The corporate investment fell from a high of 9.8 per cent of GDP in 1995-96 to 4.8 per cent in 2002-03;

(iv) The excess of gross domestic investment over gross domestic saving between the two periods, showing the extent of reliance on current account deficit, fell from 1.4 percentage points to -0.2 percentage points.

In TFC's analysis, for increasing and sustaining the growth rate at 7 per cent, an aggregate investment rate of 28 per cent is required on the assumption that the incremental capital-output ratio (ICOR) is 4. This would require, in TFC's assessment, a tangible increase in government investment and savings relative to GDP.

The combined debt-GDP ratio of the central and state governments at the end of 2002-03 was about 76 per cent of GDP, subject to some qualifications. First, the government budget documents give the centre's external debt as evaluated at the historical exchange rates, i.e. exchange rates in the years in which the debt was incurred. Since the exchange rate has depreciated over the years, it makes a difference if external debt is evaluated at the current exchange rates. This difference was as large as nearly 11 per cent in 1991-92. However, over the years, this difference has steadily come down. In 2002-03, if external debt is evaluated at the current exchange rates, about 5.6 per cent would need to be added to the debt-GDP ratio. This would take the combined debt-GDP ratio in 2002-03 to 81.6 per cent. The second qualification is that in accounting for the liabilities of the state governments, certain liabilities of reserve funds and deposits are not included. In 2002-03, about 3.4 percentage points of GDP needs to be added on this account, taking the overall debt-GDP ratio to 85 per cent. These figures do not include contingent liabilities, which amount to more than 11 per cent of GDP.

Even if we focus on the more conventional budgetary figure of debt without these qualifications, it is striking how the growth in debt-GDP ratio has accelerated since 1996-97 when it was 56.3 per cent, which was only marginally above the EFC's stipulated target. During the period of 1995-96 to 2002-03, the combined debt-GDP ratio rose from 56.3 per cent to 76 per cent in 2002-03, i.e. an increase of a little less than 20 percentage points in a span of 6 years. This is an unprecedented increase in the growth of the debt-GDP ratio in such a short span of time. One way of looking at the source of increase in the debt-GDP ratio during this period is to decompose the increase in terms of the contribution of cumulated primary deficits and that of the differential between growth and interest rates. For three consecutive years, viz., 2000-01, 2001-02, and 2002-03, the nominal growth rate fell below the effective interest rate. In these years, instead of absorbing the impact of primary deficits, the growth-interest differential, being negative, worked in the reverse by adding to the debt-GDP ratio. For the period 1996-97 to 2002-03, therefore the excess of growth over interest could not absorb any part of the impact of cumulated primary deficits, the benefit in the first three years being negated by the opposite effect in the latter three years. The entire increase therefore was due to accumulation of primary deficits, which remained unabsorbed by any excess of growth over interest rates.

High levels of debt-GDP ratio result in high interest payments relative to revenue receipts. Since interest payments are committed expenditures, revenue deficits are bound to increase when revenue receipts to GDP ratios remain sluggish. This has the effect of lowering the saving rate on the one hand and increasing the fiscal deficit on the other to maintain primary expenditures. Eventually, these changes have the potential of developing into a spiral of rising fiscal deficits, debt, interest payments, revenue deficits, and back to a higher fiscal deficit. This gives rise to the issue of sustainability of debt.

A review of the performance of different sectors in terms of the saving-investment balance provides one approach to determining the levels of permissible fiscal deficit. In India, it is the household sector that has surplus savings that are absorbed by the private corporate and government sector. These surplus savings are their savings in the financial form. The financial savings of the household sector were roughly of the same order since 1993-94, being in the range of 10-11 per cent of GDP with small variations. Comparing the trend since 1995-96, it is apparent that the public sector has been absorbing a larger part of the financial savings of the household sector. The demand for this surplus by the private corporate sector came down from 4.65 per cent of GDP in 1995-96 to 1.4 per cent in 2002-03. That is why there was no pressure on the interest rates in the late nineties. Once the private sector demand picks up, a growth augmenting scenario would emerge only if the government is able to reduce its revenue deficit. Only then would the interest rates also remain benign. Further, if the government is able to eliminate its revenue deficit, and increase its savings and capital expenditures, demand for private investment would be further strengthened. Studies have shown that government investment in infrastructure crowds-in private investment.

In the TFC scheme, the targets for revenue and fiscal deficits are essential ingredients of a restructuring program. It is assumed that the nominal growth rate (g) and the nominal effective interest rate are given and exogenous. The TFC used the following conditions for deriving the targets.

(a) The debt-GDP ratio will be stabilized at a level b* where $b^* = p\,(1+g)/\,(g-i)$.

(b) The fisc0al deficit to GDP ratio will be stabilized at f* where $f^* = p.g/\,(g-i)$.

These could also be written equivalently, indicating the ratio of revenue receipts to GDP indicated by (r), in terms of the ratio of interest payments to revenue receipts (ip)* instead of primary deficit, as follows:

(a) The debt-GDP ratio will be stabilized at a level b* where $b^* = (ip)^* r\,(1+g)/\,i$.

(b) The fiscal deficit to GDP ratio will be stabilized at f* where $f^* = (ip)^* r.g/\,i$.

In the present Indian context, the TFC argued that centre's FRBMA has fixed a fiscal deficit target for the central government at 3 per cent of GDP. Using relations (a and b), which imply [b*=f*(1+g)/g], it is seen that for this level of fiscal deficit and a nominal growth rate of 12 per cent, the debt-GDP ratio will eventually be stabilized at 28 per cent. The TFC divided the correction in the debt profile in two parts: an adjustment phase (upto 2008-09) and a stabilization phase beyond that. Since the fiscal deficit target is given by the FRBMA, as long there is an excess of growth over interest rate, a primary deficit can be maintained in the stabilization phase. For a combination of 12 per cent nominal growth rate and 7 per cent interest rate, this would be equal to 1.25 per cent of GDP. We think that a combined fiscal deficit target, relative to GDP, of 6 per cent would be consistent with the availability of savings of the household sector in financial assets, which is of the order of 10 per cent, the desirable level of current account deficit, and the requirements of the corporate sector and the non-departmental public sector undertakings. The transferable savings of the household sector of 10 per cent of GDP combined with an acceptable level of current account deficit of 1.5 per cent would be adequate to provide for a government fiscal deficit of 6 per cent, an absorption by the private corporate sector of 4 per cent, and by non-departmental public enterprises of 1.5 per cent of GDP. When the revenue deficit becomes zero, the entire fiscal deficit would lead to an augmentation of investment with the total investment as percentage of GDP touching a level in the range of 28 to 30 per cent. Of this total, the household sector could invest about 12 per cent of GDP, the private corporate sector, about 8 per cent of GDP, and the public sector, about 8 to 10 per cent of GDP.

Limiting the combined fiscal deficit at 6 per cent of GDP is also necessary to bring down the ratio of interest payments to revenue receipts from the very high levels of almost 50 per cent in 2002-03 for the centre, 26 per cent for the states, and 37 per cent on their combined account. In the proposed plan for restructuring government finances, these are to be brought down by 2009-10, respectively, to 28 per cent for the centre, 15 per cent for the states, and 22 per cent, on their combined accounts.

Given the desirable of 6 per cent of GDP as the overall fiscal deficit, as the centre has already fixed a target for its own borrowing at 3 per cent of GDP, a similar level of fiscal deficit for the states considered together was prescribed for the states. Thus, the borrowing of the public sector including the non-departmental enterprises could be of the order of 7.5 per cent. The corresponding debt-GDP ratio for the combined account is set at 56 per cent, with external debt measured at historical exchange rates, which is close to the actual level of combined debt relative to GDP at the end of 1996-97.

In the adjustment phase, the debt-GDP ratio will steadily fall as primary deficit follows a path of adjustment so that the fiscal deficit target of 6 per cent is achieved. After the debt-GDP ratio has fallen to the desirable levels, primary deficit and fiscal deficit will be stabilized.

Keeping in view these considerations, the TFC recommended that:

(i) The overall debt-GDP ratio on the combined account (with external debt measured at historical exchange rates) may be targeted to be brought down to 56 per cent of GDP over a period of time. Since the level is estimated to be as high as 81 per cent of GDP at the end of 2004-05, it should be brought down to at least 75 per cent by the end of 2009-10.

(ii) The level of combined interest payments relative to revenue receipts should be brought down from 34 per cent in 2004-05 to 22 per cent in 2009-10, and eventually to about 17 per cent.

(iii) The system of on-lending by the centre to the states should be phased out. The long term goal for the centre and state for the debt-GDP ratio should be 28 per cent each. Their fiscal deficit to GDP ratio targets should be 3 per cent each.

The plan for restructuring suggested by the TFC relies both on augmenting revenues and restructuring expenditures. The main elements in this programme are increases in the tax revenues and capital expenditures relative to GDP while attaining targeted reductions in revenue and fiscal deficits both for the centre and the states. For the combined revenue account of the central and state governments that more than 60 per cent of the adjustment comes from the revenue side. The quantum of increase in the tax-GDP ratio is stipulated to be 2.0 percentage points. The increase in the overall revenue to GDP ratio is close to 3.0 percentage points. On the expenditure side, the fall in combined revenue expenditure to GDP ratio is 1.7 percentage points. Even though total expenditure falls, primary expenditure increases as capital expenditure relative to GDP increases by about 1 percentage point. As revenue deficit is eliminated, the entire fiscal deficit supplemented by non-debt receipts in the form of loan recoveries and disinvestment proceeds can be used for capital expenditures. Since the targeted combined fiscal deficit is 6 per cent, capital expenditure would be higher than 6 per cent of GDP.

DEBT RELIEF SCHEME

In order to induce the states to undertake the necessary corrective actions for restructuring, bring out the fiscal responsibility legislation, and facilitate adjustment, the TFC recommended a major debt relief package. The main recommendation regarding debt-relief may be summarized as follows:

1. Each state must enact a fiscal responsibility legislation prescribing specific annual targets with a view to eliminating the revenue deficit by 2008-09 and reducing fiscal deficits based on a path for reduction of borrowings and guarantees. Enacting the fiscal responsibility legislation is a necessary pre-condition for availing of debt relief.
2. The central loans to states contracted till 31.3.04 and outstanding on 31.3.05 (amounting to Rs. 128795 crore) may be consolidated and rescheduled for a fresh term of 20 years (resulting in repayment in 20 equal installments), and an interest rate of 7.5 per cent be charged on them. This is, however, subject to the state enacting the fiscal responsibility legislation and will take effect prospectively from the year in which such legislation is enacted.

3. A debt write-off scheme linked to the reduction of revenue deficit of states may be introduced. Under the scheme, the repayments due from 2005-06 to 2009-10 on central loans contracted up to 31.3.04 and recommended to be consolidated will be eligible for write off. The quantum of write off of repayment will be linked to the absolute amount by which the revenue deficit is reduced in each successive year during our award period. In effect, if the revenue deficit is brought down to zero, the entire repayments during the period will be written-off. The enactment of the fiscal responsibility legislation would be a necessary pre-condition for availing the debt relief under this scheme also with the benefit accruing prospectively.
4. In respect of future lending policy, the central government should not act as an intermediary and allow the states to approach the market directly. If, however, some fiscally weak states are unable to raise funds from the market, the centre could borrow for the purpose of on lending to such states, but the interest rates should remain aligned to the marginal cost of borrowing for the centre.
5. External assistance should be transferred to states on the same terms and conditions as attached to such assistance by external funding agencies, thereby making government of India a financial intermediary without any gain or loss. The external assistance pass through to states should be managed through a separate fund in the public account.
6. (ix) All states should set up sinking funds for amortization of all loans including loans from banks liabilities on account of NSSF etc. The fund should be maintained outside the consolidated fund of the states and the public account and should not be used for any other purpose, except for redemption of loans.
7. (x) States should set up guarantee redemption funds through earmarked guarantee fees. This should be preceded by risk weighting of guarantees. The quantum of contribution to the fund should be decided accordingly.

The incentive implicit in the debt relief program has induced many states to undertake a fiscal responsibility legislation. Adjustment has been facilitated as the economy grew out of the recession in the early part of the decade and is now growing at healthy seven plus growth. Apart from the increase in the volume of grants, tax devolution is also increasing because of the improved revenue performance of the central taxes. Adjustment is eminently possible by 2008-09. If revenue deficit is brought down, as envisaged, the aggregate saving rate is bound to increase along with investment without putting any pressure on the interest rate.

FISCAL TRANSFERS: OUTSTANDING PROBLEMS

Even after twelve Finance Commissions, there are certain structural and institutional problems in the system of fiscal transfers that need to be resolved. Some of these are discussed below.

(a) Distortions Emanating From Multiple Channels of Transfers

In India, apart from the Finance Commission transfers, transfers also come through in the form of Plan grants and discretionary grants emanating from various central ministries. The combined impact of transfers from these other channels weakens the equalizing impact of the Finance Commission transfers.

The plan assistance is given to the states as consisting of grants and loans. The grant-loan ratio for the states in general is 30:70 whereas for the special category states, this ratio is 90:10. In normal central assistance, 30 per cent is earmarked for the special category states. The expenditure on state plans is met by the balance from current revenues (BCR) from the state budgets, plan assistance in the form of grants and loans by the central government, and borrowing from other sources including the market and those based on small savings. The BCRs for most states have progressively fallen and become negative. In consequence, the financing of the plan, apart from a small contribution of the plan grants from the centre, depends entirely on borrowing by the states. A large plan effectively also means larger borrowing. It becomes therefore necessary that the plan size of every state is linked to the sustainable level of debt. In the case of plan assistance, the proportion between grants and loans at 30: 70 for the general category states and 10:90 for the special category states has a counterpart in the interest rate charged by the central government on the plan loans to the states, which has been, in the past, sometimes, 300 to 400 basis points higher than the cost of funds to the centre. In other words, plan grants are not really interest-free grants. Over time, these are recovered back in the form of higher interest receipts. Plan grants should be given as genuine grants and states may be encouraged to borrow from the market directly. Such a change would require delinking of grants from loans in plan assistance. This has been recommended by the TFC.

It can be seen that the plan grants are given disproportionately in large amounts to the special category states and for the remaining states there is some progressivity in distribution but only weakly so. This weakens the equalizing content of overall transfers. The profile of shares of plan grants across states for the period 1996-97 to 1998-99, indicates that more than 37 per cent of plan grants have gone to the special category states, whereas they account for less than 5 per cent of population and only 3.3 per cent of all state GSDP. For the low-income states like Bihar, Uttar Pradesh, Orissa, Madhya Pradesh, West Bengal and Rajasthan, the share of plan grants amounted to nearly 33 per cent whereas they account for nearly 50 per cent of the population and 38 per cent of GDP. This pattern of dispensation of plan grants has led to large committed expenditures. The revenue-gap grants recommended by the Finance Commission are determined on the basis of partial application of norms. These are enough to take most special category states out of the revenue-gap grants but the special category states have such large committed expenditures that even after the application of norms, their claims are still left. This is what is left of the gap-filling approach. In EFC's case the share of the special category states in the revenue-gap grants was 82 per cent and in TFC's case, this was 87 per cent. This is the fall out of the gap-filling approach. For the special category states, since the committed expenditures have been created by the large plan grants given to them, they will have to be given support by the Finance Commission, by one route or another. Since the special category states get overwhelmingly large share here, the TFC opened the window of health and education grants to improve the equalizing content of the transfers exercise.

(b) Transmission of External Assistance to the States

External assistance used to be passed on to the states on terms and conditions that were different from the original terms of the lender. This arrangement has been called 'Additional Central Assistance' (ACA). ACA was given on the same terms as normal plan assistance. This implied for the general category states, a 70-30 loan-grant ratio of plan assistance, and for the special category states, a 10-90 loan-grant ratio. External assistance to states reflects a series of factors including priorities and targets of creditors. In this process, the character and concessionality of external assistance to states was completely transformed and a distorted pattern of cross-subsidization emerged where a poverty alleviation program given as 100 per cent grant would be given as 70 per cent loan to a general category state, which would cross-subsidise some commercial project financed by external assistance in another states. The TFC has recommended discontinuation of this practice and suggested that external assistance should passed on the state on the original terms.

(c) Challenge of Information Lag

To some extent the achieving equalization is constrained by information lags. The data on population pertains to 1971. By the time the recommendation period of the twelfth Finance Commission is over, it will be out of date by nearly 39 years. Even the data on GSDP, which serves as indicator of revenue base, will be dated by about 8 years by 2009-10. In a context where disparities are increasing, the transfers system could become regressive by the time actual transfers take place even when transfers are designed to be progressive under an equalization approach with respect to data used. It is difficult to see the relevance of 1971 population census data when population of all states was about 54 crore, when 2001 census puts the population of all states at more than 100 crore. This is out-of date by nearly 100 per cent and implies substantial changes in the relative share and pattern of population.

(d) Challenge of Hidden Transfers

In India, there are some important channels of implicit or hidden transfers. One such channel emanates from the mechanism of food subsidies. As is well known, the food subsidy serves an income-support role through the mechanism of procurement prices. If procurement by the FCI is done mainly from a limited number of states, it implicitly transfers subsidies to those states. It is also well known that then FCI procures mainly from a limited number of states like Punjab, Haryana, Maharashtra, and Andhra Pradesh. The food subsidy gets redistributed in these states, and its distribution adds to horizontal inequalities. The non-FC transfers become even more regressive when account is taken of the implicit transfers, such as those arising from procurement of food grains by the Food Corporation of India (FCI) largely from some of the better-off states [1]. In the case of special category states, the correlation is positive both for FC and non- FC transfers.

CONCLUDING OBSERVATIONS

Equity and efficiency are the main guiding principles in designing a system of fiscal transfers. An efficient fiscal transfer system should give rise to transfers that are predictable and stable. Predictability of resource flows enables the sub-national governments to plan ahead, and stability ensures that there will not be sudden shocks in the transfer arrangements. In the consideration of the issue of equity, reference is often made to its vertical and horizontal dimensions.

The equalization approach to transfers, which is followed by some of the important federal systems like Canada and Australia, is suitable for India also. This approach takes due account of resources deficiency but effectively neutralizes fiscal imprudence. Given the cost disabilities of a large number of special category states, the equalization approach should take of the cost disabilities also. In practice, the Finance Commissions have been able to follow a gap-filling approach. The main beneficiaries of this approach have been the special category states. The Finance Commission transfers exhibit a degree of progressivity. But this has been undone by a transfers that take place through various other mechanisms including plan transfers, centrally sponsored schemes, and external assistance. There are also hidden transfers that take place through the procurement mechanics of the Food Corporation of India that has implications for the distribution of food subsidies. On the whole, the transfers system has remained proportional rather than progressive.

The Twelfth Finance Commission (TFC) considered that the scheme of transfers should be designed to serve the objectives both of equity and efficiency. Fiscal transfers should also be predictable and stable. These transfers should correct both the vertical and horizontal imbalances avoid adverse incentives. Three main challenges remain in the context of fiscal transfers arising from (a) the existence of avoidable information lags including the need to use 1971 population data, (b) multiplicity in chnannels of transfers without any coordination, and (c) problems raised by hidden transfers such as those arising from central sales tax and the inter-state distribution of food subsidies linked to procurement policies of the FCI.

The TFC, apart from attending to the core duties of recommending transfers, also suggested a programme for restructuring government finances, an certain incentive linked mechanisms for correcting fiscal imbalance particularly at the state level. In particular, the proposed restructuring covers the following areas:

(i) Taxation reforms aimed at building up non-distortionary and revenue-elastic system of taxation with tax rates that are low, limited in number of rate categories, and stable;

(ii) Non-tax revenues where user charges, as a short term objective, ensure recoveries of current costs, and aim at full recovery of costs measured at acceptable efficiency levels in the longer run, in the case of services where there is no clear cut case for subsidization and ensure rates of return on investment that covers the average cost of borrowing;

(iii) Expenditure restructuring relating to both its size and sectoral allocations aimed at removing inefficiencies arising from misallocations, design and implementation of schemes, and delivery of services;

(iv) Rationalizing subsidies by reducing their overall volume, increasing their transparency by making them explicit, and improving their targeting;

(v) Public sector restructuring where, apart from natural monopolies and strategic reasons, there is a strong case for reducing government's involvement;

(vi) Fiscal transfer system where equalizing transfers are given much greater weight and extended to local bodies;

(vii) Suggesting a reformed role for the plan process;

(viii) Strengthening the role of local bodies to become a more effective instrument in the delivery of local public goods;

(ix) Role of the central government in intermediating loans for the states including the need to specify annual ceiling of borrowing for each state and implementing a hard-budget constraint; and,

(x) Suggesting institutional frameworks including ceiling on debt and deficits and mechanisms for their monitoring through state level fiscal responsibility legislation.

REFERENCES

Australian Loan Council (1993), *Future Arrangements for Loan council Monitoring and Reporting*, Canberra.

Boadway, R. and Flatters, F. (1982), "Efficiency and Equalisation Payments in a Federal System of Government: A Synthesis and Extension of Recent Results", *Journal of Economics*, 15 (4), 613-633.

Buchanan, J.M. (1950), "Federalism and Equity", *The American Economic Review*, Vol. 40.

Buchanan, J.M. and R.E.Wagner (1971), "An Efficiency Basis for Federal Fiscal Equalization" in J.Margolis (ed.), *Analysis of Public Output*, NBER, Princeton.

Commonwealth Grants Commission (1983), Equality in Diversity: Fifty Years of Commonwealth Grants Commission, AGPS, Canberra.

Commonwealth Grants Commission (2004), *Report on State Revenue Sharing Relativities, 2004 Review*, Canberra.

Collins, D.J. (2000), *The Impact of the GST Package on Commonwealth State Financial Relations*, Australian Tax Research Foundation, Research Study No. 34, Sydney.

Garnaut, R. (2002), "Equity and Australian Development: Lessons from the First Century", *Australian Economic Review*, 35(3), 227-243.

Government of India (2004), Report of the Twelfth Finance Commission, New Delhi.

Graham, J.F. (1964), "Fiscal Adjustment in a Federal Country" in R. Robertson (ed.) Inter-Government Fiscal Relationships, Canadian Tax Foundation, Toronto.

Gramlich, E.M. (1985), "Federal Fiscal arrangements" in R. Caves and L.B.Krause, The Australian Economy: A View from the North, The Brookings Institution.

Madden, J.R. (1993), "The Economics of Vertical Fiscal Imbalance", *Australian Tax Forum*, 10(1), 75-90.

Mathews, Russell (1993), "The Theory and Practice of Fiscal Equalization": A Report for the Queensland Government, Mimeo.

Mathews, Russell (1985), "Fiscal Federalism in Australia", Conference Discussion Paper on Edward M. Gramlich's Paper, The Australian National University, Canberra.

Oates,W.E.(1972), Fiscal Federalism, Harcourt Brace Jovanovich, New York.

Prud'homme, Remy (1995), "The Dangers of Decentralization", *World Bank Research Observer*", Vol. 10, No. 2.

Rangarajan, C. and D.K. Srivastava (2004), "Dynamics of Debt Accumulation: Primary Deficit, Growth and Interest Rate",

Economic and Political Weekly, No. 38, November 15-21, reproduced in Kapila, Raj and Uma Kapila(eds.), *Economic Developments in India*, Vol. 73.

Rangarajan, C. and D.K. Srivastava (2004), "Fiscal Federalism in Canada: Drawing Comparisons and Lessons", *Economic and Political Weekly*, 39, No. 19, May 8-14, and Working Paper No. 18, NIPFP, New Delhi.

Saunders, C.A. (1990), "Government Borrowing in Australia", *the Journal of Federalism*, 20, 35-52.

Scott, A.D. (1950), "A Note on Grants in Federal Countries", *Economica*, Vol. 17.

Scott, A.D. (1952), "Federal Grants and Resource Allocation", *Journal of Political Economy*, Vol. 60.

3

ISSUES AND APPROACH: AN APPRAISAL

J.V.M. Sarma

INTRODUCTION

The role of the Finance Commission in the Indian federal system is becoming more and more complex. The task of reducing the fiscal imbalances with a view to safeguarding the essence of the federal structure in the context of growing disparities among the federating units, especially without disturbing the over all objective of achieving macroeconomic stability, was a tough job given to the Twelfth Finance Commission (Twelfth Finance Commission). Although the basic approach was guided by the mandate of the constitutional provisions and the terms of reference (TOR) contained in the Presidential order, the details that needed delicate balancing of different aspects were left to be worked out by the Commission.[1]

The recommendations of the Finance Commission have profound impact on the fiscal and economic health of the country. Therefore it is pertinent to assess the methodology adopted in resolving various issues that emanated from the tasks of the Commission. Keeping in view the emphasis of this conference and the time constraints I would like to keep my attention to only selected aspects of the recommendations. They are as follows:

- Designing the federal fiscal transfers in terms of tax devolutions and grants in aid with a view to reducing the vertical and horizontal imbalances.

- Restructuring of public finances of the country as a whole to firmly keep the economy on the sustainable growth path.
- Reducing the debt burden of the centre and states and achieving fiscal consolidation.
- Designing guidelines for further decentralization and transfers to local bodies.

DESIGN OF FISCAL TRANSFERS

Fiscal transfers, in the form of tax devolution and grants, are meant to correct both the vertical and horizontal imbalances. Correcting vertical imbalance relates to transfers from the central government to the state governments taken together, whereas the correction of horizontal imbalance is concerned with the allocation of transfers among the state governments. The vertical imbalance arises since resources have been assigned more to the central government and states have been entrusted with the larger responsibilities. The horizontal imbalance has its roots in the differential capacities and needs of the states as also the differences in the costs of providing services. In India, not only the number of states is large, they differ in various respects such as area, size of population, income, tax base, and mineral and forest resources. Resource gaps may arise because states have inadequate capacities as also because the revenue effort is deficient in relative terms. While the former may need to be taken into account for correcting the horizontal imbalance, the latter should not qualify for such correction.

The Commission's endeavour was to recommend a scheme of transfers that could serve the objectives both of equity and efficiency, and result in fiscal transfers that are predictable and stable. The Commission felt that transfers should be determined on a normative basis instead of merely filling up gaps arising from the projections of revenues and expenditures based on historical trends. Under the normative approach states are assessed in terms of revenues that they ought to raise given their respective capacities and expenditures are assessed on the basis of needs consistent with an average or minimum acceptable level of service and the relevant cost norms.

VERTICAL DIMENSION

In India, resources are transferred from the central to the state governments through multiple routes and in many forms. Among these, the statutory transfers consist of sharing of central tax revenues and grants recommended by the Finance Commission. These are supplemented by grants from the Planning Commission and discretionary grants from the central ministries. Transfers under the recommendations of the Finance Commission account for about 65 per cent of the total transfers. Given the multiplicity of channels of transfers, it is important that the Finance Commission, in making its own recommendations, takes into account the overall volume of transfers. The Tenth Finance Commission's recommendations that led to the Constitution 80th Amendment, had estimated the share of the overall vertical transfers to the states in the total central gross revenue receipts to be around 37 per cent. The Eleventh Finance Commission recommended an overall share of 37.5 per cent of the centre's gross revenue receipts as transfers to states. The Twelfth Finance Commission has recommended 38 per cent as the indicative amount of overall transfers. In doing so the Commission merely tried to restore the past practice.

More appropriate would have been to measure the vertical imbalance between the centre and the states and try to restore the balance. For example, following the writings of Hunter[2], Bird[3], Grewal[4] and so on, the vertical fiscal imbalance (VFI) can be expressed as the positive difference between the Central and State level fiscal balance and accordingly, an approximate bench mark for the transfers needed from Centre to States to eliminate VFI could be $T = [(R_c - E_c) - (R_s - E_s)] / 2$, where, R_c and R_s denote revenues of Centre and States before devolution and transfers and E_c and E_s are respective total expenditures. This works out to be around 40-45 per cent under certain assumptions. Moreover, there is a case for increasing the vertical share because of non-inclusion of revenue from taxation of services, surcharges, cesses, as also the non-tax revenue.

HORIZONTAL DIMENSION

Between the two principal modes of fiscal transfers, tax devolution and grants, tax devolution has a built-in flexibility as it can increase automatically if the central taxes are more buoyant. Grants are assured as these are fixed in nominal terms. It is also easier to target grants towards states or sectors. Targeting in the case of devolution is broad and indirect and is limited by the criteria used. States generally prefer devolutions because they are unconditional. Grants in aid are mainly targeted towards achieving a degree of equalization. That is why many of the better-off states assessed to be in revenue surplus, do not get article 275 grants. As such, the transfer instruments available to the Finance Commission must include tax revenue sharing, assessed gap grants, and grants that may be earmarked for specific purposes like those meant for the local bodies or achieving certain minimum level of services. The share of grants in total transfers recommended by the Finance Commissions has been less than 15 per cent on average over the recommendation period of the Commission.

SHARING OF CENTRAL TAXES

Although significant efforts are made by the Tenth Finance Commission and Eleventh Finance Commission to bring about some amount of objectivity by integrating the system of tax devolution and enlarging the divisible pool to include all Union taxes, with regard to the horizontal revenue sharing however, not much attention seems to have been paid. One aspect that remains a source of controversy is the near-subjective identification of the criteria determining the horizontal shares, and arbitrary assignment of weights to them. The broad approach of the Finance Commissions has so far, been to specify suitable criteria that reflect the three considerations–needs, cost disability and fiscal efficiency. Successive Finance Commissions in India used several criteria for determining the horizontal shares of the tax devolution transfers. The basic criteria used so far by are (a) population, (b) transformations of income such as 'distance' and 'inverse' ('income adjusted population' as sometimes referred to), (c) developmental indicators such as poverty, backwardness and infrastructure, (d) contribution, and (e) tax effort. The criteria for determining the *inter se* shares of States have tended to converge since the Seventh Commission. Yet, the selection of a particular set of factors and the weights assigned to them for determining the shares largely remained subjective and continue to be "a gamble on the personal views of five persons, or a majority of them"[5]. In fact, the tax devolution is recommended mainly on the basis of general economic indicators and not fiscal disadvantage *per se*. The Twelfth Finance Commission essentially followed the same approach. While adopting the same criteria, the weights are slightly modified: Population 25, Income Distance 50, Area 10, Tax Effort 7.5, and Fiscal Discipline 7.5.

In my writings, I have been emphasizing the need for shedding this approach where the criteria and their weightage are imposed from above in an arbitrary way, and pleading for adopting a more rational approach. I also have suggested one such method that calls for equalizing the true fiscal gap across the states[6]. It helps in identification of the main factors and assigning weights objectively by means of their relation with the fiscal gap (before transfers). The main advantage of such an approach is that the transfer shares are determined on the basis of rational fiscal behavioral framework keeping in view the basic motivations of the federating units for coming together. The criteria and the weights for horizontal distribution of transfers in this model are derived from those factors that are responsible for variations in the basic net marginal benefit due to federation (NMBF) and not imposed from outside as has been the case so far. The NMBF (proxied by the own revenue – expenditure gap is) subdivided into three components: (a) component that varies with factors common to all the States, (b) component that varies with State-specific factors and (c) component that varies with random factors. After removing the effect of random factors the remaining two components of fiscal gap are made comparable by restricting the parameters of common factors to be uniform for all the States. The common factors are akin to the criteria and their estimated uniform parameters are similar to the weights. In this way, whatever criteria that emerge from the model are related to their respective NMBF and the weights are in accordance to the degree of their relevance to the NMBF. This method, while allowing the determining the shares, State specific factors such as cost disabilities due to geographic and climatic conditions that influence the fiscal behavior are fully taken into account in the form of State-specific 'fixed effects'. These factors are not easy to identify and not amenable for prescribing as quantifiable criteria. The model does away with the need to identify the State-specific factors although their effect is fully taken into account.

Although it was well recognized in the past that the three considerations–needs, cost disability and fiscal efficiency should form the basis in designing a suitable scheme of fiscal transfers, an objective way of striking a balance between them eluded the Finance Commissions so far. As a result, past Finance Commissions are led to devise exotic criteria such as the income-distance criteria, the inverse income criteria, the fiscal performance criteria, the tax effort criteria, poverty criteria and so on. Their form and their relevance are not easy to digest. In contrast, our model and estimation procedures automatically allow striking an optimal balance between the equity and efficiency objectives of the transfers.

The Twelfth Finance Commission was also aware of the advantages of the new approach but was cautious and did not want to be too radical in changing the sharing pattern. We have to see if the forthcoming Commissions might want to bring in more rationality.

APPROACH TO DETERMINING GRANTS

In relation to grants in aid, the Finance Commission is required to make recommendations not only to the 'principles' that should govern such grants, but also determine specific 'sums' to be paid to the states which are in need of assistance. The Twelfth Finance Commission was required to make recommendations regarding sharing of central taxes and grants for the period from 2005-06 to 2009-10 which requires making projections of resources and needs for the centre and for each individual state. The base-year was given as 2003-04. The assessment of central finances indicates the availability of funds, and the assessment of state finances provides the claim on those funds. While making the projections, the Twelfth Finance Commission followed a normative basis encompassing both the revenue and expenditure heads. These assessments took into account the likely taxation efforts of the central government and each state government as against 'targets' and 'potential' in order to improve the tax-GDP and the tax-GSDP ratios respectively for the central and the state governments.

Looking back, one feels that perhaps, the same NMBF exercise could have been extended and used for the purpose of projecting the revenues of at least the states. The fiscal gap functions that were used for determination of the tax devolution shares could be used for projecting the future fiscal gaps which would be then adjusted to obtain the post devolution version so that the sums of the grants-in-aid would be objectively estimated.

Although the Grants recommended by the Twelfth Finance Commission are largely general and unconditional in nature, the Commission also considered the case for conditional grants in respect two areas, viz., education and health including family welfare, to states that are below average in terms of per capita expenditures with a view to bringing them closer to the average. However, care was taken to see that the gap pertained only to the deficiency in fiscal capacity and not due to other factors or priorities.

RESTRUCTURING OF PUBLIC FINANCES

The Commission has taken cognizance of the prevailing fiscal and macroeconomic situation, particularly the need to sustain the growth momentum, while bringing about fiscal consolidation. The Commission, while emphasizing the need for restructuring public finances, took note of five key fiscal trends that cause serious concern. These are: decline in the tax-GDP ratio, large interest payments relative to revenue receipts, high revenue-deficit to GDP ratio, large fiscal deficit to GDP ratio, and falling levels of capital expenditure relative to GDP.

The main reasons generally given for this all round fiscal deterioration include the revision of salaries and pensions in the wake of the recommendations of the Fifth Central Pay Commission, erosion in the buoyancy of central indirect taxes, and the high nominal interest rates towards the end of the nineties. Transfers cannot be taken as a means of reducing the revenue deficit for one tier of the government by increasing it for the other. There is a need for improving the position of revenue balance both at the centre and the states.

Determining the right size of fiscal deficit and the debt in relation to GDP is important for prudent fiscal management. The central government has specified in the rules under its Fiscal Responsibility and Budget Management Act, 2003 (FRBMA), a fiscal deficit target of 3 per cent, which is to be achieved by 2008-09. The optimal level of aggregate fiscal deficit at the states' level needs to be indicated.

The Eleventh Finance Commission had also set targets for reduction of the level of debt in relation to GDP. The debt-GDP ratio of the centre and states was to be brought down by 10 percentage points so as to reach the level of 55 per cent in 2004-05. However, there was considerable slippage in achieving this target due to a rise in primary deficits as well as low growth rate in comparison to the interest rate during the three year-period 2000-2003. The Twelfth Finance Commission accordingly set long-term (2009-10) targets for tax-GDP ratio (17.6 per cent), combined debt-GDP ratio (75 per cent), fiscal deficit (3 per cent), revenue deficit-GDP ratio (0 per cent), states' salary bill–expenditure net of interest and pension (35 per cent). Some of these targets coincide with the FRBM Act.

The Commission felt that adoption of a fiscal correction and restructuring plan by the states can be facilitated and induced to some extent by built-in incentives and rewards provided for within the scheme of transfers. The reward mechanism through indicators of tax effort and fiscal efficiency was kept in tact for the same reason. In addition, a forward looking scheme was proposed along with the debt relief.

ISSUES OF DEBT RELIEF

It has become a well-established custom that finance commissions also recommend debt reliefs to states. It was observed that recommendations regarding debt relief by successive Commissions create anticipations about such measures, which has a built-in adverse incentive. Debt relief often indicates lack of fiscal discipline of the past. It could be unfair and could give significantly adverse signals if the benefit of relief is largest for the state, which was the most profligate in the past. In the literature relating to fiscal federalism, considerable attention has been given to the deleterious effects of a soft budget constraint, which refers to the relative ease with which states can borrow. This also has implications for the assessment of interest payments. If any amount of interest payments liability can be considered as legitimate claim for determining transfers, all normative assessments of current expenditures would be rendered redundant. All that a state would need to do is to borrow more in the current period and generate larger claims for the future. It is imperative that interest payments be assessed normatively and a hard budget constraint be imposed.

In this regard the conditional debt-relief package recommended by the Commission should be considered as a move in the right direction. The rescheduling of the past loans for another 20 years and reduction of interest rate to 7.5 per cent will go a long way in alleviating the debt burden of the states. More importantly the requirement that each state would enact a fiscal responsibility legislation with a view to eliminating the revenue deficit by 2008-09 and reducing fiscal deficits as also the requirement of creating a guarantee redemption fund should reform the state level fiscal management to some extent. Also, the recommendations for a back-to-back re-lending of funds from external agencies should put a stop to the allegations of centre hiking the cost of external borrowings.

DECENTRALIZATION AND TRANSFERS TO LOCAL BODIES

There is no doubt that governance decentralization efficiency augmenting as local representatives are presumed to better understand the preferences, needs, and willingness to finance the provision of the related local goods. The 73rd and 74th amendments to the Constitution do provided an effective basis for introducing local self governance in the country. Now the state governments are constitutionally required to holding of local elections, bringing out enabling legislations, transferring of functional responsibility along with the sources of revenue, and constituting the state Finance Commissions at the required intervals.

However, the reality is somewhat different. States have often been not prompt enough to constitute the state Finance Commissions with the required regularity. In many instances, after the recommendations are received, decisions have been kept pending. Even grants recommended and earmarked for the local bodies by the earlier Finance Commission, having been received into the consolidated fund of the state, have not been passed on to the local bodies in certain cases.

The Commission's approach in this regard is to strengthen the fiscal domain of the local bodies to make the local self-governance more effective. Since the local public goods have limited externalities, financing by external sources has considerable problems of adverse incentives that could lead to increasing dependence on transfers from above. Various studies do indicate that local bodies have not been enthusiastic about raising revenues. The principle of equalization, extended to the local bodies would mean that while lack of fiscal capacity, at the state level as well as the local level can be made up, lack of revenue effort should not be made up.

CONCLUDING

The system of fiscal transfers in India has been in operation for over half a century now. The transfers are channeled by multiple agencies and through multiple forms calling for more coordinated efforts. There is a need to have objectivity and stability in federal relations in general and in the system of transfers in particular. States also have to pay greater attention to policies aimed at accelerating growth and reducing intra-state regional inequalities.

What Twelfth Finance Commission has achieved is to take steps towards correcting for the fall in the volume of transfers, ensuring minimum vertical transfers while correcting a larger horizontal imbalance, ensuring minimum level of services in the case of education and health through conditional grants, encourage fiscal consolidation both for the centre and the states, and debt relief linked to monitorable achievements in regard to fiscal consolidation.

NOTES

1. Vithal B.P.R, and Sarma, J.V.M. (2002), 'Twelfth Finance Commission: Framing its Terms of Reference', Economic and Political Weekly, August 24.
2. "Vertical Intergovernmental Financial Imbalance: A Framework for Evaluation", Finanzarchiv No. 2, p. 481-92, "Federalism and Fiscal Balance (Canberra: Australian National University Centre for Research on Federal Financial Relations) (1977)
3. Bird Richard M. (1986), Federal Finance in Comparative Perspective, Canadian Tax Foundation, Toronto.
4. Bhajan Grewal (1995), "Vertical Fiscal Imbalance In Australia: A Problem For Tax Structure, Not For Revenue Sharing", Working Paper No. 2 Centre for Strategic Economic Studies, Victoria University.
5. Dissent note to the Report of the Fourth Finance Commission as quoted by Guhan (1995).
6. 'Criteria for Federal Fiscal Transfers-The Issue of Horizontal Sharing" Economic & Political Weekly, February, 1997.

4

HORIZONTAL FISCAL TRANSFERS IN INDIA AN ANALYSIS OF FINANCE COMMISSIONS' APPROACH

N. Sreedevi

INTRODUCTION

The Finance Commission, after the vertical distribution of shared taxes between the centre and the states, distributes these resources across the States-horizontal distribution. The main objective of these transfers, besides reducing the vertical fiscal imbalance, is to minimize the horizontal fiscal imbalances of the State governments. In this context, an attempt is made to discuss the basic approach of the Finance Commission in fulfilling the very purpose of this horizontal transfer. Section two discusses what theory says regarding horizontal distribution of resources in a fiscal federalism. Section three discusses whether the approaches of the Finance Commission in India in recommending the horizontal distribution of the central transfers are in consonance with the theory. It also discusses the link between the approach and the criteria adopted by the Finance Commission in the distribution of resources across the states. Last section gives the conclusions.

The study is mainly on the basis of secondary sources and mainly the reports of the various Finance Commissions.

THE HORIZONTAL FISCAL IMBALANCES: THEORETICAL ISSUES

The Horizontal Fiscal Imbalances

Buchanan (1950,1952)[1] highlights an important source of horizontal inequity in federal systems, namely, the differences in the capacity to raise resources among the States. According to him, for a given level of public service consumption, the States with lower revenue raising capacity would have to levy higher tax-rate. Alternatively, at uniform level of tax effort (tax rates) in the States with lower capacity the levels of public services would be lower. Buchanan, a staunch supporter of the equity approach, prefers unconditional transfers from people in richer States to those in poorer States to bring about horizontal equity. In Buchanan's view such an arrangement would be justified on efficiency ground also as it would prevent resource migration induced by lower public spending in poorer regions.

Bradford, Malt and Oates (1969) have shown that there can be significant differences in the unit costs of public services, thus, bringing about a divergence between levels of public expenditures and public services. If the cost differences are due to environmental factors which are beyond the control of sub-central governments, this clearly forms another important source of inequity. For example, residents in States with higher unit cost would have to bear higher tax burdens to provide a given level of public services. Le Grand (1975), therefore, argues in favour of transfer schemes to equalise purchasing power-effort ratios across the States. This issue is of particular interest when the viewpoint is on the actual intergovernmental grant programmes adopted in federal countries.

Thus the problem of horizontal fiscal inequity has to be ascribed to two sources of horizontal inequity namely, variations in taxable capacities and differences in the unit cost of providing public services.

There are two possible approaches in establishing horizontal equity in a federal system. The first is the adoption of geographically discriminating income tax rates by the Central government. Alternatively, the central government could seek to equalise the fiscal capacity of all jurisdictions by instituting a programme of unconditional grants to poorer localities. Either of these measures would result in equal treatment of equals.[2]

However, full equalisation suggests the need for unconditional grant programmes, and adjusting for spillovers requires matching grants. Fulfillment of these two goals needs various sets of grant programmes such as equalization of capacities/potentials/incentive schemes.[3]

In brief, there has been a considerable debate about the objectives of federal fiscal transfers. The two major approaches for federal fiscal transfers are equalisation and efficiency. The application of efficiency and equity principles results in four main economic reasons for grants viz. (1) inter-jurisdictional spillovers (2) fiscal gap (3) minimum standards of services and (4) differential net fiscal benefits across States.[4] Fiscal imbalances take place due to unsuitable expenditure and tax assignment, limited or unproductive tax bases accessible to lower levels of government, making tax rates incorrectly high and inter-State tax competition.[5]

The net fiscal benefits[6] vary across States for a number of reasons. Certain States own more valuable natural resources and hence they are accessible to an enlarged revenue base, while some States' relatively high income provide them to raise revenue from the existing bases. Few States suffer due to inherited higher cost disability factors or higher need factors. It is not always true that the undeveloped regions are 'resource poor'. In other words, few of these regions have abundant natural resources but under-utilization/ unutilisation of factors of production on account of unskilled labour, lack of capital and entrepreneurial skill portray the magnitude of the untapped development potential.

Measurement of net fiscal benefits which need a reasonable approximation of costs and benefits of public services provided by various States is essential. This requires advanced measures of differential revenue raising abilities and the costs of provision of public services of the States. Equalisation of net fiscal benefits could then be calculated by adopting a standard of equalisation and establishing the method of financing these transfers.

Fiscal equalisation grants are to remove or minimise the differential net fiscal benefits across the States and enhance the efficiency and equity of a federal system. *This is nothing but the role of redistribution by the federal government to strengthen the economy.* To achieve this, the distributing mechanism requires certain built-in-features as mentioned below.

Criteria for the Design of Inter-Regional Fiscal Arrangements[7]

1. Autonomy: Sub-national governments should have complete independence and flexibility in setting priorities and should not be constrained by the categorical structure of programmes and uncertainty associated with decision making at the centre.

   Tax base sharing, formula based sharing or block grants-is consistent with this objective.

2. Revenue adequacy: Sub-national governments should have adequate revenues to discharge designated responsibilities.
3. Equity: Allocated funds should vary directly with the fiscal need factors and inversely with the taxable capacity of each province.
4. Predictability: The grant mechanism should ensure predictability of Sub-national governments' shares by publishing five year projections of funding availability.
5. Efficiency: The grant design should be neutral with respect to Sub-national government choices of resource allocation to different sectors or different types of activities.
6. Simplicity: The Sub-national government's allocation should be based on objective factors over which individual units have little control. The formula should be easy to comprehend so that "grantsmanship" is not rewarded.
7. Incentive: The proposed design should provide incentives for sound fiscal management and discourage inefficient practices. There should be no specific transfers to finance the deficits of Sub-national governments.
8. Safeguard of grantor's objective: The design should ensure that certain well-defined objectives of the grantor are

properly adhered to by the grant recipients. This is accomplished by proper monitoring, joint progress reviews, and providing technical assistance, or by designing a selective matching transfer program.

The different criteria mentioned above may contradict each other and therefore a grantor may have to assign preferences to various factors in comparing policy alternatives.

The federations which have applied equity theory are Australia, Canada and Germany. The Commonwealth Grants Commission in Australia recommends general revenue sharing to offset deficiencies both in revenue capacity and variations in unit costs. (i.e., two sources of inequity are treated). In Canadian federation, unconditional transfers are recommended to offset deficiency in revenue capacity only. Inter-governmental relations in Germany are more formalised than in many other federations for various reasons. The stress is more on tax sharing laid in the Constitution itself. First, the Constitution explains the method of dividing the fiscal resources among the governments and avoids negotiations and other complications. The most important feature is the 'fraternal' rather than the 'paternal' arrangements of horizontal equalisation.

HORIZONTAL DISTRIBUTION OF CENTRAL RESOURCES: APPROACH OF THE FINANCE COMMISSIONS IN INDIA

Applicability of Equity Principle: Indian Context

The arguments/analysis of Buchanan and Scott applies to the Indian context as well. The reasons are mentioned below.

- Income differences are not reflected in resource endowments. For example, Bihar and Orissa are resource rich low income States.
- Certain factors are beyond a State's control (are called disabilities) and affect the cost at which it can provide services and its capacity for raising resources; and
- Moreover, the Central policy of 'freight pooling' transferred the natural resources from mineral rich low-income States to other parts of the Country where other States have

benefited. In other words, it is resource migration from low-income mineral rich States to high-income States. Recent policy reforms also have widened the gap further.

Functions of the Finance Commission

The Finance Commission, an important provision in the Constitution, acts as regulating machinery in the flow of resources from the Centre to the States. The principles and the bases of tax assignment and tax sharing to the States from the Union government are determined by the Finance Commission constituted by an order of the President under Article 280 of the Indian Constitution. The first Finance Commission was set up in 1951 soon after the enactment of the Constitution. So far twelve Finance Commissions have submitted their reports.

The states have a right to entitlement to their share of tax devolution in whatever manner Finance Commission may determine such a share. Most of the transfers under the Finance Commissions come under unconditional transfers (shareable taxes, grant-in-aid under Article 275 (1)) barring certain specific purpose grants and additional excise duties, which is a tax rental agreement.

The first function is to determine the share of the Centre and the State governments – vertical share. For determining the total amount to be devolved from the center to the states, the Commission would need to have some idea of the financial burden cast on the states by the responsibilities assigned to them under the constitution. Similarly the commission will have to estimate the capacity of the center to devolve the proceeds of certain taxes consistent with its own constitutional obligations. An estimate of the likely revenues and expenditures of the center and the states will, therefore, be necessary to determine these broad parameters.

The Commission's second function is allocation of the share of each state from the total amount devolved.

The Finance Commission's third function is grants-in-aid of revenues under Art.275. Article 275 of the constitution speaks of grants from the union to certain states which are in need of assistance. Such sums shall be paid out of the Consolidated

Fund of India in each year as grants-in-aid of the revenues of state such capital and recurring sums as may be necessary to enable that state to meet the costs of such schemes of development as may be undertaken by the state with the approval of the Government of India for the purpose of promoting the welfare of the Scheduled Tribes in that state or raising the level of administration of the Scheduled Areas therein to that of the administration of the rest of the areas of that state.

Vertical Distribution of Finance Commission Transfers

In order to fulfill the first function, the Finance Commission initially started at the 55% of income tax (shareable taxes that are to be distributed between center and the States). The share of net proceeds of personal income tax has been gradually raised by the later Finance Commissions (Table 1).

Table 1
States' Share in the Net Proceeds of Personal Income Tax & Union Excise Duties (%)

Finance Commission	*Personal Income Tax*	*Coverage*	*Union Excise Duties*	*Number of Dutiable Articles Covered*
I	55	Incl. CT	40	3
II	60	Incl. CT	25	8
III	66.66	Excl. CT	20	35
IV	75	"	20	All
V	75	"	20	"
VI	80	"	20	"
VII	85	"	40	"
VIII	85	"	40+5*	"
IX	85	"	40+5*	"
IX	85	"	45	"
X	77.5	"	40+7.5*	"

C.T = Corporate Income Tax

* While 40% is distributed to all States, the remaining is distributed only to the States with deficit even after distribution of all transfers.

Source: Reports of the Finance Commissions, GOI.

Article 272 of the Indian Constitution makes a permissive provision with regard to sharing of the Union excise duties with the States. Prior to April 1, 1952, the proceeds of this duty were not distributed between the Union and the States. The First Finance Commission broke new ground when it recommended that 40% of the net proceeds of the excise duties on 3 commodities should be allotted to the States.

The Second Commission added five more items to the list of divisible excise duties; while the Third Commission expanded the list to 35 items, the Fourth Commission covered all items and subsequent Commissions followed the same. The expansion of the range of commodities subjected to union excise duties was resorted to as compensation for the reduction in the share of the tax in the divisible pool. The Seventh Finance Commission steeply increased the States' share to 40%. The recent Commissions (the Ninth and the Tenth Commissions) have earmarked certain percentage for those States which have deficits after taking into account their shares from the devolution of all taxes and duties (Table 1).

With the eightieth amendment of the Constitution (80th Amendment) Act, 2000, all the Central taxes are pooled and shared between the Centre and the States. The Eleventh Finance Commission recommended 29.5 per cent of the net proceeds of all sharable central taxes to the states. The Twelfth Finance Commission enhanced the proportion to 30.5 per cent.

Criteria for Horizontal Distribution of Shared Taxes

To fulfill the second function, the First Finance Commission was initially guided by the criteria used by Sir Otto Niemeyer[8] to distribute the net proceeds of income tax shares among the individual States. But the later Commissions started altering the criteria. While doing this alteration, the successive Commissions attempted to bring different elements of equity into the distribution of the divisible pool of income tax and union excise duties. The criteria used by the various Finance Commissions are shown in the Tables 2, 3 and 4.

The Finance Commissions in India are inclined to get convinced by the importance of progressivity instead of

Table 2

Criteria for Horizontal Distribution of Income Tax (%)

Finance Commission	*Popula -tion*	*Contri- bution*	*Per capita Income Inverse*	*Per capita Income Distance*	*Poverty Ratio*	*Index of*	*Area Adjusted*	*Tax Effort*
I	80	20*	-	-	-	-	-	-
II	90	10*	-	-	-	-	-	-
III	80	20*	-	-	-	-	-	-
IV	80	20*	-	-	-	-	-	-
V	90	10#	-	-	-	-	-	-
VI	90	10#	-	-	-	-	-	-
VII	90	10#	-	-	-	-	-	-
VIII	22.5	10#	22.5	45	-	-	-	-
IX	22.5	10#	11.25	45	11.25	-	-	-
IX	22.5	10#	11.25	45	-	11.25@	-	-
X	20	-	-	60	-	5+	5	10

*Collection # Assessment @ Backwardness + Infrastructure.

Note: Under eighth and ninth Commissions, the same formula was used for '90% of income tax' and 'total of union excise duties'. Under tenth Commission same formula was used for both the taxes.

Source: Reports of the Finance Commissions.

Table 3
Criteria for Horizontal Distribution of Union Excise Duties (%)

Finance Commission	*Population*	*Index of*	*Per capita Income Inverse*	*Per capita Income Distance*	*IATP***	*Poverty Ratio sation*	*Revenue Equalited*	*Area Adjus-*	*Tax Effort*
I	100								
II	90								
III	Population major factor. Relative financial weakness of States, Disparity in levels of development, population of SCs & STs etc were also considered.								
IV	80	20*							
V	80	6.66#	13.34@						
VI	75		25						
VII	25			25	25	25			
VIII	25		25	50					
IX	25		50	12.5	12.5				
IX	25	12.5 #	33.5	12.5			16.5 for deficit States		
X	20	5 &	60					5	10

* Relative economic backwardness; @ To States whose per capita income is below the all-States average; # Index of backwardness & Index of infrastructure ; ** = Income Adjusted Total Population.

Source: Reports of the Finance Commissions, GOI.

attempting, as per the theory, to consider how fiscal capacities can be equalized. Every Finance Commission tried to introduce a host of criteria in tax devolution and each Finance Commission tries to do one better than its predecessor by appearing to be more 'progressive'. The preoccupation with progressivity in the context of federal transfers is a little misplaced. Progressivity cannot be an end in itself in deciding the allocation of federal funds among the constituent units in a federation. States with poor revenue base, should be able to get more unless their disability in this regard is offset by cost advantages.

Table 4
Criteria and Weights :Determinants of Inter se Share of the States under the Eleventh (EFC) &Twelfth Finance Commissions (TFC)

Sl. No.	*Criteria*	*EFC Weight (%)*	*TFC Weight (%)*
1.	Population	10.0	25
2.	Income (Distance Method)	62.5	50
3.	Area	7.5	10
4.	Index of Infrastructure	7.5	–
5.	Tax Effort	5.0	7.5
6.	Fiscal Discipline	7.5	7.5

Source: Report of the Eleventh Finance Commission (2000-05), June 2000,GOI, Table 6.2, p. 58.
Report of the Twelfth Finance Commission (2005-2010), Nov 2004,GOI, Table 7.2, p.133.

Thus the second function of the Finance Commission is exclusively on the basis of objective criteria. In the interests of equity and efficiency these criteria may be selected with a view to rewarding fiscal effort, or may take into account the backwardness of a state, or of its needs based on population etc. For none of these purposes a precise financial estimate of receipts and expenditures of each state is made use of.

The shared taxes constituted more than three-fourth of the Finance Commission Transfers (Table 5). Though the proportion was less than 80 per cent under first few Commissions later on its share has increased ranging 81 per cent to 93 per cent. This predominant proportion of the transfers was recommended by the Finance Commissions mainly on the basis of general economic indicators and not fiscal disadvantage of a State. Further, assigning weights to general economic indicators were arbitrary. The changes in the criteria or in the weights assigned to them are based on the discretion/justification as explained by the respective Finance Commissions in their reports. These transfers have not been designed to meet the major objective of unconditional transfers, namely, offsetting fiscal disadvantages of the States though some of the indicators reflect the backwardness factor. Twelfth Commission has followed its predecessors in this aspect.

Grants-in-aid from the Centre

The third function of the Finance Commission, according to article 275, requires the determination of 'the needs' of a state. This needs a careful estimate of the expenditure requirements of a state as well as of its resources. These resources will include its share of central taxes as recommended by the Finance Commission, i.e., one part of the recommendations of the Commission turn out to be a contribution for another part of its exercise.

According to Article 275, the grants are to aid revenues of the States which are held to be in 'need' of assistance. But there is nothing in the wording of the Article 275 which necessitates this clarification. Hence, the definition of 'need' is at the discretion of the Finance Commission.[9] This is an unconditional transfer. Hence, it is this function which demands the Finance Commission to attempt to determine 'the need' of a State for the recommendation of grants-in-aid under Article 275.

The First Finance Commission formulated the principles, which should govern the grants-in-aid to States under Article 275 and suggested that specific grants also could be given for broad purposes of national importance. The scope of grants recommended under this article gradually enlarged and are more specific in nature. They broadly include:

1. Non-plan revenue gap grants – all the Finance Commissions

2. Plan grants – (9th – 1st and 2nd Reports)
3. Up-gradation grants – 1st, 3rd, 7th, 8th, 9th (I) 10th, 11th & 12th).
4. Grants for special problems/State Specific – (8th, 9th & 10th, 11th & 12th).
5. Grants for Margin money for relief - (8th, 9th & 10th, 11th & 12th).
6. Grants for local bodies – (10th 11th & 12th Commissions).

Principles of Grants-in-aid

The principles formulated by the First Finance Commission were:

1. Budgetary needs of the States, subject to adjustments to ensure comparability with others;
2. Tax effort of a State, with due allowances for 'clear cases' of failure of States to maximise tax effort;
3. Consideration of reasonable economy in expenditure to avoid a premium upon extravagance;
4. Special assistance to States in which standards of social services are significantly lower than others;
5. Special disabilities of States; and
6. Broad purposes of national importance.

The five Finance Commissions, which followed the first Finance Commission, broadly endorsed the principles mentioned above as unexceptionable. Though the Seventh Finance Commission suggested another set of principles, they are no different from those set out by the First Commission. The Eighth Commission was in broad agreement with the principles formulated by the Seventh Finance Commission but were of the view that these principles were not intended to be exhaustive or inflexible and new problems would require new approaches.

The Ninth Finance Commission, for the first time, was asked to adopt a 'normative' approach in assessing the receipts and expenditures on the revenue account of the States and the Centre. The Ninth Finance Commission noted that the principles formulated by the First Commission were generally accepted by the later Commissions with modifications here and there, and that grants-in-aid had continued to be made largely on the basis of budgetary needs. The Tenth Commission recommended grants-in-aid to the deficit States equal to the amount of their deficits, as estimated for each of the years during 1995-96 to 1999-2000.[10] The Eleventh Commission viewed that the norms laid down by them together with the principles for the sharing of Central taxes recommended by them are expected to act as an incentive for better fiscal performance.[11] The Twelfth Finance Commission recommended grants-in-aid based on the assessment of needs and developmental concerns of the states.

All the Finance Commissions (barring the Ninth Commission) projected the 'need', based on the trend growth rates of revenue receipts and non-plan revenue expenditure. Even the Ninth Commission, though applied normative approach (cost functions to social and certain other functions), to arrive at the base year, applied the average growth rates to estimate the receipts and expenditure for the forecast period.

Thus the grants are determined on the basis of projected gaps between the non-plan revenue expenditures and the States' own revenues plus post-tax devolution revenues. Grants are given to offset the residuary fiscal disadvantages of the States as quantified by the commissions–a gap filling approach. Hence these transfers are only to few states.

Starting with the First Commission, the practice so far has been that the Finance Commissions awards covered the non-plan revenue deficit, if any, of each State, as assessed by the Commission. All the Finance Commissions (barring the Ninth Commission) have used trend growth rates either with the aid of statistical methods or other methods to forecast the Non Plan Revenue Expenditure (NPRE). But the main point that has to be kept in mind is that these trend growth rates (whether inclusive of inflation or not) will give only the picture of trend growth rate of these NPRE items in the past. It does not give whether the particular expenditure is productive or unproductive. The salary and non-salary classification of these items (as done by the recent Finance Commissions) may highlight the un-productivity of the expenditure to some extent only. The methodology adopted by the recent Finance Commissions to reassess the revenue resources and non-plan revenue expenditure is given in Appendix 1. The Commission on Centre-State Relations, headed by Justice Sarkaria, noted that "a perusal of the reports of the various Finance Commissions shows that practically all the Finance Commissions have had occasion to note that on the receipts side the norms determined by the preceding Finance Commission were seldom reached, particularly in regard to the returns from irrigation and power projects and from the State Road Transport Corporations."[12] Further, the Seventh Finance Commission asserted that they have not found the analysis of non-tax revenues and non-plan revenue expenditure particularly useful.[13]

All this cumbersome exercise to estimate the 'non-plan revenue gap' and recommend grants-in-aid only to those States with this gap even after the transfers of shared taxes and duties had validity only to a certain extent till the Sixth Finance Commission period during which the share of grants in the total Finance Commission transfers were significant in double digit. The relevance of this exercise no more exists as the proportion of gap between the grants to the total transfers under the last two Commissions reached an insignificant level at less than 9 per cent (Table 5).

Aggregate Transfers Recommended by the Finance Commissions

Of the total transfers recommended by the twelve Finance Commissions (Table 5), the shared taxes constituted 74.64% (the Fourth Finance Commission) to 92.93% (the Seventh Commission). This shows the significance of the shared taxes in the total transfers by the Finance Commission.

The non-plan revenue deficit grants ranged between 5.15% (the Seventh Finance Commission) and 24.28% (the Sixth Finance Commission). Of the total grants from the Finance Commission, the non-plan revenue deficit grants were high and the proportion of other grants were only nominal till recently. However, under the Ninth (second report) and the Tenth Finance Commissions, the proportion of other grants were higher than the non-plan revenue deficit grants. Even under twelfth Finance Commission these non-plan grants are lower than the other grants.

Table 5
Transfers Recommended by the Finance Commissions
(Rs.Crores)

Finance Commission	*Shared Taxes*	*Grants*			*Total Transfers*
		Non-plan revenue deficit	*Other Grants*	*Total Grants*	
I	370	34	72	106	476
	(77.73)	(7.14)	(15.13)	(22.27)	(100.00)
II	823	185	46	231	1054
	(78.08)	(17.55)	(4.36)	(21.92)	(100.00)
III	1068	252	35	287	1355
	(78.82)	(18.60)	(2.58)	(21.18)	(100.00)
IV	1330	423	29	452	1782
	(74.64)	(23.74)	(1.63)	(25.36)	(100.00)
V	4642	713	66	779	5421
	(85.63)	(13.15)	(1.22)	(14.37)	(100.00)
VI	8355	2683	10	2693	11048
	(75.62)	(24.28)	(0.09)	(24.38)	(100.00)
VII	21171	1173	437	1610	22781
	(92.93)	(5.15)	(1.92)	(7.07)	(100.00)
VIII	35683	2200	1569	3769	39452
	(90.45)	(5.58)	(3.98)	(9.55)	(100.00)
IX	11785	984	893	1877	13662
	(86.26)	(7.20)	(6.54)	(13.74)	(100.00)
IX	87882	6016	9001	15017	102899
	(85.41)	(5.85)	(8.75)	(14.59)	(100.00)
X	206343	7583	12717	20300	226643
	(91.04)	(3.35)	(5.61)	(8.96)	(100.00)
XI	376318	35359	23228	58587	434905
	(86.53)	(8.13)	(5.34)	(13.47)	(100.00)
XII	613112	56856	85784	142640	755752
	(81.13)	(7.52)	(11.35)	(18.87)	(100.00)

Note: Figures in the parentheses are percentages to total transfers.
Source: Reports of the Finance Commissions.

In short, more than 80 per cent of the total Finance Commission transfers are shared taxes recommended mainly on the basis of general economic indicators such as population, the per capita income and index of backwardness etc giving arbitrarily weights to them without basing on explicit objective of equity principle.

The remaining 20 per cent are grants, which are meant for the residuary fiscal gap of the States estimated by the Commission based on the reassessment of the receipts and non-plan revenue expenditure of the states. However, the methodology adopted by them has had an inherent bias against poorer States. As the projections were made by taking the existing revenues and non-plan revenue expenditures with some minor modifications as bases, the standards of services in the States with lower tax bases could not be enhanced as the budgetary gaps projected on the basis of the existing low levels of services in these States were small[14].

An overwhelming proportion of Finance Commission transfers, shared taxes, are not related to this type of reassessment of receipts and expenditures of the state governments.

Hence the approach of the Finance Commission, though has the equity objective, but is implicit and piecemeal but not objective and explicit. In India, the unconditional transfers are not relied on theoretical base (equity or efficiency) or economic rationale.

The Twelfth Finance Commission mentioned in its report that "In deciding the different criteria for transfers under tax devolution, our approach has been to keep in mind three sets of considerations, viz., needs, cost disabilities and fiscal efficiency." (para 2.22) and also stressed that "our approach to transfers comprising tax devolution and grants is guided by the equalization criterion, determined on the basis of a normative approach" (para 2.52 (ii)). But, in practice, Twelfth Commission followed its predecessors in selecting the indicators and assigning weights to them.

Now the question is about the selection of factors that should form part of a consistent formula. The basic conditions of the formula should be:

(a) The economic rationale of the formula should be to minimise the horizontal fiscal imbalances on the basis of equity principle;

(b) The objective of the distribution - minimisation of the fiscal disadvantages- should be explicit;

(c) As the low-income group States in India are the victims of historical events, Central policies and revenue and cost disadvantages, the transfers based on the equity principle should also be progressive in favour of these low-income States; and

(d) The Formula should be simple. Firm and reliable data should be available for applying the formula.[15]

CONCLUSION

A study of the Finance Commission reports reveals that their main intention of distribution is to reduce vertical as well as horizontal fiscal imbalances. The Finance Commission reassesses the receipts and non-plan revenue expenditure of the state governments–an admirable step. But the review of their methodology in forecasting these estimates remained far from reality.

Regarding horizontal distribution of shareable taxes, the set of criteria adopted by the various Finance Commissions and the basis of weightage given to each of these criteria is arbitrary and at the discretion of the Finance Commission and also independent of Commission's estimated non-plan revenue gap of the States which the Finance Commissions defined as 'need' of a State. The Twelfth Finance Commission, though used the appropriate terminology and concepts in its report, but in essence it followed its predecessors.

The cumbersome exercise of the Finance Commission is to estimate the 'non-plan revenue gap' to recommend grants-in-aid only to those States with this gap even after the transfers of shared taxes and duties lost its validity as the proportion of grants itself is insignificant. But the review of their methodology in forecasting these estimates revealed that on receipts side the norms set by them were seldom reached while the analysis of non-plan revenue expenditure was not found useful.

Here emerges the relevance of equity theory and the application in the horizontal fiscal transfers in the Indian context. This study highlights the missing link between (1) the theory and the practice; (2) measure of need and the criteria selected. The Commission should have adopted a comprehensive measure that would reflect the *triple criteria* (a) as a measure of 'need' of States and (b) as a criterion for the distribution of shared taxes and duties and also grants-in-aid and (c) based on equity principle with a theoretical base.

When there are multiple channels of central financial transfers, concentrating on only statutory transfers is not adequate. Yet one should remember that the larger the role of the Central budgetary transfers in minimizing horizontal fiscal imbalances, the greater will have to be the responsibility of a statutory body - the Finance Commission.

NOTES

1. Hemlata Rao (1981), *Centre-State Financial Relations (Criteria of Federal Transfers and Their Application in India*, Allied Publishers, New Delhi, p. 2.
2 Wallace E. Oates (1972), *Fiscal Federalism*, Harcourt Brace Jovanovich, Inc., Newyork, p. 83-84.
3. For details Richard A. Musgrave (1961), "Approaches to A Fiscal Theory of Political Federalism", in Richard A Musgrave (1986): *Public Finance in a Democratic Society*, Collected Papers Volume II, New York University Press, Washington, p. 9-29.
4. Anwar Shah (1994), *The Reform of Intergovernmental Fiscal Relations in Developing and Emerging Market Economies*, Policy and Research Series No. 23, The World Bank, p. 27-29. See also Anwar Shah and Zia Qureshi (1994): *Intergovernmental Fiscal Relations in Indonesia*, World Bank Discussion Paper.
5. Fear of losing capital, labor and business to other jurisdictions, the regional governments do not fully exploit tax potentials and thus provide lower levels of public services.
6. Net fiscal benefit (NFB) that a resident derives from his/her provincial government budget have been defined as the difference

between the benefits received through provincial expenditure and regulatory activities and taxes (the costs) that he/she pays. It is highly unlikely that all residents of al provinces will have the same NFBs regardless of the province in which they live.

7. Anwar Shah (1994): opp. cited, p. 30.
8. Sir Otto Niemeyer under the scheme of GOI Act, 1935, was appointed to make recommendations on matters which under Sections 138 (income tax) and 140 (excise duties) and 142 (grants-in-aid had to be prescribed or determined by the Order-in-Council, and on certain other ancillary matters. ...the adoption of Niemeyer's recommendations did not occur without protests and was much against the wishes of the provinces and also the Federal government. The Secretary of State for India, Lord Zetland, stated that Sir Otto Niemeyer had achieved 'as equitable a settlement between the various contestants as the case allows'. The Secretary of the State and the GOI regarded Niemeyer's report as in the nature of a quasi-arbitral award and its adoption a *fait accompli*. (BPR Vithal and ML Sastry (2001): *Fiscal Federalism in India*, Oxford University Press, New Delhi, pp. 73-74.
9. Rajkrishna (1978), A Note of Dissent "A More Equitable Distribution of Resources" in the *Report of the Seventh Finance Commission*, p. 117.
10. GOI (1994), *Report of the Tenth Finance Commission (for 1995-2000)*, Para 11-12, p. 51.
11. GOI (2000), *Report of the Eleventh Finance Commission (for 2000-05)*, para 10.5, p. 95.
12. GOI (1988), Report of the Commission on Centre-State Relations, para 10.8.20, p. 284.
13. GOI (1978), Report of the Finance Commission, p. 6.
14. Govinda Rao M. and Tapas K. Sen (1996), *Fiscal Federalism in India: Theory and Practice*, Mc Millan, p. 144.
15. GOI (1984), *Report of the Eighth Finance Commission.* Progressivity in the distribution, simplicity in the formula and reliable data availability to use this formula are stressed by experts before the Commission, para 6.24, p. 50.

REFERENCES

Anwar Shah (1994), *The Reform of Intergovernmental Fiscal Relations in Developing and Emerging Market Economies*, Policy and Research

Series No. 23, The World Bank. See also Anwar Shah and Zia Qureshi (1994): *Intergovernmental Fiscal Relations in Indonesia*,World Bank Discussion Paper.

GOI: Reports of the various Finance Commissions.

GOI (1988), Report of the Commission on Centre-State Relations.

Govinda Rao M. and Tapas K. Sen (1996), *Fiscal Federalism in India: Theory and Practice*, McMillan.

Hemlata Rao (1981), Hemlata Rao (1981), *Centre-State Financial Relations (Criteria of Federal Transfers and Their Application in India*, Allied Publishers, New Delhi.

Rajkrishna (1978), A Note of Dissent "A More Equitable Distribution of Resources" in the *Report of the Seventh Finance Commission.*

Richard A. Musgrave (1961), "Approaches to A Fiscal Theory of Political Federalism", in Richard A Musgrave (1986): *Public Finance in a Democratic Society*, Collected Papers Volume II, New York University Press, Washington.

Vithal B.P.R. and M.L. Sastry (2001), *Fiscal Federalism in India*, Oxford University Press, New Delhi.

Wallace E. Oates (1972), *Fiscal Federalism*, Harcourt Brace Jovanovich, Inc, New York.

APPENDIX - I

Reassessment of States' Own Revenues and Non-plan Revenue Expenditure by the Recent Finance Commissions

Finance	*Assessment of Own Revenues of the State Governments*	*Assessment of Non-plan Revenue Expenditure of the State Government*
Eighth	The Commission used the price elasticities and state domestic product (SDP) deflators to net out the price effect and get the real growth rate which reflects the impact of rise in income. The rates of growth have been fixed after making due adjustments to ensure that a certain minimum effort is assumed on the part of the states which have done well in the past, are not placed in a disadvantageous position.	The real growth rate of non-plan revenue expenditure by breaking it into salary (eliminating DA revision) and non-salary items (eliminating price factor). The Commission perceived that elasticity or revenue with respect to prices would take care of the rise in expenditure on account of the price factor to a certain extent. However, the Commission opted to base the forecast on the assumption of price stability in the economy.
Ninth (Report I)	Taxable capacity was estimated for 14 states using the regression approach with some modifications. To overcome the bias arising from taking 'effort' as residual, cross section observations with time-series is used. Revenue from each of the major taxes was regressed on their tax bases or their proxies to determine the average effective rates. By applying these rates on the bases of relevant taxes in different states, taxable capacity was derived.	Followed the eighth commission.
Ninth (Report II)	Taxable capacity of the states has been estimated by employing the model using pooled time-series & cross section observations. The states were	The functional classification of non-plan revenue expenditure (general, social and economic) was divided into three categories. (1) Regular and

Finance	*Assessment of Own Revenues of the State Governments*	*Assessment of Non-plan Revenue Expenditure of the State Government*
	categorized into high, middle and low-income states based on their per capita net state domestic product. The major taxes included in this methodology were Sales tax, State Excise Duty, Stamp Duty & Registration Fee, Motor Vehicle Tax & Passengers and Goods Tax &Entertainment tax. The significant determinants vary between the groups of states. However major determinants are SDP, its composition, % of urban population, road & railway length per 1000 persons /1000sq. km,inter-state price differences.	recurring for which Cost functions are estimated (2) revenue expenditure on existing stocks (physical and financial) for which engineering norms were adopted. The 3rd category do not fall under these categories The identity of the cost function is $E_i = Q_i * (C_{1i} + C_{2i})$ Assessment of non-plan revenue expenditure of the state government The normative expenditure of a state on general service is: $\bar{E}_i = \bar{Q}_i * (\bar{C}_{1i} + C_{2i})$ and for Social & economic service is: $\bar{E}_i = Q_i * (\bar{C}_{1i} + C_{2i})$ Where $\bar{Q}$ and $\bar{C}$ vectors of all-states average standard of the service and all-states average cost variable within the control of the States. Q and C_{2i} units of service and costs beyond the state control.
Tenth	The buoyancy of individual state taxes has been estimated by regressing tax revenue on nominal SDP using a double log function. By using the buoyancy coefficients and relating	Dis-aggregated the non-plan revenue expenditure into certain broad heads and applied estimated trend growth rates and other normative measures. They have provided a modest growth rate of 1.5% per

Contd....

Finance	*Assessment of Own Revenues of the State Governments*	*Assessment of Non-plan Revenue Expenditure of the State Government*
	these with the assumed rate of growth of SDP future tax yields were projected.	annum over and above the increase accounted for by prices. For certain priority sectors like elementary education and health they have provided a relatively faster growth rate of 2.5%.
Eleventh	For assessment of: 1. Tax revenue: trend growth rate 2. For non-tax revenue one of these methods whichever least was followed: (a) Trend growth rate method (b) Budget estimates of the base year (c) Average realization of three preceding years.	For assessment of the expenditure one of these methods whichever least was followed: (a) Trend growth rate method (b) Budget estimates of the base year (c) Average realization of three preceding years Expenditure was classified into salary and non-salary and also assigned growth rate for general (7%), social (15%)and economic services (11%) inclusive of 5% inflation.
Twelfth	Trend growth rate of own tax revenue of each state is estimated and applied on the latest year to arrive at the trend growth rate based base year. Prescriptive buoyancy levels are used for projection of tax revenue for the Commission's recommendation period.	The adjusted non-plan revenue expenditure of each state has been analysed under four broad categories as per functional classification. Separate projections are made for the important items such as interest payments, education health, maintenance of building s, irrigation etc specific norms are applied for rest of the heads of expenditure. In short, nine composite growth rates were worked out, three for each of the three services. For each service, the appropriate composite growth rate for a given state was applied on its base year estimates to generate the forecast levels.

Source: Reports of the Finance Commissions, Government of India.

5

FINANCE COMMISSION AWARDS HORIZONTAL EQUITY Vs. REGIONAL DISPARITY

Jagannath Lenka & Minati Mallick

INTRODUCTION

The intergovernmental transfers, their rationale, relative merits and demerits have gained wide currency in the federalism literature and are well known. The reasons commonly advocated in the theory of Public Finance so as to justify revenue transfer from the centre to the federal units may be grouped into three categories. First, What is common in federations is that transfers are needed to redress the vertical imbalance or the fiscal gap that stems from the asymmetric organisation of functions and tax powers among different jurisdictions. Second, given that sub-national activities can generate positive externalities that are not taken into account by the jurisdictions where they originate, public goods may be under produced. Specific purpose or matching grants are required to be provided by the central government so that goods in question are produced to the socially optimal level. Finally, transfers from the centre are mandated to ensure fiscal equalisation among the states in the interest of both equity and efficiency.

The present paper is a modest attempt to examine the last category of transfers that address the horizontal imbalance- 'the equalisation grants' which constitute the bulk of the transfers in many federations including India. Such transfers are supposed to be more controversial as they involve the perceived conflict between equity and efficiency and *inter se* sharing instead of being progressive often becomes more regressive and accentuates regional disparities. The paper is organised into four sections. Section-II provides materials and methodology of analysis. Results and Discussions are presented in Sec-III. In the concluding Section we summarise the findings and suggest policy implications.

DATABASE AND METHODOLOGY

The present study makes use of the secondary data collected mostly from the reports of the Finance Commissions, Economic Survey, Budgets and research papers of the scholars. Comparable data for 14 major states are considered. Simple statistical devices like percentages, ratios and proportions are used for comparative analysis and interpretation of the results.

RESULTS AND DISCUSSION

This section is divided into three parts. The first part deals with the criteria, their weightages and the formula for horizontal devolution of resources from the centre to the states. The progressiveness of devolution formula is examined in the second part. The last part discusses issues relating to regional disparities.

(Criteria, Weightage and the Formula

A major aspect of the awards of the Finance Commissions relates to the recommendations determining the inter-se allocation of the aggregate share of the states in the divisible pool. Usually this is done with the help of a formula that has two basic components such as the criteria used and the weights assigned to these criteria. The Twelfth Finance Commission (TFC) used five criteria viz- population, income distance area, tax effort and fiscal discipline in determining the shares of the states. The corresponding weights to these criteria are shown in Table 1. The overall formula used by the TFC may be stated as

$$Si = Z\,[(0.25)(Pi/\Sigma Pi) + (0.5)(Di/\Sigma Di) + (0.1)(Adj\,Ai/\Sigma Ai) + (0.075)(Ti/\Sigma Ti) + (0.075)(FSR)].$$

where Si denotes the share of state 'i' in Z that denotes the amount of tax to be shared among the states. Pi denotes the population (1971) of state 'i'. The income distance criterion (Di) is derived as (Y_{RBK}—Yi) Pi where Yi relates to per capita GSDP (1999-2000 to 2001-02). Y_{RBK} is the representative benchmark from which distances are derived and which is determined by the weighted averages of per capita GSDP of three states such as Punjab, Maharashtra and Goa. The distance of these three states is derived as a fraction of the distance of Haryana from the representative benchmark. Ai is the area of the state 'i' and the criteria is so adjusted to ensure that no state got a share of less than 2 per cent at the lower end. The tax effort criteria (Ti) is derived from the ratio of states own tax revenue to comparable GSDP (three years average from 1999-2000 to 2001-02) weighted by the square root of the inverse of per capita GSDP relative to all states tax- GSDP ratio. FSR denotes Fiscal Self Reliance criterion derived as improvement in the ratio of own revenue receipts of a state to its total revenue expenditure related to a similar ratio for all states. The base period is the average for the period from 1993-94 to 1995-96 and the reference period is from 2000-01 to 2002-03.

Table 1
Criteria and Weights for Tax Sharing Among States

%	*EFC*	*TFC*	*Change*
Population	10.0	25.0	+15.0
Income distance	62.5	50.0	- 12.5
Area	7.5	10.0	+2.5
Taxt effort	5.0	7.5	+2.5
Fiscal discipline	7.5	7.5	0.0
Infrastructure	7.5	-	-7.5
Total	100	100	

Source: TFC Report.

TFC has attempted to evolve a formula that balances equity with fiscal efficiency. Population criterion is the need for public goods and services within the state, the income distance reflects differentials in revenue capacity while the area criterion measures cost disability of the regions. The remaining two criteria tax effort and fiscal self-reliance are indications of fiscal efficiency. Table 1 shows the criteria and the corresponding weights assigned to these criteria for determining *inter se* determination of shares of the states.

TFC has increased the weightage of population to 25 but reduced the weightage of per capita income distance to 50.0 as against 10 and 62.5 assigned by the Eleventh Finance Commission (EFC) respectively. The weightage assigned to tax effort has marginally increased to 7.5 but fiscal self-reliance weightage bas been retained by TFC. However, the infrastructure criterion has been dropped by TFC on the ground that it is correlated with income distance criterion and can be better used in an ordinal way.

How Progressive is the Devolution Formula ?

An important issue relating to the inter se distribution of tax revenue is the progressiveness of the formula utilised for determining the shares of the states. A progressive formula based on equity considerations awards more resources to the poorer states enabling them to overcome the differential in revenue capacity and better meet the needs for public goods and services. The formula introduced by the TFC do not appear to adversely affect the degree of progressiveness associated with EFC and in fact seem to have marginally improved in terms of gain to low-income states. A close examination reveals that TFC award has redistributed away from the middle income states to both low and high income states as compared to EFC awards. Moreover, if TFC would have persisted with the formula of EFC that would have clearly benefited the low income states primarily at the expense of the high income states. Thus, retention of EFC formula would have been better and more progressive compared to that of TFC.

Regional Disparities

The gain or loss to individual states due to change in the formula by TFC may be observed from table 2. It is seen that, there has been diversion of shares from the low income states to middle and high income states for which the former category states have incurred loss whereas the latter category states have gained. The gains in share to the high income states stand in the order of 1.55 for Maharashtra, 0.55 for Gujarat, 0.41 for Punjab and 0.32 for Haryana. All middle-income states except West Bengal are found to have gained from the change. On the other hand, all the low income states have lost their shares and the loss is found to be highest for the poorest state Bihar. This has accentuated the magnitude of regional disparity existing between richer and poorer states.

Table 2
Gain/Loss in Shares of States Due to Change in Formula Between the EFC and TFC Awards

States	*EFC Share*	*TFC Share*	*EFC in TFC*	*Gain (+)/ Loss (-)*
(1)	(2)	(3)	(4)	(5) = (4-3)
High Income States	9.54	10.95	8.12	2.83
Maharashtra	4.63	5.00	3.45	1.55
Gujarat	2.82	3.57	3.02	0.55
Panjab	1.15	1.30	0.89	0.41
Haryana	0.94	1.08	0.76	0.32
Middle Income States	29.19	26.86	24.99	1.87
Tamil Nadu	5.83	5.31	4.54	0.77
Karnataka	4.93	4.46	4.04	0.42
Kerala	3.06	2.67	2.26	0.41
Andhra Pradesh	7.70	7.36	7.04	0.32
West Bengal	8.12	7.06	7.11	- 0.05
Low Income States	53.77	54.73	59.41	- 4.68
Rajasthan	5.47	5.61	5.67	- 0.06
Madhya Pradesh	8.84	9.37	9.76	- 0.39
Orissa	5.06	5.16	5.57	- 0.41
Uttar Pradesh	19.80	20.20	22.09	- 1.89
Bihar	14.60	14.39	16.32	-1 .93

Note: Undivided MP, UP and Bihar are taken for analysis.
Source: Computed from FC reports.

CONCLUSION

In the light of the above discussion it may be concluded that the TFC has paid less attention to the issues relating to equity.

Equity considerations necessitate greater utilisation of criteria that takes care of the variations in the level of regional development. A progressive formula based on equity considerations awards more resources to the poorer states, which would enable them to overcome at least partly the differential in fiscal capacity and better meet the needs for public goods.

The TFC no doubt started with an objective of a more egalitarian distribution of resources across the states that is contained in para 2.51 of TFC report that 'Growing disparities in fiscal capacities and levels of services require larger and more progressive transfers'. But contrary to the expectations, the devolution of resources has become less progressive due to a change in the sharing formula that defeats the very objective of the Commission. It is seen that the four biggest gainers from the TFC on the transfer front are the richest states: Maharashtra, Gujarat, Punjab and Haryana. The states that are adversely affected are the low income states: UP, MP, Orissa, Bihar and Rajasthan. It is to be noted that there is an apparent discrepancy between what the TFC set out to do and what it actually did.

The question that may be raised is that if the share of the poorer states in central revenue is enlarged as much as normative approach would require and that of richer states reduced will that not be discriminatory against the better performing states and thus be detrimental to the growth of the economy? While the argument looks persuasive, it overlooks the possibility that improvements in the regions that are lagging behind may unleash the growth potential of the country. Keeping these regions poor also may not be in the larger interest of the nation or even the best interest of the states that are already advanced. It would of course not be reasonable to expect all regions to attain the same level of development irrespective of their endowment. However, equalising the fiscal level is necessary to prevent migration lured by better living conditions in the richer states and also as a matter of 'Categorical Equity' as Musgrave (1999) insists. The better off states should not complain the flow of larger central funds to the poorer states. The task of fiscal transfers is therefore to provide a level playing field. What is required is not giving less to the poor because they are poor but to see that they come up by using the transfers properly.

REFERENCES

Bagchi, A. (2002), "Equalisation as Goal of Centre-state Transfers"; *EPW* July 6.

Bagchi, A. and Chakraborty, P. (2003), "Towards a Rational System of Centre-State Revenue Transfers in India: An Exploration", Conference on Issues before the Twelfth Finance Commission, New Delhi, September.

Bird, Richaard M. and Smart, M. (2002), "Intergovernmental Fiscal Transers: International Lessons for Developing Countries", *World Development* 30 (6).

Boadway, Robin (1997), "The Economics of Equalisation: An Overview", in Robin Boadway and Paul Hobson (eds) *Equalisation: Its Contribution to Canada's Economics and Fiscal Progress.* John Deutsch Institute, Queen University, Canada, Kingston, Ontario.

Chakraborty, P. (2003),"Unequal Fiscal Capacities Across Indian states: How Corrective the Fiscal Transfer Mechanism, Paper presented at the World Institute of Development Economic Research, United Nations, University Conference on Spatial Inequality in Asia, Tokyo.

Chaubey, P.K. (2003), *Fiscal Federalism in India,* Deep & Deep Publications, New Delhi.

Courchene, T. (1998), "Renegotiating Equalisation: National Polity, Federal state, International Economy", C.D. Howe Institute, Toronto.

Dholakia, Ravindra H. (2003), "Measurement Issue in Comparing Fiscal Performance of States", *EPW*, March, 8 pp. 991-94.

Godbole, Madhav (2001), "Finance Commissions in a cul-de-sac", *EPW* 36(I), pp. 29-34.

Greaul, Bhajan S. (1999), "Federalism and Fiscal Equalisatin : Should India Follow the Australian Path?", in Ian Copland and John Rickard (eds) *Federalism, Comparative Perspectives from India and Australia*, Monohar, New Delhi 244-68.

Hower, Stephen and Prasad, M. (2005), "Reforms to the India's Federal Transfer and Government Regime Proposed by the Twelfth

Finance Commission: What will they mean for the States". Presented in the seminar on Recommendations of the Twelfth Finance Commission and their implication for the states, 6-7 May 2005, Giri Institute of Development studies, Lucknow.

Khemani, Stuti (2003), "Partisan Politics and Intergovernmental Transfers in India", Policy Research Working Paper 3016, The World Bank.

Kumar, T. Ravi (2005), "Tax Devolution and Regional Disparities", *EPW*, Vol. XL, No. 20, May-14-20, pp. 2020-2022.

Kumar, T. Ravi (2001), "Regional Development Criteria and Horizontal Devolution under the Finance Commission Awards", *EPW*, Vol. 36 (50), Dec. 15-21, pp. 4671-75.

Lenka, J. (2003), 'Federal Transfers to states: Searching Actual weight to Devolution Criteria in P.K.Choubey (ed) *Fiscal Federalism in India*, Deep & Deep Publications, New Delhi.

Martinez-Vazguez; Jorge and Boex, J. (2002), "The Design of Equalisation Grants: Theory and Application", World Bank Institute, Washington DC. The World Bank.

Musgrave, R.A. (1999), "Fiscal Federalism" in John M. Buchanan and R.A. Musgrave, 155-175, *Public Finance and Public Choice Two Contrasting Versions of the states*, Mass, USA MIT Press.

Oates Wallace (1999), "An Essay on Fiscal Federalism", *Journal of Economic Literature* ,Vol. XXXVII, pp. 1120-49.

Petchi, Jeffery, Perry, Shapiro and Cliff, Walsh (1997), "Transfers in Federal System: A Critical Survey" in Ronald C. Fisher (ed.), *Intergovernmental Fiscal Relations*, Mass. USA. Kluwer.

Reports of the 11th and 12th Finance Commission

Rangarajan C. (2005), "A Synoptic view of the Twelfth Finance Commission's Recommendations". Inaugural Address, at the 16th Biannual Conference of the state Finance Secretaries, Reserve Bank of India Mumbai on April, 8, 2005.

Rao, M. Govinda (1997),"'Invisible Transfers in Indian Federalism" *Public Finance/ Finances publique*, 3-4 (52), pp. 429-448.

Rao, M. Govinda and Sen,T.K. (1996), *Fiscal Federalism in India: Theory and practice*, Macmillan, New Delhi.

Rao, M.G. and Singh, N. (2002), "Fiscal Transfer in a Developing Economy: The Case of India" Paper presented at a Seminar in Birmingham.

Raskhit, Mihir (2000), "On Correcting Fiscal Imbalance in the Indian Economy: Some Perspectives", *Money and Finance* July-Sept. 2000, pp. 19-58.

Romanik, Clare. et.al. (1999), "Romania: Winners and Losers: The Impact of Refrom of Intergovernmental Transfers", Urban Institute, Washington DC.

Sen T.K.and Trebesch, C. (2004), "The Use of Socio Economic Criteria for Intergovernmental Transfers: The Case of India", Working Paper 10, NIPFP, New Delhi.

Shaw, Anwar (1996), "A Fiscal Needs Approach to Equalisation", *Canadian Public policy*, Vol. XXII.

Srivastavá, D.K. (2003), "Intergovernmental Fiscal Transfers in Asia: Current Practice and Challenge for the Future", Manila, Asian Development Bank, pp. 83-137.

World Bank (2004), *State Fiscal Reforms in India : Progress and Prospects* Macmillan.

6

STATE LEVEL FISCAL REFORMS AND THE RECOMMENDATIONS OF THE TWELFTH FINANCE COMMISSION—A NOTE

A.C.K. Nambiar

INTRODUCTION

The Indian federation is not only characterized by profound economic imbalance among the constituent states but also diversity of all kinds. Finance Commission is the key pillar in the Indian federal structure to bridge the economic imbalances among the states. As envisaged in the Constitution the Finance Commission has to help to redress the twin economic imbalances–vertical and horizontal-that India faces. Over the years this task of the Commission is getting more and more complex. One significant development is the Constitution 73rd and 74th amendments, which required addressing the financial position of local governments. Another sphere where the Finance Commission has to apply its mind is how to redeem the deteriorating financial health of the states. Here there is a strong body of opinion that to a certain extent this is the creation of the finance commissions that the scheme of providing grants in aid under Article 275 for states to meet the non-plan revenue gap has led to financial profligacy on the part of the states. It is also a fact that the finance commissions were pre occupied with the equity objective and disregarded the efficiency of states in terms of revenue mobilization and its utilization in its transfer schemes. In fact it has generally been agreed that a system of fiscal transfers should satisfy the criteria of adequacy, autonomy, economic efficiency, fiscal discipline and equity. Now a days the reform process too has put further pressure for the proper management of the finances of the states. In the liberalized era it is the private sector investment that determines the development prospects of states. One of the crucial determinants of private sector investment is infrastructure availability. In infrastructure provision the states have big responsibility. Precisely the states have to find more resources for developing the infrastructure by proper management of their finances. Starting from mid 1980's there was deterioration in the finances of the states and the question of containing the deficit for strengthening the finances of the states and macro economic stability has attracted widest attention. Thus the finance commissions are now a days entrusted with the task of recommending "plan by which the governments, collectively and severally may bring about restructuring of public finances restoring budgetary balance, achieving macro economic stability and debt reduction along with equitable growth"(Rao and Jena 2005:3409). To start with the Tenth Finance Commission first emphasized the importance of maintaining fiscal balance by the states and subsequently for the first time in the history of finance commissions in India an item of fiscal restructuring explicitly appeared in the terms of reference of the eleventh finance commission. Accordingly the commission has evolved a fiscal reform incentive scheme. This was more articulated in the terms of reference of the twelfth finance commission as Item 4 explicitly related to "restructuring of public finances of states and center to restore the budgetary balance and maintain macro economic stability". The commission has also broken new grounds in several key areas in its recommendations. Its proposal for restructuring of the finances of the center and states, new borrowing regimes for states and debt relief measures are notable ones. Thus schemes for fiscal correction have come to stay in the transfer schemes of the Finance Commissions in India. Specifically tax effort and fiscal discipline has been given weightage in the resource sharing formulae suggested by the Commissions for the horizontal sharing of resources besides other incentive schemes.

While the eleventh finance commission gave 12.5 per cent weightage this has been raised to 15 per cent by the twelfth finance commission in the distribution scheme. So also the debt reduction strategy of the commission is linked to fiscal discipline. To administer such an efficient transfer system there is the need for evolving sound criteria for the monitoring of the fiscal discipline of the states. Here skepticisms have been expressed on the soundness of the criteria followed by the finance commissions (Archana 2005). In this context this paper while taking note of the criteria followed by the finance commissions makes an attempt to evolve an alternative criteria to monitor the finances of the states. So also the paper after taking note of the debt reduction strategy examines how far the scheme is beneficial to the debt prone states. The reference period of the study is the ten-year period starting from 1993-94, as actual budgetary data is available upto 2002-03. We consider the case of 14 major states of India. The data is drawn from the Reserve bank of India publications on the finances of states.

MEASURES OF FISCAL DISCIPLINE

As part of the terms of reference it was the eleventh finance commission that evolved a measure of fiscal discipline and that was Fiscal Self Reliance and Improvement Index (FSRII). In the distribution formulae 7.5 per cent weight was also given by the Commission. FSRII is constructed by relating own revenue receipts (RR) to own revenue expenditure (REX). So also the EFC came out with a scheme called Fiscal Reform Facility and this is based on one single indicator Revenue deficit/Revenue receipt (RD/RR). There are a number of limitations in adopting a single indicator and hence the need for a composite index is well articulated in the literature on federal finance. Resource mobilisation effort and its utilization pattern are important in assessing the fiscal prudence of states. Here we construct a composite index considering the resource mobilization effort, resource utilization pattern and the problem of deficit. For the purpose 3 separate indexes are constructed such as revenue effort index, expenditure index and deficit index. These three indexes are combined to derive an overall index of fiscal performance. Each of these three indexes is worked out with reference to few ratios as outlined below.

Revenue Effort Index: The index attempts to measure to what extent a state makes effort in mobilizing resources on its own and strives to be self sufficient. This is measured with reference to two ratios such as:

1. Own revenue/revenue expenditure ratio- higher the ratio higher the self-sufficiency.
2. Own revenue/Gross State Domestic Product (GSDP) ratio– the ratio measures the revenue effort of the state and higher the ratio higher the revenue effort.

Expenditure index: Prudential fiscal practice requires that the available resources have to be utilized for productive and development purposes. This is examined with reference to four ratios.

1. Plan expenditure/total expenditure
2. Development expenditure/total expenditure
3. Capital expenditure/total expenditure
4. Non plan non development expenditure/total expenditure

The plan, capital and development expenditure are more productive in nature and hence higher the ratio better the fiscal management. Where as the fourth ratio is non developmental in nature and hence lower the ratio better the management of finance. Deficit index- Sound fiscal policy requires that except for economic stablilisation purpose deficit budget policy should no be followed. Even if budget deficit is incurred the deficit finance has to be used for productive purposes and has to be kept within safe limits. This is examined with reference to two ratios:

1. Fiscal deficit/GSDP-lower the ratio better the fiscal discipline
2. Revenue deficit/fiscal deficit-prudent financial practices requires that borrowed funds should not be used for current expenditure and hence lower the ratio better the fiscal discipline.

For working out the index we have used the methodology developed by Morris and MCAlpin (1982). Accordingly we first identified the worst and best values of each indicator during the period. We defined the best and worst values in such a way that all the indexes became unidirectional and could be horizontally combined to form the FPI.

Before looking into the comparative fiscal performance of states based on the indexes let us consider the revenue effort, expenditure pattern and the deficits of the states.

REVENUE EFFORT OF STATES

To know the revenue effort we consider the ratio of own revenue/ revenue expenditure and own revenue/NSDP ratios. The same is shown in Table 1. In considering the own revenue we have excluded from the revenue expenditure the states expenditure on lottery and in revenue only net revenue from lottery i.e. revenue minus expenditure on lottery was only considered. So also in considering the total expenditure and total revenue, expenditure on lottery is excluded. As can be seen from the table among the states the sufficiency ratio varied from the lowest 33.4 per cent of Bihar to 73.4 per cent of Maharashtra. Poorer states Orissa, Bihar Rajasthan and UP are having big shortages as they were not able to meet even 50 per cent of their revenue expenditure out of their own revenue. Most paradoxically the better off West Bengal too belonged to this category as it own revenue constituted only 40.2 per cent of its revenue expenditure and was considerably lower than Rajasthan. Richer states were able to meet more than 65 per cent of their revenue expenditure out of their own revenue and Karnataka placed in the middle-income category is placed in this respect in the group of richer states. Coming to the revenue mobilization effort the best effort was made by Karnataka (10.4 per cent) and the least effort was by West Bengal (5.3 per cent). Here again the richer states made best effort and the performance poor states were less impressive. The middle-income state of Kerala also made substantial effort at resource mobilization. On the whole it emerges that revenue effort of richer states were more and that they were more self-sufficient compared to poor states with some notable exceptions.

Table 1
Revenue Effort of States

State	*Sufficiency ratio*	*Revenue GSDP ratio*
Andhra Pradesh	58.9	8.8
Bihar	33.4	6.3
Gujarat	69.2	10.1
Haryana	72.9	9.6
Karnataka	67.4	10.4
Kerala	58.5	9.5
MP	53.1	8.2
Maharashtra	73.4	9.1
Orissa	34.5	6.9
Punjab	64.0	9.7
Rajasthan	49.4	8.2
Tamil Nadu	65.3	9.8
Uttar Pradesh	39.9	6.3
West Bengal	40.2	5.3

EXPENDITURE PATTERN OF STATES

The pattern of expenditure is shown in Table 2. When we consider the plan expenditure as can be observed from the table the size of plan expenditure varied from the lowest 17.1 per cent of Punjab to the highest 30.1 per cent of Karnataka. Orissa (30 per cent) followed by Andhra Pradesh (28.5 per cent) and Madhya Pradesh (28.1 per cent) maintained higher plan outlay. Whereas the allocation pattern of Tamil Nadu (20 per cent), Uttar Pradesh (21.1 per cent), Bihar (20.3 per cent) Maharashtra and Gujarat (21.8 per cent) appears as less impressive. Thus most of the richer states were not able to allocate more resources to plan. Coming to development expenditure the share varied from the lowest 49.3 per cent of Punjab to the highest 68 per cent of Gujarat. On this front the allocation of Gujarat (68 per cent), Haryana (66.2 per cent) and Karnataka (65.4 per cent) was better. Compared to better off states like West Bengal and Kerala poor states Rajasthan and Madhya Pradesh maintained higher outlay for development. The capital expenditure also varied from the lowest 12.9 per cent of Tamil Nadu to the highest

20.9 per cent of Andhra Pradesh. Performance of Rajasthan, Orissa, Uttar Pradesh, Punjab, Gujarat and Haryana was better. At the same time besides Tamil Nadu the performance of Kerala, Bihar and Madhya Pradesh was poor. Many developed states have not been able to maintain higher capital outlay.

Table 2
Pattern of Expenditure

(% of total expenditure)

State	*Development expenditure*	*Plan expenditure*	*Capital expenditure*	*Non-plan non-development revenue Expenditure*
Andhra Pradesh	66.0	28.5	20.9	27.0
Bihar	54.7	20.3	14.3	35.3
Gujarat	68.0	21.8	18.1	25.4
Haryana	66.2	24.6	18.2	27.6
Karnataka	65.4	30.1	17.2	27.2
Kerala	58.6	24.3	13.6	35.3
MP	61.5	28.1	14.5	27.5
Maharashtra	62.0	21.8	17.2	31.1
Orissa	59.0	30.0	19.5	31.9
Punjab	49.3	17.1	18.8	40.0
Rajasthan	62.7	27.1	20.8	30.7
Tamil Nadu	61.0	20.0	12.9	29.5
Uttar Pradesh	51.4	21.1	18.5	35.8
West Bengal	57.1	22.1	16.8	34.6

Coming to the non-plan non-development expenditure the share is widely varying as the share varied from the highest share of 40 per cent incurred by Punjab to the lowest 25.4 per cent of Gujarat. Bihar, Uttar Pradesh, West Bengal and Kerala spent nearly 35 per cent of total expenditure for non-plan non-development expenditure. It was relatively low in the case of Andhra Pradesh, Madhya Pradesh, Haryana and Karnataka. The expenditure pattern bears no relation to the level of development as some of the developed and less developed states incurred high level of non-plan non-development expenditure.

DEFICIT PROBLEM OF STATES

The deficit ratios are given in Table 3. As can be observed from the table gross fiscal deficit (GFD) as per centage of gross state domestic product (GSDP) ranged from the lowest 3 per cent of Tamil Nadu to the highest 6.9 per cent of Orissa. Deficit problem was more acute in the case of West Bengal, Rajasthan, Punjab and Uttar Pradesh as the ratio was more than 5. The problem was moderate in the case of Madhya Pradesh, Maharashtra, Haryana and Karnataka as the ratio was less than 4. Many states used debt finance for meeting current expenditure and to this category belonged Punjab (65.5 per cent), West Bengal (63.8 per cent), Kerala (58.6 per cent), Orissa (56.2 per cent), Uttar Pradesh (56.2 per cent) and Tamil Nadu (56.4 per cent). Karnataka spent less (29.7 per cent) and this was followed by Gujarat (37.6 per cent), Andhra Pradesh (39.6 per cent) and Maharashtra (40 per cent).

Table 3
Deficit Ratios

State	*Rev.deficit/fiscal deficit*	*GFD\GSDP*
Andhra Pradesh	39.6	3.9
Bihar	49.5	4.7
Gujarat	37.6	4.0
Haryana	45.7	3.4
Karnataka	29.7	3.6
Kerala	58.6	4.8
MP	49.8	3.1
Maharashtra	40.0	3.4
Orissa	56.2	6.9
Punjab	65.5	5.3
Rajasthan	44.7	5.5
Tamil Nadu	56.4	3.0
Uttar Pradesh	56.2	5.1
West Bengal	63.8	5.5

FISCAL PERFORMANCE OF STATES-A COMPARISON

Based on the above ratios let us consider the performance of the states on the fiscal front considering the ten-year period.

Three indexes and a composite index were worked out and the same is shown in Table 4. Effort index was high in the state of Karnataka, Haryana, Gujarat, Maharashtra and Tamil Nadu. It was low in the case of West Bengal, Bihar followed by Uttar Pradesh, Orissa and Rajasthan. Thus clearly the poor states were less self sufficient in finance and their revenue effort is low. Quite paradoxically the more developed West Bengal also belonged to this category. In expenditure index Andhra Pradesh ranked first followed by Karnataka, Rajasthan, Haryana and Gujarat in order. The richest state Punjab recorded worst performance followed by poorest states of Bihar and Uttar Pradesh. Performance of Kerala and Tamil Nadu was also poor. Deficit problem was least in the case of Karnataka followed by Maharashtra, Gujarat, Andhra Pradesh and Haryana. The problem was severe in the case of Orissa, Punjab, West Bengal, Uttar Pradesh and Kerala. When considered the composite index it can be seen that Karnataka ranked first in fiscal performance followed by Andhra Pradesh, Gujarat, Haryana and Maharashtra in order. West Bengal and Bihar were the worst performers followed by Uttar Pradesh, Punjab, Orissa and Kerala.

Table 4
Fiscal Performance Indexes

State	Effort index	Exp. index	Deficit index	Composite index
Andhra Pradesh	67 (7)	92 (1)	76 (3)	81 (2)
Bihar	10 (11)	26 (12)	51 (7)	28 (12)
Gujarat	92 (2)	75 (4)	76 (3)	80 (3)
Haryana	92 (2)	75 (4)	73 (4)	78 (4)
Karnataka	93 (1)	82 (2)	93 (1)	87 (1)
Kerala	73 (6)	37 (10)	37 (9)	46 (8)
MP	53 (8)	64 (6)	71 (5)	63 (6)
Maharashtra	88 (3)	55 (7)	81 (2)	69 (5)
Orissa	18 (10)	73 (5)	13 (12)	44 (9)
Punjab	82 (5)	19 (13)	21 (11)	35 (10)
Rajasthan	49 (9)	78 (3)	47 (8)	63 (6)
Tamil Nadu	84 (4)	39 (9)	63 (6)	56 (7)
Uttar Pradesh	18 (10)	36 (11)	36 (10)	31 (11)
West Bengal	9 (13)	42 (8)	21 (11)	28 (12)

(Figures in parentheses indicates the rank of the state)

Now a comparison can be made of the performance of states based on the composite index and the FSRII of the finance commission. FSRII was worked out with reference to 1993-97 and 1998-03 periods. In respect of the composite index the change in the composite index for the same two sub periods was considered and states were ranked. The ranks of the sates are shown in Table 5. When the ranks of the states for the whole ten year period is compared with the change in the rank of states during the two sub periods it can be seen that there are notable variations. In terms of change in the composite index Karnataka which ranked first as per the index worked out for the whole 10 year period now gets pushed down to 8th rank and Bihar which ranked low now emerges as 3rd. UP which ranked 11th for the whole period now emerged as the first. At the same time AP and Haryana made consistent performance as per the two indexes. Now when we compare the FSRII rank of states and the rank as per the composite index change it is interesting to note that while there is close correspondence in the ranks of a number of states there are notable divergences too. Thus while the ranks of Orissa, Kerala and West Bengal were the same in the case of AP, Karnataka, MP, and UP the ranks differed by a very low margin. Among them while according to composite index AP, Karnataka, and MP ranked lower than FSRII UP got ranked higher. The most notable divergences were in the case of Gujarat, Maharashtra, Rajasthan and Tamil Nadu. While Gujarat ranked high in accordance with the composite index (6th against 11th) Maharashtra, Rajasthan and Tamil Nadu ranked considerably lower. As to the question of best indicator of fiscal performance a few questions can now be posed. Is the fiscal performance of Gujarat lower than that of Maharashtra? Is the performance of Rajasthan better than Gujarat and that of Tamil Nadu better than Karnataka. Take the case of Gujarat and Maharashtra. As per FSRII Gujarat got ranked 11th and as per the composite index change 6th. On the other hand as per FSRII Maharashtra got ranked 6th and as per composite index change 12th. It has to be noted that during the 1997-03 period Gujarat on an average is able to allocate more for developmental purposes and its non-plan non-development

Table 5
FSRII and Composite Index Ranks of States

State	*FSRII rank*	*Composite index rank*
Andhra Pradesh	1	2
Bihar	5	3
Gujarat	11	6
Haryana	2	4
Karnataka	7	8
Kerala	10	10
MP	4	5
Maharashtra	6	12
Orissa	5	5
Punjab	9	7
Rajasthan	8	11
Tamil Nadu	3	9
Uttar Pradesh	2	1
West Bengal	12	13

expenditure was considerably lower than Maharashtra. Revenue effort is also high though deficit indicators are little unfavourable. Gujarat is less developed than Maharashtra when considered the per capita GSDP. Looked form these perspectives performance of Gujarat was better and this is reflected in the composite index. Now compare Rajasthan with Gujarat. Gujarat is ranked lower than Rajasthan as per the FSRII and higher as per the composite index change. It can be seen that plan and capital outlays of both the states are comparable. Development outlay is high in Gujarat and its non-plan non-development expenditure very low. Revenue effort is high of Gujarat and its fiscal deficit low compared to Rajasthan. Thus it is irrational to place Rajasthan above Gujarat as per FSRII. Now consider the case of Tamil Nadu and Karnataka. According to FSRII Tamil Nadu ranked 3rd and Karnataka 7th. Where as in accordance with the composite index Karnataka (8th rank) got placed above Tamil Nadu (9th rank). Except marginally higher placed in size of fiscal deficit, the performance of Karnataka is far better than Tamil Nadu in revenue mobilisation and expenditure allocation. What all this highlights is that the single indicator based approach has limitations and there is need for considering other aspects of the finances of the states in assessing the fiscal performance. The composite index used here appear as better.

FISCAL PERFORMANCE AND GRANT IN AID

Now to what extent the grant in aid recommended to the states takes into account the fiscal performance can be examined for which we have considered the per capita grant in aid and the change in the composite index rank. The same is shown in Table 6. It can be seen from the table that highest per capita transfer goes to Punjab whose fiscal performance rank is 7th. The best-performed state of Uttar Pradesh is receiving Rs. 1242 while Orissa gets Rs. 1437, which is ranked, fifth in fiscal performance. So also it can be noted that in fiscal performance Orissa and MP gets the same rank but MP's per capita receipt is only 61 per cent of Orssa's receipt. Similar observations can be made of several other states too. On the whole when we consider the composite index the grant in aid does not show close correspondence with the fiscal performance of states.

Table 6
Grant in aid of the Twelfth Finance Commission

State	*Per capita grant in aid (Rs)*	*Fiscal performance rank*
Andhra Pradesh	689	2
Bihar	1003	3
Gujarat	733	6
Haryana	685	4
Karnataka	769	8
Kerala	1024	10
MP	879	5
Maharashtra	571	12
Orissa	1437	5
Punjab	2022	7
Rajasthan	822	11
Tamil Nadu	666	9
Uttar Pradesh	1242	1
West Bengal	944	13

DEBT RELIEF MEASURES

The twelfth finance commission apart from introducing new borrowing regimes for states has recommended substantial debt relief measures to states. The proposal in this regard is four fold: (a) Cessation of lending by the center and requiring the states to go through the market for borrowing. (b) On lending of external loans on a back-to-back basis. (c) Rescheduling of all outstanding central loans of the states for a fresh period of 20 years carrying only 7.5 per cent rate of interest as against an average of 10.5 per cent at present and (d) A debt write off scheme for remission of states debts payable to the center during 2005-10 linked to implementation of fiscal reform. The benefit of debt consolidation is conditional on the state's enacting a fiscal responsibility law (FRL) with some basic features. For the debt write off the states must start reducing revenue deficit for its total elimination by 2008-09 and contain their fiscal deficit to no more than 3 per cent of GDP. While recommending these schemes the TFC has scrapped the Medium Term Fiscal Facility Fund, which was set up on the recommendations of the report of the EFC. To what extent the debt relief measures are fair can now be examined The incentive for potential debt write off varies considerably across the states. As stated one of the condition for debt write off is to wipe out the revenue deficit. There are states with high and low revenue deficits. For high deficit states it will be prudent to wipe out the deficit if only incentives are high say what is the debt write off compared to the deficit. To examine this the potential debt write per Re. of revenue deficit is shown in Table 7. Among the states the incentive varied from the lowest Re 0.18 per rupee of revenue deficit of Rajasthan to Rs. 2.09 of MP i.e. by reducing Re. 1 of fiscal deficit while MP will get write off of Rs. 2.09 Rajasthan will get only Re. 0.18. Incentives are more to AP, Orissa and Bihar while it is low to Punjab, Maharashtra, West Bengal and Tamil Nadu. It is also very interesting to note from the table that in respect of debt GSDP ratio Orissa is the most indebted state (65.4 per cent) its incentive is only Re. 1.11 considerably lower than MP which is less indebted (30.9 per cent). Also

Table 7
Debt Write off

State	*Debt write off per Re. of reve. Deficit (Rs)*	*Debt GSDP ratio*	*Per capita GSDP 2003 (Rs.)*	*Fiscal perfor-mance index*	*Debt write off as % of central loans and advances 2003*
Andhra Pradesh	1.25	30.6	21583	2	19.9
Bihar	1.05	49.6	8242	3	14.5
Gujarat	0.73	31.2	27879	6	16.9
Haryana	0.85	28.2	31362	4	10.9
Karnataka	0.78	26.3	22782	8	17.2
Kerala	0.26	38.3	25518	10	16.3
MP	2.09	30.9	14011	5	19.5
Maharashtra	0.21	20.7	30529	12	8.6
Orissa	1.11	65.4	12090	5	18.3
Punjab	0.20	50.3	30327	7	6.4
Rajasthan	0.18	50.2	15126	11	6.6
Tamil Nadu	0.35	25.2	24976	9	14.9
Uttar Pradesh	0.91	40.6	12169	1	13.8
West Bengal	0.25	43.1	20700	13	9.8

indebtedness of Punjab and Rajasthan is very high (50.3 per cent and 50.2 per cent respectively) still their incentive comes very low, Re. 0.20 and Re. 0.18 respectively. Debt relief also does not bear any relation to the development of the states. Thus for e.g. incentive for Bihar which is the poorest state in India in terms of per capita GSDP the incentive is only Re. 1.05 while AP which is comparatively more developed the incentive is Re. 1.25. Rajasthan's per capita GSDP is more or less half of Haryana while the incentive to Rajasthan is less than one fourth of Haryana. The incentive also does not bear any relation to the fiscal performance of states. For e.g. AP ranks second in fiscal performance according to composite index change but its incentive is only Re. 1.25 and MP which ranks 5th is getting an incentive of Rs. 2.09. Also the worst performer was West Bengal in fiscal matters and it gets an incentive of Re. 0.28 while Rajasthan and Kerala ranked high gets lower incentive. All this indicates that debt relief measures have not taken into account the indebtedness, level of development and the fiscal performance of states. So also as can be seen from the table the share of potential debt write off as percentage of centeral loans and advances varied from the lowest 6.4 per cent share of Punjab to the highest 19.9 per cent of AP. Relatively the share of MP, Orissa, Gujarat Karnataka and Kerala were high and those of Maharashtra, West Bengal and Haryana low.

CONCLUSIONS

Of late the need for fiscal reforms at the state level have been recognised and incentive schemes for reform have also been suggested by the finance commissions. To administer such schemes there is need for evaluating the fiscal performance of the states. The finance commissions have been adopting a single indicator based approach for measuring fiscal performance. This has limitations. While assessing the fiscal performance of states the resource mobilization effort and utilisation pattern too need to be considered. Taking into account these factors we have constructed an index of fiscal performance. A comparison of the same with the index of finance commission showed that though there is close correspondence between the two ranks in the case of few states there are large divergences also. A composite index appears as a better measure of fiscal performance of states. Our analysis also indicates that the grant in aid pattern do not take into account the performance of sates when considered the composite index. Debt relief measure is one of the other significant recommendations of the finance commission. Here too the level of indebtedness of the sates or fiscal performance is not considered.

REFERENCES

Academic Foundation (2005), Reports of the Finance Commissions of India- First Finance Commission to the Twelfth Finance Commission, New Delhi.

Archana Dholakia (2005), Measuring Fiscal Performance of States-An Alternative Approach, Economic and Political Weekly, July 30.

Morris M.D. and M.B. McAlpin (1982), Measuring the Conditions of Poor, A Physical Quality of Life Index, Promila and Company Publishers, New Delhi.

Rao Govinda M. and Jena Pratap R. (2005), Balancing Stability, Equity and Efficiency, Economic and Political Weekely. July 30.

Reserve Bank of India (2004), Handbook of Statistics on State Government Finances, Mumbai.

Reserve Bank of India (2005), State Finances–A Study of Budgets of 2004-05, Mumbai.

7

DEVOLUTION OF TAX REVENUE –A REVIEW OF THE FINANCE COMMISSIONS

G. Satyanarayana & M. Reddi Ramu

Finance Commission is constituted to define financial relations between the Centre and the States. Under the provision of the Article 280 of the Constitution, the president appoints a Finance Commission for the specific purpose of devolution of non-plan revenue resources. This article, in addition to analyse the implications of twelfth Finance Commission, is aimed to present a brief review of the Twelve Finance Commissions constituted and implemented in India. The functions of the Commission are to make recommendations to the president with respect to:

1. The distribution between Union and the States of the net proceeds of taxes which are to be, or may be, divided between them and the allocation between the states of the respective share of such proceeds.
2. The principle which should govern the grants-in-aid of the revenue of the States out of the consolidated fund of India; and
3. Any other matter referred to the commission by the president in the interests of sound finance.

In above context so far 11th Finance Commission have been appointed.

All the 12 Commissions have submitted their reports. The recommendations of the various commissions can be divided under three heads according to Table 1.

Table 1
Finance Commissions in India

Finance Commission	*Year of Establishment*	*Chairman*	*Operational Duration*	*Year of submitting Report*
I	1951	K.C. Niyogi	1952-57	1952
II	1956	K. Santhanam	1957-62	1956 &1957
III	1960	A.K. Chanda	1962-66	1961
IV	1964	P.V. Rajamannar	1966-69	1965
V	1968	Mahaveer Tyagi	1969-74	1968 & 1969
VI	1972	Brahma Nand Reddy	1974-79	1973
VII	1977	J.M. Shellet	1979-84	1978
VIII	1983	Y.B. Chawan	1984-89	1983 & 1984
IX	1987	N.K. P.Salve	1989-95	1989
X	1992	K.C. Panth	1995-2000	Nov.26,1994
XI	1998	A.M. Khusro	2000-05	7th July, 2000
XII	2003	C. Ranga Rajan	2005-2010	2004

Source: Report paper on finance commission.
(a) Division and distribution of Income tax and other taxes ;
(b) Grants-in-aid; and
(c) Loans to the states by the centre.

A BIRD'S EYE-VIEW OF FINANCE COMMISSION'S IN INDIA

While the estimated quantum's of transfers by way of tax devolution are staggering and should cause concern in the light of the revenue trends of the Central Government one must not that the Finance Commissions recommended the States share as a percentage of net proceeds of Central Taxes and Duties, and the transfers by the Centres to the States may turn out to be lower than the amounts indicated in the Reports on the basis of their own revenue projections.

Available evidence suggest that Tenth and the Eleventh Finance Commissions had over estimated the resources of the Union Government and under estimated its expenditure commitments. It is significant that the Tax/GDP ratio of Centre has been going down from 9.4 per cent in 1995-96 to 8.2 per cent in 2001-02 with marginal improvement to 8.8 per cent in 2002-03. Eleventh Commission had in its report also drawn specific attention to the secular decline in buoyancy rate of Central Revenues from 1.38 in the fifties to 0.91 in the nineties.

Emphasis on tax reform by way of reduction in rates in the hope of ensuring greater compliance has resulted in lower revenue realization compared to budgetary projections. But in absolute terms the Gross tax revenue of the Centre had increased by 15.6 per cent in 2002-03 and 17.9 per cent in 2003-04. It is possible that Twelfth Commission has persuaded itself to go by the rather ambitious 24.6 per cent revenue growth projections made in the Union Budget of 2004-05 and has recommended higher transfers to the states.

Table 2
Finance Commission Transfers

(Rs. in crores)

Finance Commissions	*Devolution*	*Grants*	*Total*	*Increase over PFC (%)*	*% of Total Transfer*	
					Devolution	*Grant*
I FC (1952-57)	362	50	412	–	88	12
II FC (1957-62)	852	197	1049	120	81	19
III FC (1962-66)	1068	244	1312	25	81	19
IV FC (1966-69)	1323	422	1745	33	76	24
V FC (1969-74)	4605	711	5316	205	87	13
VI FC (1974-79)	7099	2510	9609	70	74	26
VII FC (1979-84)	19233	1610	20843	117	92	8
VIII FC (9184-89)	35683	3769	39452	89	90	10
IX FC (1989-90),	11785	1877	13662	–	–	–
(1990-95)	87882	18154	106036	303	83	17
X FC (1995-2000)	106343	20300	226643	89	91	9
XI FC (2000-05)	376318	58587	434905	92	87	13
Total	108431	860984	–	87	13	–
XII FC (2005-10)	613112	142639	755751	74	81	19
Grant Total	1365665	251070	1616735	–	84.6	15.4

Source: Report paper on finance commission.

The criteria set for each Finance Commission keeps on changing as seen in Table 2 and Table 3. Where one can perceive that the percentage composition of total transfer consisting of the percentage of Tax Revenue and Grants keeps on changing from one Commission to another. For instance the total devolutions in the 1st Finance Commission was Rs. 412 crores. Which went up to Rs. 7,55,751 crores in the XII Finance

Commission and the percentage increase in total transfers from Central pool to the States over the Eleventh Finance Commission was just 74. While the same was 205 per cent and 303 per cent over their corresponding previous Finance Commissions in the V Finance Commission and IX Finance Commission respectively.

Table 3
Criteria for Inter-State Distribution and Weightage

Item	*X FC*	*XI FC*	*XII FC*
Population	20.0	10.0	25.0
Income (distance)	60.0	62.5	50.0
Area	5.0	7.5	10.0
Index of Infrastructure	5.0	7.5	Nil
Tax Effort	10.0	5.0	7.5
Fiscal discipline	0	7.5	7.5
Total	100.00	100.00	100.00

Source: Report of the Twelfth Finance Commission.

Another contentious issue in Federal Fiscal Transfer has been the criteria for determining the share of individual States, in the total States share. A dominant objective of the various Finance Commissions has been the need to raise the level of public services in the poorer States and providing the required resources to these States. In pursuit of the objective Finance Commissions have devised their own formulae for determining the share of individual states. Population size, State's contribution to Central Taxes, and poverty levels have been among the core criteria adopted by the earlier Commissions while geographical are and fiscal performance criteria have been added by recent Commissions.

For determining the share of the State in income tax, the first Seven Finance Commissions had taken population and contribution has the main criteria and the Eighth and Ninth Finance Commissions introduced poverty level as criteria. As for share in excise duties, population was an important factor for all the ten Commissions but per capital income of the States came to be adopted as criteria from the sixth Finance Commission onwards though the weightage assigned by each

Commission varied. Tenth Finance commission brought about a qualitative shift in the Fiscal Transfer Scheme, by moving away from specified Central Taxes to the total tax revenue of the Centre. It may be useful to briefly review the various criteria adopted and weightage assigned by the Tenth, Eleventh and Twelfth finance Commissions indicated in Table 3.

While the Tenth commission added a newly computed index of infrastructure, which was also adopted by the Eleventh Commission, the Twelfth Commission has dropped it. The Tenth Commission gave a high weightage of 10 per cent, without any reference to fiscal discipline, the Eleventh reduced the weightage to tax effort from 10 to 5 and added a new criteria of fiscal discipline with a weightage of 7.5 per cent, thus increasing the weightage for fiscal performance to 12.5 per cent in the total. The XII Commission has increased this to 15 per cent with 7.5 per cent each for tax effort and fiscal discipline.

FINANCIAL IMPLICATIONS OF THE TWELFTH FINANCE COMMISSION

Twelfth Finance Commission

In pursuance of the provision of Article 280 of Constitution of India and of the Finance Commission (Miscellaneous Provisions) Act, 1951, the Twelfth Finance Commission has been constituted with Dr. C. Rangarajan, as Chairman, with three other members. The Commission will make recommendations on the distribution of the divisible pool of net proceeds of taxes between the Union and the States and the allocation between the States of such proceeds, principles governing grants-in-aid of the revenues of the states out of the Consolidated Fund of India and grants under Article 275 of the Constitution, and the measures needed to augment the Consolidated Fund of a State to supplement the resources of the panchayats and munipalities. The Commission is mandated to review the state of finances of the Union and the States and suggest a plan by which the Governments collectively and severally may bring about a restructuring of public finances, restoring budgetary balances, achieving macro-economic stability and debt restructuring along with equitable growth. In addition, the commission is also required to review the fiscal reforms facility introduced by the Central government on the basis of the recommendations of Eleventh Finance Commission and suggest measures foı effective achievements of its objective. The Commission has been asked to submit its report by July 31, 2004 covering a period of five years commencing on April 1, 2005.

From the reforms measures underlined by the States in their MTFRP for revenue augmentation, expenditure compression, reducing debt burden, restructuring of PSEs, Power Sector reforms and budgetary reforms. One can reasonable come to the conclusion that the States have been sensitized to the need for fiscal consolidation. A menu of reform measures under taken by the States include:

(i) Increasing the tax rates and widening the tax base. A consensus on floor rates;

(ii) Better tax administration and introduction of VAT;

(iii) Indexation of user charges in services such as Road Transport Undertakings, Irrigation ect;

(iv) Ban on recruitment and abolishing of vacant posts;

(v) Freezing of grant-in-aid;

(vi) Reprioritisation of expenditure;

(vii) Capping of borrowing and reduction in the plan size to sustainable levels of debt.

(viii) Restructuring SEBs and setting up of SERCs;

(ix) 100 per cent mattering at 11 KV levels and securitistion of SEB debt;

(x) Making the budget documents more transparent by including details of number of employees in the roll of state government, the expenditure incurred on their salaries and terminal benefits and the expenditure on subsidies;

(xi) Computerization of treasury records and day-to-day functioning; and

(xii) Introduction of debt swaps mechanism.

To keep the process of reform on rail, the Ministry of finance has been interacting with the State Governments to review their reform matrix at regular intervals. This also enables the States to revise the MTFRP targets keeping in view the actual performance and necessary corrections in macro economics assumptions.

Financial Implications of Twelfth Finance Commission

(i) The states will during 2005-10, get as their share 30.5 per cent of the net proceeds of all Central taxes and duties, a marginal set-up from 29.5 per cent recommended by the Eleventh Finance Commission for 2000-2005. The estimated Twelfth Finance Commissions transfer of Rs. 7,55,751 crores (Tax devolution of Rs. 6,13,112 crores and Grants of Rs. 1,42,639 crores) will mean a 74 per cent increase over the Eleventh Finance Commission recommended transfer of Rs. 4,34,905 crores (devolution Rs. 3,76,318 crores and grant of Rs. 58,587 crores).

(ii) A significant reduction in their debt servicing burden ad account of the recommended consolidation of debt contracted up to March 2004,estimated at Rs. 1,28,795 crores as outstanding on march 31st, 2005, rescheduling for 20 years, with a revised rate of interest of 7.5 per cent against the contracted levels of 13 per cent, and later reduced to 9 per cent in the recent budget. Debt write-off will be linked to fiscal reforms and enactment of fiscal responsibility and budget management bill.

(iii) Cessation of loan component of Central Assistance for State Plan with all Central assistance taking the form of grants to the states, and facility for States to resort to open market borrowings within the framework of Article 293 of the India Constitution.

(iv) Central Government passing on all external assistance on back to back basis, and managing it through separate fund in Public Account, subject to the condition that service cost and exchange rate fluctuations also be passed to the States.

TFC's recommendations involve a major demand on Centre's resources, despite the Union Government's well-known fragile capacity to maintain its fiscal balance. The dimensions of increasing demands on Centre's resources can be gauged from the fact that during the five decades covered by the first ten Finance Commissions, the total transfer recommended from Centre to the States was Rs. 4,25,989 crores (tax devolution Rs. 3,76,235 crores and Grant Rs. 49,844 crores). Eleventh Finance Commissions, (EFC) recommended transfer of Rs. 4,34,905 crores over five years between 2000-2005 exceeded the total transfers made in the previous five decades. Twelfth Commission has added to this Rs. 7,55,751 crores. In effect, between 2000-2010 Ctntre may need to mobilize resources not only to meet its expenditure commitments but also provide to the states Rs. 11,90,656 crores, 3.5 times the sum of Rs. 3,32,679 crores recommended for the nineties by the Ninth and Tenth Finance Commissions put together.

CONCLUSION

The criteria adopted for Inter State distribution and weightage Twelfth Finance Commission is highly improvised one when compared to X FC and XI FC. But even its recommendations, with an attempted balance of increased weightage to population and lower weightage for poverty, appear to somewhat favour States with high population and low per capita income like Uttar Pradesh, Bihar and West Bengal. Grants for health and education sectors seems to be an indirect way of providing additional assistance to the states which had received substantial transfers from the Eleventh Commission. While it was expected that the states which are perceived as good fiscal performers may benefit to some extent by the increase in weightage for tax effort, and the emphasis on efficiency, their shares in total transfer of resources recommended by the Commission, do not reflect such a change. It does appear that while the Twelfth Commission attempted to balance the considerations of equalization and efficiency in its deliberations, the emphasis of the new government at centre on assistance to the backward states seems to have influenced the Commission's final recommendations. The Commission has also admitted that it has not been possible to implement full the equalization approach consistent with both equity and efficiency.

REFERENCES

Ruddar Datt & K.P.M. Sundharam, "Indian Economy", S.Chand & Company Ltd., Ram Nagar, Ned Delhi-110055.

GOI Reports of the Ministry of Finance, New Delhi, (1993-98).

S.K. Misra & V.K. Puri, "Indian Economy", Himalaya Publishing House, Pooja Apartments, 4-B, Murari Lal Street, Ansari Road, Darya Ganj, New Delhi-110002.

GOI (1995) Ministry of Finance, Report of the Tenth Finance Commission, New Delhi.

GOI (2000) Ministry of Finance, Report of the Eleventh Finance Commission, New Delhi.

GOI Ministry of Finance, November 2004.

GOI Ministry of Finance, Report of the Twelfth Finance Commission, (2005-10), New Delhi.

Rangarajan, C. (2004), "Issues Before the Twelfth Finance Commission", Economic and Political Weekly, June 26th.

Rangarajan, C. (2005), "Twelfth Finance Commission: Approach and Recommendations", Economic and Political Weekly, Vol. XL, No. 3, July 30, August 5.

GOI "Commission on Centre-State Relations", Part-I, Printed by the General Manager, GOI (1998), Press Nasik.

Bagchi, Amaresh, Bajaj, J.L. and William, A. Byrd (1992), "State Finances in India", Vikash Publishing House, (1992), New Delhi.

RBI Annual report (2003-04), Supplemented to RBI Bulletin, Sept. 2004.

RBI Bulletin, May 2005.

8

GRANTS–IN–AID UNDER TWELFTH FINANCE COMMISSION IN INDIA

Chandraiah Miriyala, Appala Naidu Gullipalli & Suryanarayana N.

INTRODUCTION

The political setup existed in India on the eve of independence was federal in nature and it was working under the Government of India Act 1935. In the financial field, the Indian constitution has very elaborate provisions. Such are not found in other Federal Constitutions. As far as financial resources are concerned, the Indian Constitution adopted the salient features of the 1935 Act. Let us now discuss the Union–State financial relations that are given in the Constitution of India.

The present paper presents "The recommendations of the Twelfth Finance Commission with reference to Grant in Aid to States and Grants to Local Bodies".

In fact, by providing for the establishment of Finance Commission for the purpose of allocating and adjusting the receipts from certain sources, the Constitution has made an original contribution in this extremely complicated aspect of federal relationship. The Indian Constitution lays down a broad scheme for this distribution of revenue resources between the Union and the States.

FINANCIAL COMMISSION'S (ARTICLE 280 & 281) FORMATION

The Constitutional requirement of setting up a Financial Commission is an original idea. According to this, the president should, within two years from the inauguration of the constitution and thereafter on the expiry of every fifth year or at such earlier intervals as he thinks necessary, constitute a Finance Commission. The commission will consist of a chairman and four other members who are all to be appointed by the President. As the commission has to be constituted at regular intervals, ascertain measure of continuity in the work of these commissions is ensured.

According to Article 280, the Finance Commission has to make recommendation to the President on two specific matters and "any other matter referred to the Commission by the President in the interests of sound finance.

It shall be the duty of the commission to make recommendations to the President as to:

(i) The distribution between the Union and the States of the net proceeds of taxes which are to be or may be divided between the Union and the States and allocation between the States of the respective shares of such proceeds.

(ii) The principles which should govern the grants – in – Aid of the revenues of the States out of the Consolidated Fund of India.

(iii) The measures needed to augment the consolidated Fund of State to supplement the resources of the panchayats in the State.

(iv) The measures needed to augment the consolidated Fund of a State to supplement the resources of the Municipalities in the state; and

(v) Any other matter referred to the Commission by the President in the interests of sound finance.

The President, after considering the recommendations of the Finance Commission with regard to income tax, prescribes by order the percentages and the manner of distribution. Parliament is not directly concerned with the assignment and distribution of income tax.

GRANTS–IN–AID (ARTICLE 275) ORIGIN

Federalism is not only a unifying, but also a leveling – up force. Among the constituent States of the union are some which are developed and advanced while others are undeveloped or underdeveloped and backward. One of the results expected of a federal union is the opportunity that it should provide for the socially and economically backward units to better their lot. A common method adopted for this purpose the system of the Union giving grants to the needy States. Article 275 provides for this by empowering parliament to pay, out of the consolidated Fund of India, certain sums every year as Grants in Aid to the revenues of such States, to the extent that such assistance is adjudged as necessary. The grants so fixed are based upon the recommendations of the Finance Commission. It is not necessary that every State should get Grant–in–Aid every year.

GRANTS IN–AID–TO THE STATES–DIFFERENT FINANCE COMMISSIONS

Under Article 275 of the Indian Constitution, the Finance Commission have to decide about the grants–in–aid to states corresponding to each five year plan. A summary of the recommendations of the Finance Commission on the grants–in–Aid is given below:

Finance Commission	*Grant – in – Aid*
First	(i) Grants were given for 7 states, to cover deficits during the period 1951 – 56 (ii) Grants were given for 8 states to improve primary education facilities.
Second	Large grants–in–Aid for meeting developmental needs of States were given
Third	(i) Grants were given about Rs. 550 Crores to all Sates except Maharashtra to cover part their revenue expenditure (ii) About Rs. 45 Crores of Grants were given for improvement of communication.

Contd....

Finance Commission	*Grant – in – Aid*
Fourth	Grants of about Rs. 610 Crores were given to cover deficits during the period 1966 – 71,
Fifth	Grants of about Rs. 638 Crores were given to cover deficits during the period 1969 – 74.
Sixth	Grants of about Rs. 2,510 Crores were given for 14 out of 21 states to cover their non-plan deficits during the period, 1974 – 79.
Seventh	About Rs. 1,600 Crores of Grants were given to cover deficits of a few poor states during 1980– 85 and also to upgrade the standards of Administration.
Eighth	(i) A small grant of Rs. 1,556 Crores was given for the period 1985-90 to cover deficits. (ii) A grant of Rs. 915 Crores was given to certain States to upgrade the standards of Administration.
Ninth	(i) Grant of Rs. 15,017 Crores was given to cover deficits on plan and non-plan revenue account during 1990 – 95. (ii) A special annual grant of 603 Crores was given towards the centre's Administration to the Calamity Relief Fund – totaling Rs. 3,015 Crores for the 5 year period, 1990-95. (iii) A grant of about Rs. 122 Crores was given to Madya Pradesh towards the expenditure on rehabilitation and relief of victims of Bhopal gas leak.
Tenth	(i) Grant–in–Aid was given of about Rs. 7,580 Crores to cover deficit on revenue account during 1995 – 2000. (ii) Grants of about Rs. 1,360 Crores were given for such selected items as police, fire service, jails, promotion of girls education, additional facilities for upper primary schools, drinking water facilities in primary, etc. (iii) Grants of about Rs. 1,250 Crores were given to solve the special problems of States. (iv) Calamity relief of Rs. 4,730 Crores; (v) Grants of about Rs. 5,380 Crores to Local Bodies, Viz. panchayats and Municipalities.

Finance Commission	*Grant – in – Aid*
Eleventh	Grants of about Rs. 63891.25 Crores were given to cover Local Bodies, Centre's share in Calamity Relief, Non-plan revenue deficit, upgradation and special problems and Centre's share of Incentive Fund.
Twelfth	Grants of about Rs. 1,42,639.60 were given to cover Local Bodies and others which are explained in this paper in detailed in ensuring sections.

PURPOSE OF GRANTS–IN–AID

As important welfare and development functions are entrusted to the States gaps between their revenue and expenditure have to be corrected through transference of resources from the Centre. This is done partly by arrangements for tax sharing. But the Grants–in–Aid by the Union for specific purpose or general aid have come to occupy an important place in Union – State financial relation in India. The grants also serve the purpose of correcting inter-state disparities in resources. They also help in the coordination over essential Welfare Services and development programmes in different states.

Grants–in–Aid means transfer of resources from the Centre to the States. Thus, grants are given to cover the gap between the revenues and expenditure of the States. Grants are also given to remove inter–state disparities in resources. Grants are also given to bring about a balanced development of the Country. Thus, Comparatively more grants are granted to Backward and under –developed Areas/States. Both general and specific grants are used as part of the financial assistance to States, in addition to shared taxes. Besides, grants–in–aid are also given in lift of export duty on jute and jute products under Article 273 of the Constitution.

TWELFTH FINANCE COMMISSION AND GRANTS–IN–AID

On 1st November 2002 under the chairmanship of Dr. C. Ranga Rajan, President of India has appointed the Twelfth Finance Commission. The statewise estimation of share in Central taxes and specific amount of grants recommended by the commission has been brought out. In this paper the Grants–in–aid to states and grants to Local Bodies are presented.

The Non-plan grants under Article 275 of the constitution as per Twelfth Finance Commission are significantly higher when compared with the Eleventh Finance Commission recommended Non-plan grants for the period of 2000–2005. The Non-plan grants as per the Former Commission has been Rs. 1,42,639.60 where as it was Rs. 63,891.25 as per the latter commission. There are several grants being provided by the Union to the states. Those grants are Non-plan revenue deficit grants, grants for Education and Health, grants for maintenance of Rods & Bridges, Public Building and Forests, Grants for Heritage Conservation, Grants for states specific needs and Grants for Local Bodies. These grants are explained briefly as below.

Non-Plan Revenue Deficit Grant

The total non-plan revenue grant of Rs. 56,855.87 Crore has been recommended by TFC during the period 2005–2010 for fifteen states. During the first year of the award period, non-plan revenue deficit grant has been recommended by the Commission for fifteen states amounting to Rs. 15,091.86 Crore. By the last year of the Award period, only nine states will get Rs. 9,528.14 Crore as Non-plan revenue deficit grant. Except four non-special category states like Kerala, Orissa, West Bengal and Punjab, the Non-plan revenue deficit grants are recommended by the commission for the special category states.

Grant for Education and Health

Under Twelfth Finance Commission, Eight states have been recommended for grants amounting to Rs. 10,171.65 Crores over the award period for the education, with a minimum of Rs. 20 Crores in a year for any eligible state. Seven states have been recommended for grants amounting to Rs. 5,887.08 Crores over the selected period for the health sector with a minimum of Rs. 10 Crores in a year for any eligible state.

Grants for Educational and Health sectors are additional, over and above the normal expenditure to be incurred by the states in these sectors. The commission has recommended that these grants should be utilized only for the respective sectors based on certain conditions specified by the commission. Monitoring of the expenditure relating to these grants will rest with the state government concerned.

Grants for maintenance of Roads & Bridges, Public Building and Forests

The Commission has recommended grants separately, for maintenance of roads and bridges and building and forests as under:

(i) A grant of Rs. 15,000.00 Crores over the award period has been recommended for maintenance of roads and bridges.

(ii) An amount of Rs. 5,000 Crores is recommended as grants for maintenance of public buildings.

(iii) The Commission has recommended grants of Rs. 1,000 Crores spread over the award period of 2005–10 for maintenance of Forests.

(iv) The maintenance grants are additionally over and above the normal maintenance expenditure to be incurred by the states. These grants are to be released and spent in accordance with certain conditionalities specified by the commission.

Grants for Heritage Conservation

A grant of Rs. 625 Crores spread over the Award period has been recommended for heritage conversation. The grant will be used for preservation and protection of historical monuments archaeological sites, public libraries, museums and archives and also for improving the tourist infrastructure to facilitate visits to these sites.

Grants for State Specific Needs

The grant recommended by the Commission for State specific needs is on the pattern of the grant recommended by Eleventh

Finance Commission for the special problems of the states. The grant recommended by the latter for the special problems of states was Rs. 1,129.00 Crores. The former (12) Commission has recommended an amount of Rs. 7,100 Crores as grant for state specific needs. While these grants have been phased out equally over the last four years. Commission has observed that this phasing should be taken an indicative in nature. These states may communicate the required phasing of grants to the Central Government.

CONCLUSION

For solving the economic disparities among all states over the country, the grants–in–aid are very essential. So in making its recommendations on various matters, the commission will take the base of population figures as of 1971, in all such cases where population is a factor for determination of devolution of taxes and duties and grants–in–aid.

REFERENCES

B.P. Tyagi, "Public Finance"

Dutt and Sundaram (2005), "Indian Economy"

Misra and Puri, "Indian Economy"

9

STATES DEBT BURDEN, TWEFTH FINANCE COMMISSION AND DEBT RELIEF

V.P. Gupta

The present paper is divided into three sections. First section examines briefly the problem of state's debt burden. Section second describes in short the debt relief measures recommended by the various finance commissions. In third section, an appraisal of the likely impact on the states of the debt relief measures recommended by the Twelfth Finance Commission has been made along with concluding observations.

SECTION - I

The debt burden of the States is growing phenomenally. The outstanding public debt of state governments in India was only Rs. 1, 00,289 crore at the end of March 1991. It has increased to Rs. 9,13,103 crore at the end of March 2005 reflecting a nine-fold increase during this period. The public debt of state governments in India is mounting due to large mismatches between revenue receipts and revenue expenditure, poor financial working of the state public sector undertakings, poor recovery of cost for provision of social goods, mismatches between cost and user charges of the products and due to implementation of the recommendations of Fifth Pay Commission.

COMPOSITION OF STATE GOVERNMENTS DEBT

The public debt of state governments in India prior to 1972-73 was classified in terms of permanent debt, floating debt, loans from the centre, unfunded debt and other debt. The classification of state's debt has undergone changes as per recommendations contained in the second part of the team on reforms in the structure of budget and accounts. Now, state's debt has been reclassified into internal debt, loans and advances from the central government and provident funds etc. Internal debt comprises of minor heads of accounts such as market loans, compensation and other bonds, ways and means advances from the RBI and loans from banks and other institutions. The share of outstanding internal debt in total outstanding debt has been sharply rising during the period 1981 to 2005. It was 18.5 per cent in 1981. It increased to 36.4 per cent in 2001 and is budgeted to rise to 62.7 per cent at the end of March 2005.

The share of central loans and advances in total state's outstanding liabilities has been continuously declining during this period and of provident funds etc. has been rising. The share of Central loans and advances in total outstanding liabilities has come down steadily from 71 per cent in 1981 to 22 per cent in 2005 and the share of provident funds etc has increased from 10.6 per cent in 1981 to 15 per cent in 2005. These trends categorically reveal that the state's indebtedness to the central government has been declining and the burden of internal and provident funds on state governments has been continuously rising. Table 2 shows these trends.

The loans and advances are given by the central government to state governments for plan and non-plan schemes. Plan loans are given by the central government to states for meeting their expenditure on state plan schemes, central plan schemes and centrally sponsored schemes. On the other hand, non-plan loans are given by the centre to states for meeting expenditure on natural calamities and in the form of ways and means advances and small savings loans given prior to 1st April 1999, when the National Small Savings Fund (NSSF) was created. One of the factors for the gradual decline in the state's indebtedness to the centre is that the borrowings against small savings are maintained in the NSSF public account with effect from 1st April 1999 and the other reason for decline is the debt-swap scheme announced by the central government. The states indebtedness to centre

Table 1
Outstanding Liabilities of States Governments (As on March 31st)

Year	*Market Loans*	*Compensation and other Bonds*	*WMA from RBI*	*Loans from Banks and other Institutions*	*Special Securities issued to NSSR*	*Internal debt (2+3+4+5+6)*	*Loans and Advances from Central Government*	*State Provident funds*	*Insurance & pension fund trust and endowments, small Savings Etc*	*Total Provident Funds etc. (9+10)*	*Total liabilities (7+8+9)*
(1)	(2)	(3)	(4)	(5)	(6)	(7)	(8)	(9)	(10)	(11)	(12)
1981	2988	59	482	914		4443	16980	2185	351	2536	23959
1982	3328	54	1750	1051		6182	19080	2571	439	3010	28272
1983	3735	50	617	1205		5607	23557	3163	576	3739	32903
1984	4323	48	812	1357		6540	26979	3830	720	4550	38069
1985	5101	43	1640	1539		8323	30555	4846	671	5517	44395
1986	6104	41	286	1618		8049	38786	5743	1082	6825	53660
1987	7271	36	214	1544		9065	43702	6699	1256	7955	60722
1988	8793	10	129	1922		10854	49534	7994	1589	9583	69971
1989	10765	2	325	2121		13213	56222	9625	1960	11585	81020
1990	13063	-2	589	2544		16194	64139	11514	2377	13891	94224
1991	15618	8	679	2906		19211	74117	14002	2959	16961	110289
1992	18923	6	891	3157		22977	83491	16357	3513	19870	126338
1993	22426	-16	708	3156		26274	92412	19347	4145	23492	142178
1994	26058	-2	746	3507		30309	101945	22996	4826	27822	160077
1995	30133	-4	-1228	6321		35221	116705	26783	5818	32601	184527
1996	36021	-3	-24	7225		43217	131505	30984	6519	37502	212225

Contd...

Year	Market Loans	Compen-sation and other Bonds	WMA from RBI	Loans from Banks and other Institutions	Special Securities issued to NSSR	Internal debt (2+3+4+5+6)	Loans and Advances from Central Govern-ment	State Provi-dent funds	Insurance & pension fund trust and endow-ments, small Savings Etc	Total Provi-dent Funds etc. (9+10)	Total liabilities (7+8+9)
(1)	(2)	(3)	(4)	(5)	(6)	(7)	(8)	(9)	(10)	(11)	(12)
1997	42536	-4	638	8425		51595	149053	35556	7322	42878	243525
1998	49816	0	1288	10847		59375	172729	40823	8280	49103	281207
1999	60283	3	2940	13893		77119	203786	50827	10245	61072	341978
2000	72947	1	5493	20132	26416	124989	216194	65600	13349	78949	420132
2001	85466	-2	4724	32235	59022	181445	224590	76446	15609	92056	498092
2002	102715	-5	7584	43916	94670	248880	235564	84423	17819	102242	586687
2003	131199	-5	677	61132	146914	339918	234632	91618	20487	112105	686655
2004 (RE)	176318	18750	709	66330	208151	470258	213181	101341	22452	123692	807131
2005 (BE)	203867	21256	849	74086	271888	571946	204945	111660	24552	136211	913103

would further decline during 2005-10 as per recommendations of the 12th Finance Commission. The 12th Finance Commission recommended that the central government would not act as an intermediately and allow the states to approach the market directly. The recommendations of 12th Finance Commission have been accepted by the Central Government.

Table 2
Composition and Share of Outstanding Liabilities of State Governments at the end of March 31st

Year	*1981*	*1991*	*2001*	*2002*	*2003*	*2004*	*2005*
(1)	(2)	(3)	(4)	(5)	(6)	(7)	(8)
Internal debt	18.5	17.4	36.4	42.4	49.5	58.3	62.67
Loans and advances from Centre	70.9	67.2	45.1	40.7	34.2	26.4	22.4
Provident Funds etc.	10.6	15.4	18.5	17.4	16.3	15.3	14.92

INTER-STATE VARIATIONS IN DEBT LEVELS

There are large inter-state variations in the magnitude of outstanding public debt of state governments in India. The magnitude of outstanding debt of Goa was the lowest and of Uttar Pradesh was the highest as on 31st March 2005. In case of Uttar Pradesh, it was around 30 times more than that of Goa. The states like West Bengal, Maharashtra, Andhra Pradesh and Gujarat have huge outstanding public debt ranging from Rs. 60,408 crore to Rs. 95,246 crore at the end of March 2005. Rajasthan is the sixth largest indebted state among the non-specialized category states. These trends are clearly evident from Table 3. The burden of internal debt is the largest on Uttar Pradesh followed by West Bengal and is the minimum on Goa among non-special category states. State's indebtedness to the centre in absolute terms in case of Uttar Pradesh is the maximum followed by Andhra Pradesh. The relative position of Rajasthan was eleventh in this respect. The burden of provident fund is the largest on Uttar Pradesh followed by Kerala as can be easily seen from Table 3.

Table 3
Inter-State Various in Outstanding Liabilities at the End of March2005 (BE)

State	*Internal Debt*	*Of which Special Securities Issued to NSSF*	*Loans and Advances from the Centre*	*Provident Fund etc.*	*Total debt*
(1)	(2)	(3)	(4)	(5)	(6)=(1)+(4)+(5)
1. Andhra Pradehs	41214	13912	20134	5045	66392
2. Bihar	29676	15617	18094	78844	55654
3. Goa	2293	1289	970	548	3811
4. Gujarat	41547	26488	14910	3950	60408
5. Haryana	13349	7115	2995	5563	21907
6. Karnataka	22594	10327	12351	6704	41649
7. Kerala	18840	5507	6651	14929	40420
8. Madhya Pradesh	32072	11914	12100	9204	53376
9. Maharashtr	55312	32230	19002	9800	84114
10. Orissa	18396	3734	10505	9183	38085
11. Punjan	30708	15593	6984	8504	46196
12. Rajasthan	36429	18290	8281	11869	56580
13. Tamil Nadu	33639	13124	12656	7593	53887
14. Uttar Pradesh	69494	30508	29319	15924	114737
15. West Bengal	75545	42027	15025	4677	95246
16. NCT Delhi	16860	16860	-308	-	16552

DEBT SERVICES

Table 4 reflects the increasing size of debt-services of governments in India. The share of debt services of states in gross transfers of the state governments on aggregate basis has been rising. It was 32.7 per cent in 1999-2000. It increased to 62 per cent by the end of 2003-04. There are however, wide inter-state variations in the ratio of debt services to gross transfers. There are some states like Go, Haryana, Punjab and Delhi where whole of the receipts from gross transfers are absorbed by debt services in recent years.

Table 4
Ratio of Debt Services of States to Gross Transfers

State	1992-93	1999-2000	2000-01	2001-02	2002-03	2003-04(RE)	2004-05(BE)
(1)	(2)	(3)	(4)	(5)	(6)	(7)	(8)
1. Andhra Pradesh	19.5	31.0	39.5	32.2	49.5	45.6	39.7
2. Bihar	20.9	24.7	24.1	26.2	26.7	23.0	25.0
3. Chatisgarh	-	-	27.9	25.0	29.4	34.0	25.2
4. Goa	38.9	68.8	48.0	52..3	89.8	100.4	100.5
5. Gujarat	42.6	58.5	57.0	54.4	84.2	116.1	38.9
6. Haryana	34.3	60.0	75.0	70.2	61.1	123..2	113.9
7. Jharkhand	-	-	-	22.0	14.4	22.8	21.4
8. Karnataka	23.9	33.5	31.8	27.5	48.9	58.1	32.2
9. Kerala	28.6	35.0	37.9	39.0	47.0	51.9	43.8
10. Madhya Pradesh	20.6	24.3	20.5	21.5	33.5	36.2	36.1
11. Maharasthra	37.2	79.4	89.6	80.1	88.2	91.0	55.1
12. Orissa	19.5	14.1	32.0	38.4	39.0	39.1	35.0
13. Punjab	19.0	125.1	83.8	100.8	158.0	127.9	128.6
14. Rajasthan	19.4	59.1	32.4	46.5	60.5	63.2	70.2
15. Tamil Nadu	19.3	36.3	36.2	40.5	57.0	53.2	30.9
16. Uttar Pradesh	20.0	35.8	35.4	33.1	47.7	52.3	34.2
17. West Bengal	30.5	57.8	43.6	46.3	51.2	111..3	82.5
18. NCT Delhi		78.6	119.9	147.1	229.6	473.7	497.4

Table 5
Major Deficit Indicators of State Governments (Consolidated)

Year	Gross Fiscal Deficit	Net Fiscal Deficit	Revenue Deficit	Conventional Deficit	Primary Deficit	Net RBI credit to States
(1)	(2)	(3)	(4)	(5)	(6)	(7)
1990-91	18787	14532	5309	-72	10132	420
	(3.3)	(2.6)	(0.9)	(0.0)	(0.1)	(0.1)
1991-92	18900	15746	5651	156	7956	-340
	(2.9)	(2.4)	(0.9)	(0.0)	(1.2)	(-0.1)
1992-93	20891	15769	5114	-1829	7681	176
	(2.8)	(2.1)	(0.7)	(-0.2)	(1.0)	(0.0)
1993-94	20596	16263	3813	462	4795	591
	(2.4)	(1.9)	(0.4)	(0.1)	(0.6)	(0.1)
1994-95	27596	23507	6156	-4468	8284	48
	(2.7)	(2.3)	(0.6)	(-0.4)	(0.8)	(0.0)

Contd....

Year	*Gross Fiscal Deficit*	*Net Fiscal Deficit*	*Revenue Deficit*	*Conven-tional Deficit*	*Primary Deficit*	*Net RBI credit to States*
(1)	(2)	(3)	(4)	(5)	(6)	(7)
1995-96	31426	26695	8201-2849	9494	16	(0.1)
	(2.7)	(2.5)	(1.2)	(0.5)	(0.9)	
1996-97	37251	33460	116114	7041	11675	898
	(2.7)	(2.5)	(1.2)	(0.5)	(0.9)	(0.1)
1997-98	44200	39135	16333	-2103	14087	1543
	(2.9)	(2.6)	(1.1)	(-0.1)	(0.9)	(0.1)
1998-99	74254	66209	43642	3520	38381	5579
	(4.2)	(3.8)	(2.5)	(0.2)	(2.2)	(0.1)
1999-2000	91480	79309	53797	3113	46309	1312
	(4.7)	(4.1)	(2.7)	(0.2)	(2.4)	(0.1)
2000-01	89532	98254	53569	2733	37830	
	(4.3)	(4.0)	(2.6)	(0.1)	(1.8)	
2001-02	95994	87903	59188	2417	33488	
	(4.2)	(3.6)	(2.6)	(0.1)	(1.5)	
2002-03	102123	91680	55111	-4611	31981	
	(4.1)	(3.7)	(2.2)	(-0.2)	(1.3)	
2003-04(RE)	141010	133626	72126	11671	57042	293
	(5.1)	(4.8)	(2.6)	(0.4)	(2.1)	(0.0)
2004-05(BE)	111852	104318	43718	-1049	20994	
	(3.6)	(3.3)	(1.4)	(-0.0)	(0.7)	

RE: Revised Estimates, BE: Budget Estimates; Not Available.

1. Overall surplus or deficit referred to here as conventional deficit represents the difference between aggregate disbursements and aggregate receipts. Aggregate receipts include (i) Revenue receipts(ii) Capital receipts excluding ways and means advances and overdrafts from RBI and (iii) Net receipts under Public Accounts excluding withdrawals from Cash Balance Investment Account and Cash Balances. Aggregate disbursement include (i) Revenue expenditure and (ii) Capital disbursement excluding repayments of ways and means advances and overdrafts from RBI; additions to Cash Balance are excluded.
2. Revenue deficit is the difference between revenue expenditure and revenue receipts.
3. GFD is the difference between aggregate disbursements net of debt repayments and recovery of loans and revenue receipts and non-debt capital receipts.
4. Net fiscal deficit is the difference between gross fiscal deficit and net lending.
5. Primary deficit is FGD less of interest payments.
6. Figures in brackets are percentages to GDP at current prices.
   (-) indicates surplus
   All figures are rounded off.

Source: Budget Documents of State Government and Reserve Bank Record.

FISACL DEFICIT AND REVENUE DEFICIT

The Fiscal health of state governments has been worrisome as revealed from Table 5. As a proportion of GDP, gross fiscal deficit of states after declining from 3.3 per cent in 1990-91 to 2.4 per cent in 1993-94 has been consistently increasing in the later years and has reached to an unsustainable level of 5.1 per cent in 2003-04. The fiscal deficit of states is budgeted to decline to 3.6. per cent of GDP in 2004-05. As a proportion of GDP, revenue deficit of state governments in India declined from 0.9 per cent in 1990-91 to 0.4 per cent in 1993-94 but thereafter it has been growing and reached to a peak level of 2.7. per cent of GDP in 1999-2000. It declined to 2.2. per cent of GDP in 2002-03 but again mounted to 2.6 per cent of GDP in 2003-04 (RE). The revenue deficit of states is budged to come down to1.4. per cent of GDP in 2004-05.Recognising the urgent necessity of fiscal consolidation at states level, a number of states had initiated an array of reforms in the late nineties covering taxation, user charges on public services, public sector under takings, expenditure management and the enactment of fiscal responsibility legislation.

DECOMPOSITION AND FINANCING OF GFD

There are three components of gross fiscal deficit of state viz., revenue deficit, capital outlay and net lending. It is striking to note that the share of capital outlays as well as net lending in GFD has been declining and of revenue deficit has been sharply increasing. The share of revenue deficit which was around 25 per cent on an average during the first half of the nineties has increased to 51 per cent in 2003-04 (RE). On the other hand, the share of capital outlay has declined from 55 per cent to 43.6 per cent and the share of net lending has fallen from 20 per cent to 5.3. per cent during this period. There is an urgent need to step-up the share of capital outlay in fiscal deficit via reducing and eliminating the share of revenue deficit in gross fiscal deficit.

Gross Fiscal Deficit is financed through borrowings. There is structural change in the composition of financing pattern of GFD of states during the last one and half decade. The role of small savings loan, market loans, loans from financial institutions, reserve funds deposits has been accelerating in financing GFD and of central loans and state provident funds has been decelerating. This is clearly evident from Table 6. The negative financing of GFD from central loans began with effect from 2003-03 depicting that repayments of loans from the states to the centre have surpassed the gross loans from the centre to states.

Table 6
Decomposition and Financing Pattern of Gross Fiscal Deficit of State Governments (Consolidated)

Item	*1990-95 (Average)*	*1995-2000 (Average)*	*2000-02*	*2002-03*	*2003-04 (RE)*	*2004-05 (BE)*
(1)	(2)	(3)	(4)	(5)	(6)	(7)
De-Composition						
1. Revenue Deficit	24.7	44.7	60.7	54.0	51.1	39.1
2. Capital Outlay	55.3	43.2	34.2	35.8	43.6	54.2
3. Net lending	20.0	12.1	5.1	10.2	5.3	6.7
4. Gross Fiscal Deficit(1+2+3)	100	100	100	100	100	100
Financing of GFD						
1. Small savings	-	5.8	36.8	51.2	43.4	57.0
2. Market borrowings	16.0	16.1	16.0	27.9	32.0	24.6
3. State Provident Fund	14.3	13.4	10.2	7.0	6.8	9.3
4. Central Loans	49.0	40.6	13.5	-0.9	-15.2	-7.4
5. Others**	20.7	24.0	23.6	14.8	33.0	16.5

** Includes reserve funds, deposits, loans from banks and other institutions.

INTEREST PAYMENTS

One of the important components of revenue expenditure of state governments in India is interest payments. The share of interest payments in revenue expenditure of states irrespective of whether developed or developing has been increasing over tome to unsustainable levels. West Bengal has biggest ratio of interest payments to revenue expenditure among all non-special category states. The ratio of interest payments to revenue expenditure on an average of all the states including special category was 20.9 per cent during 2003-04. The ratio was large to all states average during 2003-04 in case of Andhra Pradesh, Bihar, Gujarat, NCT Delhi, Orissa and Rajasthan. The ratio was the lowest in Chattisgarh during 2003-04. Jharkhand follows next at 13.6 per cent Karnataka, Madhya Pradesh, Tamil Nadu, Maharashtra and Goa have displayed lower levels of the ratios of interest payments to revenue expenditure around 16 to 18 per cent during 2003-04. Table.10 reflects these trends.

SECTION - II

The issue of mounting state's indebtedness to the centre has been referred by the President of India to the successive Finance Commissions. The successive Finance Commissions have tried to grapple with this issue every fifth year or so but the problem is still looming large. The share of outstanding central loans in state's indebtedness had been remaining large. The mounting state's indebtedness to the centre in turn has created a severe problem of debt servicing in the form of repayment of principle amount and interest payments. It is realized in every sphere that there is an urgent need to reduce significantly the mounting state's indebtedness. This issue was also referred to the 12th Finance Commission. In its terms of reference, the 12th Finance Commission was required to assess the debt position of state governments in India and to suggest corrective measures that are consistent with macro economic stability and debt sustainability.

The state's indebtedness to the centre has been mounting because there is limit on borrowing programmes of state governments per Article 193 of the Constitution of India, state governments are not empowered to borrow from the market without the approval of the central government so long as they are indebted to the centre. In practice, all state governments, whether developed or developing are heavily indebted to the centre. The state governments re required to take prior permission from the central government for their borrowing programmes. Moreover, there are limits for states on ways and means advances from the RBI. However, the limits on ways and means advances have been raised by the RBI from time to time for facilitating the management of temporary mismatches in receipts and payments of the state governments. In recent years, the state government are borrowing from the RBI exceeding the permissible limits of ways and means advances leading to unauthorized overdrafts of some states.

The state governments had been increasingly demanding debt-relief on outstanding central loans from the Finance Commissions because their financial position is not in good health. There are wide mismatches between revenue receipts and revenue expenditure of state governments in India. Revenue expenditure has been far greater than revenue receipts. As result, the state governments have fallen in a trap of revenue and fiscal deficits which are enlarging from year to year.

The second finance commission was the first one to deal with the issue of debt relief. The commission was required to examine the modifications in the rates of interest and the terms of repayment of loans. The second commission objected the policy of providing free loans or concessional loans to states. The commission was of the opinion that the revenue budgets should reflect the actual interest burden and any assistance to it be given, should be given in the form of subsidy. However, the commission recommended for consolidation of loans given by the central government to states except for rehabilitation of displaced persons and interest free loans. The commission was of the view that the centre should not deal with the states as if it were a commercial banker. Both are partners in the process of development. The commission was of the view not to undercharge or overcharge he states from the true cost of borrowing. The central government did not accept the recommendations f the commission regarding postponing the repayment periods well as for charging uniform rate of interest from every state irrespective of purposes for which loans were taken. The Centre's contention was that implementing the recommendations of the commission would reduce the size of central resources for financing state projects either for plan purpose or outside the plan.

The fourth commission was required to assess the extent of assistance required by the states owing to any further expenditure likely to devolve upon the states for servicing of their debt. The fourth commission admitted the gravity of the problem of states indebtedness but being unable to examine the issue comprehensively recommended it to be examined by an independent expert body.

One of the terms of reference of the fifth finance commission was to examine the problem of unauthorized overdrafts of some states with the RBI and the procedure for avoiding such overdrafts. Providing debt relief to states was not an issue for the commission.

The Sixth commission was asked to undertake a general review of the state's debt position with particular reference to central loans advanced to states and suggest changes in the terms of repayments. The commission neither favoured the demands of the states to write-of-their debt liabilities nor to turn the small savings loans into debt in perpetuity. The commission for providing debt relief to states analyzed the purpose wise distribution of union loans to the states. The commission recommended debt-relief to the extent of Rs. 1969.62 crore to the states out of which Rajasthan got the maximum amounting to Rs. 258.14.

The seventh finance commission as like the sixth finance commission did not recommend scaling down or writing-off of the outstanding central loans to states. The commission recommended to write-off the unproductive loans given by the centre to the states on the ground that the states do not get any return from these loans which would enable them to meet their interest liability. The commission recommended to write-off Rs.942.82 crore on this account. The commission also recommended to convert small savings loans into loans in perpetuity. This recommendation was no0t accepted by the central government. The commission recommended that loans used for productive purposes by the states should be paid over 15 years and for semi-productive purposes be repaid over the period of 50 years.

The eight finance commission was of the view that the relationship between the centre and the states is one of partnership and not as creditor-debtor relationship and the repayment of the loans to the centre is essential for redeployment of the funds for the benefit of the same state or some other states. Therefore, in general, the finance commission was not in favour of write-off loans. The eight commission recommended debt relief to states to the extent of Rs.2285.39 crores. Around 30 per cent of the total debt relief was obtained by two states viz., Bihar and Uttar Pradesh. The commission did not favour the idea of conversion of small savings loans into the debt in perpetuity. The commission recommended to write-off the loans given by the centre to states for relief and rehabilitation of displaced persons, repatriates etc. The commission recommended debt-relief to different states on a progressive basis.

The Ninth Finance Commission recommended debt relief to different states on the basis of performance to two sector viz., power and road transport. Larger debt relief was provided to those states where the rate of return was more and less to those where rate of return was low. The Ninth commission was the first one who initiated the process of linking debt-relief to performance parameters. The ninth commission recommended lesser amount of debt relief as compared to eight commission. It recommended only Rs. 975.6 crores amount as debt-relief.

The Tenth Finance commission recommended general debt relief on the basis of fiscal performance of the states and specific relief to states with high fiscal stress. The finance commission measured improvement in fiscal performance by comparing the ratio of revenue receipts to revenue expenditure in a given year with the average of corresponding ratio in the three immediately preceding years. According to the recommendations of the commission, if a state improve performance by 2.5 percentage points, the relief would be Rs. 565.5 crores. The commission recommended debt relief to high fiscal stress states viz. Bihar, Orissa and Uttar Pradesh. For measuring fiscal·stress, the commission took the ratio of interest payments to revenue expenditure and according to the commission high fiscal stress are those states which have more than 17 per cent of this ratio.

The Eleventh Finance Commission was required to consider the issue of long term sustainability of debt both for the cenre and the states. For debt sustainability point of view the commission recommended that the ratio of interest payments to revenue receipts should not exceed 18 per cent. In terms of this criteria, 17 out of 28 states have unsustainable levels of debt viz. Orissa, Punjab, West Bengal, Himachal Pradesh, Rajasthan, Uttar Pradesh, Andhra Pradesh, Bihar, Gujarat, Haryana, Kerala, Goa, Jharkhand, Karnataka, Madhya Pradesh, Maharastra and Tamil Nadu. The Eleventh Finance Commission did not consider any special debt-relief for the fiscally stressed states but continued the general debt relief scheme linking it to the improvement in performance in the ratio of revenue receipts of revenue expenditure. The performance indicator expected each state to achieve a minimum improvement of 5 percentage points in the ratio of revenue receipts to revenue expenditure. The estimated debt relief was between Rs.600 to 700 crore but the states qualified for Rs. 131.77 crore only by the end of September 2004. This reflects that most of the states were unable to improve the ratio of revenue receipts to revenue expenditure.

The Twelfth Finance Commission was of the view that unless concrete and immediate measures are taken to tackle the debt problem of state governments, fiscal sustainability of states cannot be achieved. The Twelfth Finance Commission recommended debt relief from two angles viz., (i) to eliminate revenue deficit of states and (ii) for bring9ng states on the path of debt sustainability. For this purpose, both qualitative and quantitative measures were prescribed by the commission to check the future growth of states debt beyond sustainable levels. The precondition laid down by the commission for granting debt-relief to a state is to enact fiscal responsibility legislation prescribing specific annual targets for bringing down their revenue and fiscal deficit and providing for a ceiling along with a path for reduction of borrowings and guarantees. The commission did not recommend linking of debt relief to the performance of human development and investment climate as desired by some states. The commission was of the view that debt swap scheme of the central government has given sufficient relief to the states. Therefore the focus of the commission was to improve the finances of state governments in India. According to the recommendations of the commission, if a state achieves a zero revenue deficit by 2008-09, it will have the facility of having all the repayments due from 2005-10 on central loans contracted up to 31.3.2004 and consolidated by the commission written off. The amount of debt relief on this count is around 32,200 crore if all states eliminate their revenue deficit by 2008-09. The magnitude of write-off depends upon the reduction in the absolute amount of revenue deficit. Further more, if a state enacts a fiscal responsibility legislation, then, the central loans to that state contracted till 31.3.2004 and outstanding on 31.5.2005 will be consolidated and rescheduled for a fresh period of 20 years on the rate of interest of 7.5. per cent. If all states enact fiscal responsibility legislation, it will amount to Rs. 128795 crore relief. Nothing has been laid down by the finance commission about provisions if a state fails completely or partially achieve the standards set by the FRI.

SECTION - III

The issue of providing debt relief had been referred to various Finance commissions by the President of India. The twelve finance commissions constituted so far have recommended debt-relief in the form of (i) consolidation of loans and reduction in interest rates, (ii) revision in terms of (i) consolidation of loans and reduction in interest rates, (ii) revision in terms of repayment of loans (iii) moratorium on interest payments and repayment of principal amount, (iv) write-off certain categories of loans and (v) introduction of debt-relief schemes linked to fiscal performance. The scheme of linking debt-relief to performance was first recommended by the ninth finance commission and thereafter each successive finance commission including the Twelfth Finance Commission has followed the scheme though somewhat in a different way in terms of criteria of performance.

State finances have reached to such an alarming stage that the strategic conditionalities such as enactment of Fiscal Reforms legislation, reduction in the absolute amount of revenue deficit yearly and to achieve revenue balance by 2008-09 imposed by the Twelfth Finance Commission on states for providing debt relief seems to be reasonable for bringing fiscal discipline among the states. The magnitude of debt relief to be provided to states by the Twelfth Finance Commission is substantial and significantly higher than that provided by the earlier Finance Commissions. Some of the poorer states where investment climate is not healthy and the level of social and economic infrastructure is poor will be tempted in order to comply with the tight conditionalities of the commission for reducing their deficit by steeply decreasing their plan expenditure which would adversely affect the rate of growth of different sectors of the economy.

A historical and path-breaking recommendation of the Twelfth Finance Commission has been to eliminate the old-long intermediary role of the central government lending to the states. The recommendation of the commission will undoubtedly reduce the fiscal deficit of the central government because to that extent the market borrowing programme of the central government would be reduced. Besides, state's indebtedness to the center would be significantly reduced. But, it would in no way help reducing the absolute size of the magnitude of states debt. The recommendation will radically change the composition of state's debt. The proportion of the size of internal debt of the states in the total state's debt would go up significantly along with reduction in the ratio of the state's debt indebtedness to the center in the forthcoming years. The burden of market borrowings on the states would grow in leaps and bounds. Besides, the poorer states would face problems in raising resources from the market. There had already been some instances of under-subscription to the state government issues despite easy liquidity conditions in the market.

By the time, the Twelfth Finance Commission submitted its report 13 states had set-up sinking fund for amortization of debt recommended by the earlier three commissions. The Twelfth Finance Commission has also endorsed the recommendation of the earlier three commissions. A true sinking fund is that which is fed from the tax revenue of the concerned state. The present fiscal scenario of states reveals that it would be a herculian task for the states to maintain true sinking fund in the immediate future. Sinking funds maintained from additional market borrowings by states will increase unnecessarily the size of interest burden due to locking of borrowed funds for a considerable period for amortization without yielding any return.

REFERENCES

Gupta V.P. (2003), *"Federal Finance in India"*, University Book House, Jaipur.

Stephen Howes, Ashok K.Lahiri and Nicholas Stern (2003), *"State-Level Reforms in India"*, Mac Millan India Ltd.

Reserve Bank of India, *"State Finances"*, Study of Budgets of Various Years.

Reports of Various Finance Commissions viz., Second, Fourth, Fifth, Sixth, Seventh, Eighth, Ninth, Tenth, Eleventh and Twelfth.

EPW Research Foundation, *"Finances of State Governments: Deteriorating Fiscal Management"*, May 1-7, 2004.

10

IMPORTANT RECOMMENDATIONS OF THE TWELFTH FINANCE COMMISSION

E. Nagabhusana Rao, M. Chandrayya,
M. Sankara Reddi & M. Ramesh

INTRODUCTION

In all federal Governments, some degree of vertical and horizontal fiscal imbalances exists. This is the case with India too. The framers of our Constitution of India had anticipated that the States would be in deficits while Union Government would have the surplus in its budgets. So under Article 280, the President of India appointment Finance Commission at an interval of five years or earlier to make recommendations pertaining to the sharing of income tax and excise taxes and grant-in-aid of state revenues. It is a quasi-judicial body whose recommendations, once accepted by the Government become binding on it. Further the institution of Finance Commission is a unique feature of our constitution. It is no parallel to any other federation, old or new. Ninth Finance Commission has adopted "normative" approach. This led to speculation of discrimination in the treatment in its application between the Centre and the States and the possibility of further erosion of autonomy of states.

President appointed the Twelfth Finance Commission (TFC) on 1st November 2002 under the Chairmanship of Dr. C. Rangarajan. The Terms of Reference of the Commission are at *Annexure-I.* Summary of the recommendations of the TFC are placed at Annexure-II.

SALIENT FEATURES OF TWELFTH FINANCE COMMISSION (TFC) RECOMMENDATIONS

Total Transfers Recommended

- The 12th Finance Commission has recommended a total transfer of Rs. 7,55,751.62 crore (share in central taxes and duties Rs. 6,13,112.02 Crore + Grants-in-aid Rs. 1,42,639.60 crore) to States during 2005-10 as against Rs. 4,40,209.26 crore (Rs. 3,76,318.01 crore as share in central taxes and duties + Rs. 58,587.39 crore as grant-in-aid + Rs. 5,303.86 crore as Centre's share of Incentive Fund) by 11th Finance Commission for the five years period 2000-05, showing an increase of 71.68% over TFC award period.

Grant in Aid of States' Revenues

The Non-plan grants under Article 275 of the constitution as per 12th Finance Commission are significantly higher when compared with the corresponding grants for the period of 11th Finance Commission 2000-05 as shown below: (Rs. in crore)

Sl. No.	*Purpose of Grant*	*During 2000-05 (11th FC)*	*During 2005-10 (12th FC)*
1.	Local Bodies grants	10,000.00	25,000.00
2.	Centre's share in Calamity Relief	8,255.69	16,000.00
3.	Non-Plan revenue deficit grants	35,359.07	56,855.87
4.	Grant for education	Nil	10,171.65
5.	Grant for heath	Nil	5,887.08
6.	Grant for maintenance of roads and bridges	Nil	15,000.00
7.	Grant for maintenance of public buildings	Nil	5,000.00
8.	Grant for maintenance of forest.	Nil	1,000.00
9.	Grant for heritage conservation.	Nil	625.00
10.	Grant for State-specific needs	Nil	7,100.00
11.	Up gradation and special problem grants.	4,972.63	Nil
12.	Centre's share of Incentive Fund	5303.86	Nil
	Total Non Plan Grants	63891.25	1,42,639.60

Under the scheme of transfer recommended by the TFC, the share of grants in the total transfer is 18.9 per cent, whereas it was 8.1%, 11.1%, 13.8%, 10.3% and 14.5% as per the recommendations of last five commissions.

Share in Central Taxes

The share of the States in the net proceeds of shareable central taxes would be 30.5 per cent during 2005-10 (during 2000-05 it was 29.5%). For this purpose, additional excise duties in lieu of sales tax on textiles, tobacco and sugar are treated as a part of the general pool of central taxes. If the tax rental arrangement for these three commodities is terminated and the States are allowed to levy sales tax (or VAT) on these commodities without any prescribed limit, the share of the States in the net proceeds of shareable central taxes shall be reduced to 29.5 per cent.

Criteria and Relative Weights for determining Inter-se shares of States by 11th Finance Commission and 12th Finance Commission has been as under:

Sl. No.	*Criterion*	*Relative Weight (per cent)*	
		11th Finance Commission	*12th Finance Commission*
1.	Population	10.0	25.0
2.	Income (Distance Method)	62.5	50.0
3.	Area	7.5	10.0
4.	Index of infrastructure	7.5	0.0
5.	Tax effort	5.0	7.5
6.	Fiscal Discipline	7.5	7.5

Commission has recommended that if any legislation is enacted in respect of service tax after the eighty eighth Constitutional amendment is notified, it must be ensured that the revenue accruing to a State under the legislation should not be less than the share that would accrue to it, had the entire service tax proceeds been part of the shareable pool.

Overall Transfers to States

The Commission has recommended that indicative amount of over all transfer to States may be fixed at 38 per cent of the central gross revenue receipts, as against 37.5% of the gross revenue receipts of the Central Government recommended by EFC for 2000-05

Non-plan Revenue Deficit Grant

A total non-plan revenue deficit grant of Rs. 56,855.87 crore is recommended during the award period for fifteen States. During the first year of the award period, non-Plan revenue deficit grant has been recommended for fifteen States amounting to Rs. 15091.86 crore. By the last year of the award period, only nine States would get non-Plan revenue deficit grant amounting to Rs. 9,528.14 crore. Non-plan revenue deficit grants are largely for special category States, except four non-special category states of Kerala, Orissa, West Bengal and Punjab.

Grant for Education and Health

- Eight States have been recommended for grants amounting to Rs. 10171.65 crore over the award period for the education sector, with a minimum of Rs. 20 crore in a year for any eligible State.
- Seven states have been recommended for grants amounting to Rs. 5887.08 crore over the award period for the health sector, with a minimum of Rs. 10 crore in a year for any eligible State.
- Year-wise allocation for each State in the grants for education and health.
- Grants for the education and health sectors are additional, over and above the normal expenditure to be incurred by the States in these sectors. The Commission has recommended that these grants should be utilized only for the respective sectors (non-Plan) based on certain conditionality specified by the Commission. Monitoring of the expenditure relating to these grants will rest with the State government concerned.

Grants for Maintenance of Roads & Bridges, Public Buildings and Forests

The 12th Finance Commission has recommended grants separately for maintenance of roads and bridges, maintenance of buildings and forests as under:

- A grant of Rs. 15,000.00 crore over the award period has been recommended for maintenance of roads and bridges.
- An amount of Rs.5000 crore is recommended as grants for maintenance of public buildings.
- The Commission for maintenance of forests has recommended Grant of Rs.1000 crore spread over the award period 2005-10.
- State-wise and year-wise allocations for these three grants.
- The maintenance grants are additional, over and above the normal maintenance expenditure to be incurred by the states. These grants are to be released and spent in accordance with certain conditional ties specified by the Commission.

Grants for Heritage Conservation

A grant of Rs. 625 **crore** spread over the award period has been recommended for heritage conservation. This grant will be used for preservation and protection of historical monuments, archaeological sites, public libraries, museums and archives, and for improving the tourist infrastructure to facilitate visits to these sites.

Grants for State Specific Needs

The grant recommended by the TFC for State specific needs is on the pattern of the grant recommended by EFC for the special problems of the States. The grant recommended by EFC for the special problems of States was Rs. 1,129.00 crore. TFC has recommended an amount of Rs. 7,100 crore as grant for States' specific needs. While these grants have been phased out equally over the last four years, Commission has observed that this phasing should be taken as indicative in nature. The States may communicate the required phasing of grants to the Central government.

Grants for Local Bodies

- The Commission's mandate was to recommend as to the measures needed to augment the Consolidate Fund of a State to supplement the resources of the Panchayats and the Municipalities in the State based on the recommendations made by the Finance Commission of the State.
- The Commission has recommended a sum of Rs. 25, 000 crore for the period 2005-10 as grants-in-aid to augment the consolidated fund of the States to supplement the resources of the municipalities and the panchayats. This is equivalent to 1.24 per cent of the shareable tax revenue and 0.9 per cent of gross revenue receipts of the Centre as estimated by the Commission during the period 2005-10.
- The Commission has also recommended that amount of Rs. 25000 crore may be divided between the panchayats and the municipalities in the ratio of 80:20.
- A total grant of Rs. 20,000 crore for the panchayati raj institutions and Rs. 5,000 crore for the urban local bodies may be given to the States for the period 2005-10 with inter-se distribution.

Weight Adopted for Working Out Inter-se Allocation of the Grant

Sl. No.	*Criterion*	*Relative Weight (per cent)*	
		11th Finance Commission	*12th Finance Commission*
1.	Population	40.0	40.0
2.	Geographical area	10.0	10.0
3.	Distance from highest per capita Income	20.0	20.0
4.	Index of decentralization	20.0	0.0
5.	Revenue effort of which	10.0	20.0
	(a) With respect to own revenue of States		10.0
	(b) With respect to GSDP		10.0
6.	Index of deprivation	0.0	10.0

Financing of Relief Expenditure

Calamity Relief Fund (CRF)

The Commission has made the following recommendations regarding Calamity Relief:

- The scheme of CRF is continued in its present form with contributions from the Centre and the States in the ratio of 75:25.
- The size of the CRF for TFC's award period is Rs. 21,333.33 crore (Centre's share of Rs. 16000 crore + State's share of 5,333.33 crore).

Under the recommendations of EFC for the 2000-05 the size of the CRF was Rs. 11007.59 crore (Centre's share Rs. 8,255.69 crore and Rs. 2,751.90 crore as States share). The size of CRF as recommended by TFC is much larger than what was recommended by EFC even after indexation for inflation.

National Calamity Contingency Fund (NCCF)

- The TFC has recommended that the scheme of NCCF may continue in its present form with core corpus of Rs. 500 crore. The outgo from the fund may continue to be replenished by way of collection of National Calamity Contingent Duty and levy of special surcharges.
- The definition of natural calamity, as applicable at present, may be expanded to cover landslides, avalanches, cloud burst and pest attacks.
- The Center may continue to make allocation of food grains to the needy States as a relief measure, but a transparent policy in this regard is required.
- A committee consisting of scientists, flood control specialists and other experts are set up to study and map the hazards to which several States are subject to.
- The provision for disaster preparedness and mitigation needs to be built into the State plans, and not as a part of calamity relief.

Fiscal Reforms Facility

The 12th Finance Commission felt that the Fiscal Reform Facility introduced by the government based on the EFC recommendations did not play a significant role in bringing about an improvement in the State's fiscal position. Accordingly, the Commission has recommended that the scheme of Fiscal Reform Facility may not continue over the period 2005-10, as the scheme of debt relief as recommended by it obviates the need for a separate Fiscal Reform Facility.

Debt Relief

The Commission's mandate was to make an assessment of the debt position of the States as on 31st March 2004, suggest such corrective measures, as are deemed necessary, consistent with macro-economic stability and debt sustainability. Such measures recommended will give weight-age to the performance of the States in the field of human development and investment climate. The Commission has made the following recommendations:

- Each State must enact a fiscal responsibility legislation prescribing specific annual targets with a view to eliminating the revenue deficit by 2008-09 and reducing fiscal deficits based on a path for reduction of borrowings and guarantees. Enacting the fiscal responsibility legislation will be necessary pre-condition for availing of debt relief.
- Debt relief may not be linked with performance in human development or investment climate.
- The Central loans to States contracted till 31.3.04 and outstanding on 31.3.05 (amounting to Rs. 1,28,795 crore) may be consolidated and rescheduled for a fresh term of 20 years (resulting in repayment in 20 equal installments), and an interest rate of 7.5 per cent be charged on them. This will be subject to the State enacting the fiscal responsibility legislation and will take effect prospectively from the year in which such legislation is enacted.
- The debt relief during the award period for all the States put together, works out to Rs. 21,276 crore in interest payments and Rs.11,929 crore in repayments.

- A debt write-off scheme linked to the reduction of revenue deficit of States may be introduced. Under the scheme, the repayments due from 2005-06 to 2009-10 on central loans contracted up-to 31.3.04 and recommended to be consolidated will be eligible for write off.
- The quantum of write off of repayment will be linked to the absolute amount by which the revenue deficit is reduced in each successive year during the award period. The reduction in the revenue deficit must be cumulatively higher than the cumulative reduction attributable to the interest relief recommended. Also, the fiscal deficit of the State must be contained at least to the level of 2004-05. In effect, if the revenue deficit is brought down to zero, the entire repayments during the period will be written off. The enactment of the fiscal responsibility legislation would be a necessary pre-condition for availing the debt relief under this scheme also with the benefit accruing prospectively.
- The Central Government should not act an intermediary for future lending and allow the States to approach the market directly. If some fiscally weak States are unable to raise funds from the market, the Centre could borrow for the purpose of on lending to such States, but the interest should remain aligned to the marginal cost of borrowing for the Centre.
- External assistance may be transferred to States on the same terms and conditions as attached to such assistance by external funding agencies, thereby making Government of India a financial intermediary without any gain or loss. The external assistance passed through to States should be managed through a separate fund in the public account.
- The moratorium on repayments and interest payments on the outstanding special term loans amounting to Rs. 3,772 crore as on 31.3.2000 given to Punjab may continue for another two years i.e. upto 2006-07, by which time the Central Government must finalise the quantum of debt relief to be allowed in terms of the recommendations of the EFC.

- In respect of relief and rehabilitation loans given to Gujarat from ADB and World Bank through the Central Government, the Central Government may, if the Government of Gujarat so desires, alter the terms and conditions of these loans, so that these are available to Gujarat on the same terms on which the external agencies have extended these loans.
- States should set up sinking funds for amortization of all loans including loans from banks, liabilities because of NSSF etc. The fund should be maintained outside the consolidated fund of the States and the public account and should not be used for any other purpose, except for redemption of loans.
- States should set up guarantee redemption funds through earmarked guarantee fees. This should be preceded by risk weighting of guarantees. The quantum of contribution to the fund should be decided accordingly.

Sharing of Profit Petroleum

The issue of sharing of Profit Petroleum was added to the terms of reference of the Commission in October 2003. The Commission was required to make recommendation as to whether the non-tax revenue of 'Profit Petroleum" arising out of contractual provision, be shared with the States from where the mineral oils are produced, and if so, to what extent. Accordingly, the Commission has made the following recommendation:

The Union should share the Profit Petroleum from NELP areas with the States from where the mineral oil and natural gas are produced. The share should be in the ration of 50:50.

- There need not be sharing of profits in respect of nomination fields and non-NELP blocks.
- The revenues earned by the Central Government on contracts signed under the coal bed methane policy may be shared with the producing States in the same manner as Profit Petroleum.

- In respect of any mineral, if a loss of revenue is anticipated for a State in the process of implementation of a policy, which involves production sharing, a similar compensation mechanism should be adopted by the Central Government.

Contents of Fiscal Responsibility Legislation

Each State should enact a fiscal responsibility legislation, which should, at a minimum, provide for:

- Eliminating revenue deficit by 2008-09;
- Reducing fiscal deficit to 3 per cent of GSDP or its equivalent, defined as the ratio of interest payment to revenue receipts;
- Bringing out annual reduction targets of revenue and fiscal deficits;
- Bringing out annual statement giving prospects for the State economy and related fiscal strategy; and
- Bringing out special statements along with the budget giving in detail the number of employees in government, public sector, and aided institutions and related salaries.

Status of Releases Made Against Recommendations of XI FC

A statement indicating the allocations made by EFC and the grants released during 2000-05 are stated in a table.

Status on the Issuance of Guidelines

To operationalise the various recommendations under Twelfth Finance Commission, following guidelines have been issued. Release and Utilisation of grants-in –aid other than local bodies and CRF-NCCF Local Bodies Grants Calamity Relief Fund.

CONCLUSION

There is a need to reconstitute National Development Council under Article 263 as Economic and Development Council. Further, it is right time to implement Sarkaria Commission and Ramamurthy Commission recommendations.

ANNEXURE - I

Terms of Reference of Twelfth Finance Commission

The President vides the notification dated 1st November 2002 mandated the Commission to do the following:

The Commission shall make recommendations as to the following matters:

1. The distribution between the Union and the States of the net proceeds of taxes which are to be, or may be, divided between them under Chapter I Part XII of the Constitution and the allocation between the States of the respective shares of such proceeds;
2. The principles which should govern the grants-in-aid of the revenues of the States out of the Consolidated Fund of India and the sums to be paid to the States which are in need of assistance by way of grants-in-aid of their revenues under article 275 of the Constitution for purposes other than those specified in the provisions to clause (1) of that article; and
3. The measures needed to augment the Consolidated Fund of a State to supplement the resources of the Panchayats and Municipalities in the State based on the recommendations made by the Finance Commission of the State.

The Commission shall review the state of the finances of the Union and the States and suggest a plan by which the governments, collectively and severally, may bring about a restructuring of the public finances restoring budgetary balance, achieving macro-economic stability and debt reduction along with equitable growth.

In making its recommendations, the Commission shall have regard, among other considerations, to:

1. The resources, of the Central Government for five years commencing on 1st April, 2005, on the basis of levels of taxation and non-tax revenues likely to be reached at the end of 2003-04;
2. The demands on the resources of the Central Government, in particular, on account of expenditure on civil administration, defense, internal and border security, debt-servicing and other committed expenditure and liabilities;
3. The resources of the State Governments, for the five years commencing on 1st April, 2005, on the basis of levels of taxation and non-tax revenues likely to be reached at the end of 2003-04;

4. The objective of not only balancing the receipts and expenditure on revenue account of all the States and the Centre, but also generating surpluses for capital investment and reducing fiscal deficit;
5. Taxation efforts of the Central Government and each State Government as against targets, if any, and the potential for additional resource mobilization in order to improve the tax-Gross Domestic Product (GDP) and tax-Gross State Domestic Product (GSDP) ratio, as the case may be;
6. The expenditure on the non-salary component of maintenance and upkeep of capital assets and the non-wage related maintenance expenditure on plan schemes to be completed by the 31st March, 2005 and the norms on the basis of which specific amounts are recommended for the maintenance of the capital assets and the manner of monitoring such expenditure;
7. The need for ensuring the commercial viability of irrigation projects, power projects, departmental undertakings, public sector enterprises etc. in the States through various means including adjustment of user charges and relinquishing of non-priority enterprises through privatization or disinvestments.

In making its recommendations on various matters, the Commission will take the base of population figures as of 1971, in all such cases where population is a factor for determination of devolution of taxes and duties and grants-in-aid. The Commission shall review the Fiscal Reform Facility introduced by the Central Government on the basis on the recommendations of the Eleventh Finance Commission, and suggest measures for effective achievement of its objectives.

The Commission may, after making an assessment of the debt position of the States as on the 31st March 2004, suggest such corrective measures, as are deemed necessary, consistent with macro-economic stability and debt sustainability. Such measures recommended will give weightage to the performance of the States in the fields of human development and investment climate. The Commission may review the present arrangements as regards financing of Disaster Management with reference to the National Calamity Contingency Fund and the Calamity Relief Fund and make appropriate recommendations thereon. The Commission shall indicate the basis on which it has arrived at its findings and make available the State-wise estimates of receipts and expenditure. In addition to the above, through a subsequent notification dated 31st October 2003, the

Commission was asked to make recommendations on the following matters:

- Whether non-tax income of profit petroleum to the Union, arising out of contractual provisions, should be shared with the States from where the mineral oils are produced; and If so, to what extent.

ANNEXURE - II

SUMMARY OF RECOMMENDATIONS

Plan for Restructuring Public Finances

1. By 2009-10, the combined tax-GDP ratio of the center and the States should be increased to 17.6 per cent, primary expenditure to a level of 23 per cent of GDP and capital expenditure to nearly 7 per cent of GDP. (Para 4.52).
2. The combined debt-GDP ratio with external debt measured at historical exchange rates should, at a minimum, be brought down to 75 per cent by the end of 2009-10. (Para 4.45).
3. The system of on lending should be brought to an end over time and the long-term goal for the center and States for the debt-GDP ratio should be 28 per cent each. (Para 4.45).
4. The fiscal deficit to GDP ratio targets for the center and the States may be fixed at 3 per cent of GDP each. (Para 4.45).
5. The center's interest payment relative to revenue receipts should reach about 28 per cent by 2009-10. In the case of States, the level of interest payments relative to revenue receipts should fall to about 15 per cent by 2009-10. (Para 4.54).
6. The revenue deficit relative to GDP for the center and the States, for their combined as well as individual accounts should be brought down to zero by 2008-09. (Para 4.51)
7. States should follow a recruitment and wage policy, in a manner such that the total salary bill relative to revenue expenditure net of interest payments and pensions does not exceed 35 per cent. (Para 4.63).
8. Each State should enact a fiscal responsibility legislation, which should, at a minimum, provide for:
    - Eliminating revenue deficit by 2008-09;

- Reducing fiscal deficit to 3 per cent of GSDP or its equivalent, defined as the ratio of interest payment to revenue receipts;
- Bringing out annual reduction targets of revenue and fiscal deficits;
- Bringing out annual Statement giving prospects for the State economy and related fiscal strategy; and
- Bringing out special Statements along with the budget giving in detail the number of employees in Government, public sector, and aided institutions and related salaries. (Para 4.79)

9. Sharing of Union Tax Revenues

10. The share of the States in the net proceeds of shareable central taxes shall be 30.5 per cent. For this purpose, additional excise duties in lieu of sales tax are treated as a part of the general pool of central taxes. If the tax rental arrangement is terminated and the States are allowed to levy sales tax (or VAT) on these commodities without any prescribed limit, the share of the States in the net proceeds of shareable central taxes shall be reduced to 29.5 per cent. (Para 7.22).

11. If any legislation is enacted in respect of service tax after the eighty eighth Constitutional amendment is notified, it must be ensured that the revenue accruing to a State under the legislation should not be less than the share that would accrue to it, had the entire service tax proceeds been part of the shareable pool. (Para 7.22).

12. The indicative amount of over all transfers to States may be fixed at 38 per cent of the central gross revenue receipt. (Para 7.22).

13. The States should be given a share as specified in the following table in the net proceeds of all the shareable Union taxes in each of the five financial years during the period 2005-06 to 2009-10. (Paras 7.35, 7.36).

Sl. No.	*State*	*Share (all shareable taxes excluding service tax) (per cent)*	*Share of Service Tax (per cent)*
1	2	3	4
1.	Andhra Pradesh	7.356	7.453
2.	Arunachal Pradesh	0.288	0.292
3.	Assam	3.235	3.277

Contd...

Sl. No.	*State*	*Share (all shareable taxes excluding service tax) (per cent)*	*Share of Service Tax (per cent)*
1	2	3	4
4.	Bihar	11.028	11.173
5.	Chhattisgarh	2.654	2.689
6.	Goa	0.259	0.262
7.	Gujarat	3.569	3.616
8.	Haryana	1.075	1.089
9.	Himachal Pradesh	0.522	0.529
10.	Jammu & Kashmir	1.297	0.000
11.	Jharkhand	3.361	3.405
12.	Karnataka	4.459	4.518
13.	Kerala	2.665	2.70
14.	Madhya Pradesh	6.711	6.799
15.	Maharashtra	4.997	5.063
16.	Manipur	0.362	0.367
17.	Meghalaya	0.371	0.376
18.	Mizoram	0.239	0.242
19.	Nagaland	0.263	0.266
20.	Orissa	5.161	5.229
21.	Punjab	1.299	1.316
22.	Rajasthan	5.609	5.683
23.	Sikkim	0.227	0.230
24.	Tamil Nadu	5.305	5.374
25.	Tripura	0.428	0.433
26.	Uttar Pradesh	19.264	19.517
27.	Uttaranchal	0.939	0.952
28.	West Bengal	7.057	7.150
	All States	100.000	100.000

LOCAL BODIES

1. A total grant of Rs,.20,000 crore for the panchayati raj institutions and Rs.5,000 crore for the urban local bodies may be given to the States for the period 2005-10 with inter-se distribution as indicated in Table 8.1. (See Annexure-XI) (Para 8.38).

2. The PRIs should be encouraged to take over the assets relating to water supply and sanitation and utilize the grants for repairs/ rejuvenation as the O&M costs. The PRIs should, however, recover

at least 50 per cent of the recurring costs in the form of user charges. (Para 8.40).

3. Out of the grants allocated for the panchayats, priority should be given to expenditure on the O&M costs of water supply and sanitation. This will facilitate panchayats to take over the schemes and operate them. (Para 8.41).
4. At least 50 per cent of the grants provided to each State for the urban local bodies should be earmarked for the scheme of solid waste management through public-private partnership. The municipalities should concentrate on collection, segregation and transportation of solid waste. The cost of these activities, whether carried out in house or out sourced, could be met from the grants. (Para 8.42).
5. Besides expenditure on the O&M costs of water supply and sanitation in rural areas and on the schemes of solid waste management in urban areas, PRIs and ULBs should, out of the grants allocated, give high priority to expenditure on creation of data base and maintenance of accounts through the use of modern technology and management systems, wherever possible. Some of the modern methods like GIS (Geographic Information Systems) for mapping of properties in urban areas and computerization for switching over to a modern system of financial management would go a long way in creating strong local Governments, fulfilling the spirit of the 73rd and 74th Constitutional amendments. (Para 8.43).
6. The States may assess the requirement of each local body based on the principles Stated by us and earmark funds accordingly out of the total allocation re-commended by us. (Para 8.43).
7. Grants have not been recommended separately for the normal and the excluded areas under the fifth and sixth schedule of the Constitution. The States having such areas may distribute the grants recommended by us to all local bodies, including those in the excluded areas, in a fair and just manner. (Para 8.51).
8. The Central Government should not impose any condition other than those prescribed by us, for release or utilization of these grants, which are largely in the nature of a correction of vertical imbalance between the center and the States. (Para 8.52).
9. The normal practice of insisting on the utilization of amounts already released before further releases are considered may continue and the grants may be released to a State only after it

certifies that the previous releases have been passed on to the local bodies. The amounts due to the States in the first year of our award period i.e. 2005-06 may be released without such an insistence. (Para 8.52).

10. State Governments should not take more than 15 days in transferring the grants to local bodies after these are released by the Central Government. The center should take a serious view of any undue delay on the part of the State. (Para 8.53)
11. The Central Government should take note of our views on the issues listed in para 8.23, while formulating or revising various policy measures. In particular, action may be taken to raise the ceiling on profession tax. (Para 8.23).
12. The State should adopt the best practices listed in para 8.19 to improve the resources of the panchayats.
13. The suggestions made by us in respect of State finance commissions in paras 8.29 to 8.37 and 8.54 should be acted upon with a view to strengthening the institution of SFCs, so that it may play an effective role in the system of fiscal transfers to the third tier of Government.

CALAMITY RELIEF

1. The scheme of CRF is continued in its present form with contributions from the center and the States in the ratio of 75:25. (Paras 9.10, 9.11)
2. The size of the CRF for our award period is worked out at Rs. 21333.33 crore. (Para 9.11).
3. The scheme of NCCF may continue in its present form with core corpus of Rs. 500 crore. The outgo from the fund may continue to be replenished by way of collection of National Calamity Contingent Duty and levy of special surcharges. (Paras 9.16, 9.17).
4. The definition of natural calamity, as applicable at present, may be expanded to cover landslides, avalanches, cloud burst and pest attacks. (Para 9.12).
5. The centre may continue to make allocation of food grains to the needy States as a relief measures, but a transparent policy in this regard is to be put in place. (Para 9.18).
6. A committee consisting of scientists, flood control specialists and other experts are set up to study and map the hazards to which several States are subject to. (Para 9.14).

7. The provisions for disaster preparedness and mitigation need to be built into the State plans, and not as a part of calamity relief. (Para 9.14).

11

TWELFTH FINANCE COMMISSION AND INCENTIVES FOR FISCAL REFORM PROGRAM OF BACKWARD STATES IN INDIA: A STUDY OF ORISSA

Bhagabata Patro

Since the later part of the nineties, state level fiscal reform process is under implementation due to the imposition of conditionality by the Ministry of Finance to release central assistance to the states. The fiscal stress witnessed by the states by the end of the nineties was such that there is no option for the states at that time. Due to careless policies pursued by theses government for about two earlier decades, their loan burden was unmanageable, establishment expenses uncontrollable and revenue yield was unachievable.

Fiscal sector reform at the national level came to the country along with other reforms like financial sector reform, industrial reform and labour policy reform. At the state level, the application of fiscal sector reform was taken up in the year 99-00. This is due to inability of the states to mobilize more resources to meet the hike in salary and pension of the government employees as a result of 5th pay commission recommendation. Mismatch between receipt and expenditure in the revenue account to a smaller extent (19 crores) originated in 90-91 but expanded its size thereafter at a rapid pace in Orissa. By the end of the nineties it is around 40 per cent of the states own revenue.

STATE LEVEL FISCAL REFORM

Fiscal sector reform has brought discipline in the fiscal management of almost all the states in India. The Ministry of Finance, Government of India; the Planning Commission and the Finance Commissions have acted in unison on the state governments and practically compelled them to toe their line of thinking. As a result, the state governments gradually adopted privatization of certain services and reduction of some other services. The eighties and the nineties see decline in the growth rate of seven states. These are A.P. Bihar, Haryana, Orissa, Punjab, Rajastan and U.P. Only Gujarat and Maharastra grew at the rate of 8 to 9 per cent. The other five states in the non-special category recorded 5-7 per cent growth rate. (Howes, Lahiriand Stern; 2003) The reform process of the 99-00 accentuated this process by supporting the already buoyant economies of developed states at the cost of backward ones. The 10th, 11th and 12th Finance commissions have come out with a methodology supportive of affluent states. The Finance Commissions have concentrated on 'no problem in governance' criterion ignoring the fact that surplus in the revenue account will determine the development effort of a state. Three things happened in the period between 1999-00 and 04-05 with regard to state fiscal systems in the country:

(i) The share of central participation in state development initiatives declined;

(ii) The states have emphasized more on reducing public expenditure to bring fiscal balance;

(iii) The states made less effort to raise revenue as it is likely to have adverse impact on their political prospects.

This paper intends to examine the role of the finance commissions in general and the 12th finance commission in particular on the public investment situation due to their emphasis on fiscal reform programs. The backward states have no option but to accept the central advise of rationalizing their income and expenditure ignoring their consequence on growth and employment level in the economy. Reduced public expenditure has resulted in slow growth of the state economy, particularly in Orissa as private sector investment in the state is very marginal.

TREND OF PUBLIC EXPENDITURE IN ORISSA

The main emphasis of the state government in the year 99-00 is to draw a comprehensive programme for fiscal and governance reform in the state. Under this, each state is expected to take effective steps for revenue augmentation and expenditure compression over the period from 2000-05. The MOU signed by the state with the centre promises expenditure reduction measures like ban on creation and filling up of posts, reduce the size of the government machinery and start recruiting employees on contract basis. At present about thirty per cent of the primary school teachers in the state are working on contract basis on a paltry sum of Rs. 1500/- which is much les than the minimum wage declared by the government. The slogan of the government is to 'right size the bureaucracy' and this is mostly confined to the posts in the lower cadres of class three and class fourth employees. In an effort to reduce public expenditure, the state government has gone for liquidating, disinvesting and closing 38 PSUs causing misery to thousands of employees. Even the government sold away the profit-earning IDCOL cement at Bargarh to ACC at a very nominal price. It appears that the psychology of the government is that everything government is bad and requires privatization. It is surprising to note that the government has come out with the results of the high schools for 2003 and 2004 to make out a point that such investment in school is unproductive. In far flung tribal areas of the state, education is precious and getting passed in the examination is no measurement of productivity of education. In the health sector, the state has practically remained stagnant with respect to number of health institutions, number of beds available per lakh population etc. Even there is rise in the population covered by one health institute from 12984 to 13932. Most of the health schemes are either sponsored by the centre or under external assistance. Only very few schemes are state government's own scheme. In economic services, the state has withdrawn substantially from many areas and this led to decrease of share of economic services in the stat budget. Table 1 below gives the pattern of growth of public expenditure in Orissa.

Table 1
Growth of Public Expenditure in Orissa

Year	*Rev. Exp.*	*Capital Exp*	*Total Exp*	*Increase*	*% rise*
1995-96	4698	865	5563		
1996-97	5117	1193	6310	745	11.8
1997-98	5535	1317	6852	542	7.9
1998-99	6817	1823	8640	1788	20.7
1999-00	8459	1751	10210	1570	15.4
Average					14.9
2000-01	8834	2213	11047	837	7.6
2001-02	9881	2187	12068	1021	8.5
2002-03	10015	3252	13267	1199	9.0
2004-05	12372	4964	17336	1771	10.2
Average					10.1

Source: Orissa Budget 2005-06 At a Glance, Finance Department, Government of Orissa, Bhubaneswar.

Between 1995-00, the growth of public expenditure was around 15 per cent per annum and declined to 10 per cent for the period 2000-05. The worst causality of this decline is the 'development expenditure'(includes expenditure on social and economic services) which constituted 61 per cent in 95-96 of the total expenditure and reduced to 47 per cent in 03-04.The state government, however, boldly declared, "there should not be any impression in any quarter that these reforms are induced by any external agency or for obtaining any aid or loan assistance". Because of all these tight fiscal measures, the state became eligible for structural adjustment loan of Rs. 3000 crores from the international funding agencies. To receive 3000 crores the state reduced the developmental expenditure to the tune of 14 per cent (61-47) which constitutes on an average about Rs. 2500 crores (Assuming the total state expenditure at Rs. 20,000 crores per annum). Table 2 gives this information for the period 1995-96 to 2003-04.

Table 2
Nature of Public Expenditure in Orissa

Year	*Non-developmental Spending*	*Developmental Spending*	*Others*	*Total*
1995-96	1667	3656	691	6013
	28	61	12	
1996-97	1995	4088	2236	8319
	24	49	27	
1997-98	2328	4186	2932	9446
	25	44	31	
1998-99	2877	5149	2980	11005
	26	47	27	
1999=00	3096	6608	4338	14043
	22	47	31	
2000-01	4093	6041	6073	16207
	25	37	37	
2001-02	5036	5958	7587	18582
	27	32	41	
2002-03	5257	7327	7961	20545
	26	36	39	
2003-04	6215	8039	2629	16883
	37	48	16	

Source: Orissa Budget 2005-06 At a Glance, Finance Department, Government of Orissa, Bhubaneswar.

GROWTH OF REVENUE RECEIPT

On the revenue front, Orissa has tried to improve its performance but could not achieve any substantial growth in tune with the requirement of the state. Revenue receipt has two components. One is the central devolution and the other is the state's own effort to mobilize more resources. In the reform period, the state could manage to achieve elasticity in the tax revenue but not in case of non-tax revenue.

Between 1995-96 to 99-00, the revenue effort of the state was severely impaired due to the super cyclone in 1999.The annual average growth of revenue receipt was close to 10 per cent in the first period but has gone up to nearly 13 per cent in the second period. Going by the requirement of the state, it should have been close to 15 per cent to fill the gap in the receipt –expenditure difference.

Table 3
Trend of Revenue Receipt of Orissa

Year	*OTR*	*ONTR*	*ST*	*GIA*	*TOTAL*	*% Rise*
95-96	1137	628	1285	850	3890	
96-97	1343	482	1566	897	4287	9.3
97-98	1421	541	1514	1106	4632	7.4
98-99	1758	558	1695	815	4825	4.0
99-00	1704	716	1748	1715	5884	18.0
Average						9.7
00-01	2184	685	2603	1428	6902	
01-02	2467	692	2649	1241	7047	16.2
02-03	2872	961	2806	1800	8439	16.5
03-04	3301	1094	3327	1716	9440	10.6
04-05	4177	1346	3946	3978	2350	20.3
Average						12.7

Source: Orissa Budget 2005-06 At a Glance, Finance Department, Government of Orissa, Bhubaneswar.

DISPARITY IN PER CAPITA INCOME

Public investment programme of a state has the ultimate objective of raising the per capita income of the people. However, a look at the statistics on per capita income of Orissa and India shows no signs of convergence. The situation in the growth of NSDP/GSDP for the above period reflects that the reduction in the incremental public investment programme has resulted in slow growth of the state economy. The annual average NSDP growth of the state during 1995-00 was more than 10per cent while in the period of 2000-05 it is around 9 per cent. Barring the year 03-04, all other years do not reveal encouraging growth situation.

Table 3
Disparity in Per Capita Income of India and Orissa

(Rs. In crores)

	95-96	*99-00*	*03-04*	*% Rise (99-00 over 95-96)*	*%rise (03-04 over 99-00)*
India -	10149	15625	20988	53	34
Orissa -	6985	9486	12388	36	31

Source: Economic Survey, Government of India, 2004-05.

INCENTIVE SCHEME AND THE FINANCE COMMISSIONS

The 10th and 11th Finance Commissions have started the incentive linked grant/debt relief schemes in India. This is based on the logic of efficiency in public expenditure across the states. The 11th FC started a separate Fiscal Reform Facility (FRF) by drawing 15 per cent of non-plan revenue deficit grant and contribution from the central government. By assuming 99-00 as the base year, it is envisaged that the revenue deficit as percentage to revenue receipt of the states will improve by 5per cent every year. The revenue deficit is inclusive of the contingent liabilities and indirect subsidies of the PSEs. Till Mid-November, 2004, only Rs. 5029 crores was released out of the incentive fund which consists of Rs. 10608 Crores. Orissa got 263 crore under this head out of the total availability of fund to the tune of Rs. 315 crores. The 12th FC discontinued the FRF scheme on the ground that it provides inadequate incentive, uniform target of 5 per cent reduction in revenue deficit is unjustified and the scheme is based on 'arbitrary flexibility' shown to some states. The Commission, however, reformulated the debt relief scheme which includes the objectives of FRF scheme.

Table 4
Release from Incentive Fund to Orissa in the 11th Finance Commission Period

(Rs. in Crores)

	Part-A	*Part-B*	*Total*
2000-01	53.77	24.18	77.95
2001-02	5.46	42.07	47.53
2002-03	41.80	45.54	87.34
2003-04	–	50.91	101.82
Total	100.03	162.70	263.73

Source: Report of the 12th Finance Commission, p. 469.

The emphasis of the 12th Finance Commission on incentivising the fiscal performance and linking it with debt relief will lead to negative effect on the public capital investment in Orissa. The state govt. with huge debt liability will not show any interest to go for additional borrowing as it will go against the fiscal performance.

Table 5
Debt Relief under Incentive Scheme of 12th Finance Commission for Orissa (Proposed)

(Rs. in Crores)

		Orissa	*Total*
1.	Total Repayment		
	Due before consolidation	2624	44127
2.	Outstanding debt		
	As on 31.03.05	36615	881349
3.	Debt servicing dues		
	Repayment	873	11929
	Int.	1008	21276
	Total	1881	33204
4.	Relief repayment due		
	After consolidation	1751	32199

Source: Report of the 12th Finance Commissin.

The likely benefit out of the 12th FC award is presented in Table 5. The total debt servicing liability of the state before consolidation and restructuring comes to 2624 crores. After consolidation and restructuring, it got reduced to Rs. 1751 crores. The incentive–linked debt relief package of the 12th FC gives Orissa a coefficient of 0.71. This means, if Orissa satisfies all the requirement of the incentive scheme, it will get the benefit to the extent of around Rs. 1200 crores.

CONCLUSIONS

Orissa now has a number of steel industries in the pipeline. This necessitates huge infrastructure investment to satisfy and attract the private investors. Absence of such investment will cause great harm to the state economy. What is necessary now, is to follow prudent norms for more current capital investments and examine viability and feasibility of such programmes. It is necessary to allow the state to get more market resources by adopting a flexible stipulation on debt-revenue receipt condition. The state also deserves to be supported with more non-plan revenue grant to have a reasonable amount of revenue surplus to have a bigger plan size of not les than Rs. 5000 crores. It is also necessary for the Finance commission in the coming years to look into the problem of non-revision of mining royalty which is a major source of non-tax revenue of the state. Any delay in such matters should involve a penalty devolution to account for the loss the state is suffering.

REFERENCES

Howes, Stephen; Lahiri, A.K. and Stern, Nicholas (2003), State–Level Reforms in India; Towards more Effective Government; Macmillan India Ltd. Delhi.

Report of the 12th Finance Commission.

Report of the 11th Finance Commission.

Report of the 10th Finance Commission.

Economic survey, Government of India, 2004-05.

Orissa Budget 2005-06 At a Glance, Finance Department , Government of Orissa, Bhubaneswar.

Orissa Budget 2004-05 At a Glance, Finance Department, Government of Orissa, Bhubaneswar.

Economic Survey, 2005-06, Government of Orissa, Directorate of Economics and Statistics, Bhubaneswar.

12

PROBLEMS AND PROSPECTS OF CENTRAL GRANTS FOR DEBT SUSTAINBALE, DEFICIT STABLE AND MAXIMUM GROWTH: A CASE STUDY OF ORISSA

S.S. Rath

INTRODUCTION

Article 280 of the constitution describes the duties of the Finance Commission relating to sharing of central taxes under article 270 and determination of grants for the states as provided for under article 275. Finance Commissions' endeavour has been to recommend a scheme of transfer that could serve the objective both of equity and efficiency, and result in fiscal transfers that are predictable and stable. These transfers in the form of tax devolution and grants are meant to correct both the vertical and horizontal imbalances. Correcting vertical imbalance relates to transfer from the central government to the state governments taken together, whereas the correction of horizontal imbalance concerned with the allocation of transfers among the state governments. The vertical imbalance arises since resources have been assigned more to the central government and states have been entrusted with the larger responsibilities. The horizontal imbalance has its root in the differential capacities and needs of the states as also the differences in the cost of providing services.

In the relevant literature also in practice in many, federal countries, the concept of equalization is considered to be a guiding principle for fiscal transfers as it promotes equity as well as efficiency in resource use equalization transfers aim at providing citizens of every state a comparable standard of services provided their revenue effort is also comparable. In other words, equalization transfers neutralize deficiency in fiscal capacity but not in revenue effort. Under such an approach, transfers should be determined on a normative basis instead of merely filling up gaps arising from the projections of revenues and expenditures based on historical trends. There are adverse*

incentives associated with a 'gap filling' approach where the case for larger transfers would depend merely on a larger gap in the past without reference to whether available revenue capacity was adequately exploited or whether there was an undue growth in expenditures. The normative approach can effectively neutralize such adverse in terms of revenues that they ought to raise given their respective capacities. Similarly, expenditures are assessed on the basis of needs consistent with an average or minimum acceptable level of service and the relevant cost norms and not driven by the past history of expenditures.

Vertical transfers refer to the total transfers from the central government to the states. There are many forms and routes in this connection. Among these, the statutory transfers consist of sharing of central tax revenues and grants recommended by the Finance Commission. These are supplemented by grants from the Planning Commission and discretionary grants from the central ministries. In the present scheme of transfers, tax devolution plays a dual role of correcting vertical as well as horizontal imbalance. Grants-in-aid are mainly targeted towards achieving a degree of equalization. That is why many of the better-off states assessed to be in revenue surplus do not get article 275 grants. Grants are the more effective transfer instrument for state-specific and purpose-specific targeting. As such the transfer instruments available to the Finance Commission must include tax revenue sharing, assessed gap grants, and grants that may be earmarked for specific purposes like those meant for the local bodies or achieving certain minimum level of services.

In relation to grants, there are two duties cast upon the Finance Commission conjointly by article 280(3)(b) and 275. Article 280(3)-(b) requires the Commission to make recommendations as to the "principles" which should govern such grants-in-aid. Following from article 275(i), specific sums are to be recommended to be paid to the states, which are assessed, to be in "need of assistance". Thus, while article 270 speaks of percentage share, article 275 refers to specific 'sum' and that these grants should be given to states which are in need of assistance. In this context, the services that should be covered should be limited to the services that can be interpreted as public goods like general administration and law and order and merit goods like education and health services provided by the state governments. In considering the expenditure requirements, account can also be taken of particular circumstances of a state that may result in higher per capita costs.

The First Finance Commission had considered the 'principles' of determining grants at length and had opined that both unconditional and specific purpose grants can and should be considered by the Finance Commission under article 275 read with article 280(3) b. The Second Finance Commission had observed that grants-in-aid should be a residuary from of assistance given in the form of general and unconditional grants. However, it also agreed that grants for broad purposes may be given and, in respect of these, states should be under obligation to spend the whole amount in furtherance of the broad purposes indicated. Most of the subsequent Finance Commission had generally agreed to the principles listed by the First Finance Commission but have by and large followed the procedure adopted by the Second Finance Commission. In respect of two areas such as education and health including family welfare, states that are below average in terms of per capita expenditure should be brought closer to the average.

The plan assistance given to states consists of grants and loans. The grant-loan ratio for the states in general is 30:70

whereas for the special category states, this ratio is 90:10. In normal central assistance, 30 percent is earmarked for the special category states. The expenditure on state plans is met by the balance from current revenues (BCR) from the state budgets, plan assistance in the form of grants and loans from the central government and borrowing from other sources including the payment in the form of non-plan expenditure as committed liabilities. This leads to the convergence of both plan and non-plan expenditure practically considering the distinction between the two as irrelevant.

Of the different transfer types, the Finance Commission transfers are the most progressive (negatively correlated with the income level of states), while other Government of India (GOI) transfers are less so. The combined effect is a distribution of central transfers that is negatively correlated with, but much less varied than, state income. The per capita income of the richest state is more than 4-5 times of the poorest but the per capita transfer to the poorest state is a little less than double that of the richest. While the richest states clearly get less than the poorest, some middle income states get more for example, Tamil Nadu, Kerala and Andhra Pradesh all received at least as much in central transfer per capita as Uttar Pradesh during 1995-2000 (World Bank Report, 2005). Transfers through the Planning Commission (Block Plan Grants) are the grant components of a mixed grant loan transfer under the Gadgil formula are not as equalizing as the statutory transfer through the Finance Commission. Block grant transfers make up about 20 percent of total transfers and just less than 1 percent of GDP. The nature of resource flows to states changed greatly in the 1990s with fall in grants and a rise in loans. From 1998-94 onwards borrowed resources supplement a state's own revenues at least as much as central revenue transfer do. Not surprisingly this development has generated considerable fiscal stress. Following the award of the Eleventh Finance Commission (2000-2005), some have argued that center-state transfers are not adequately progressive to address the widening imbalances between states, while others have complained that the high-income stated are being punished rather than being awarded for performance. For all the disagreement, there is also a clear and shared recognition of the need for change. Traditionally states policy objectives of center-state fiscal arrangements, namely inter-regional equity and efficiency in the use of public resources, have been joined by a new set of objectives-fiscal responsibility, sustainability and public finance accountability which have gained prominence in recent years.

CENTRAL GRANTS TO ORISSA: AN ANALYSIS

The study is based on secondary data collected from Orissa Budget at Glance, Handbook of Statistics on State Government Finances, R.B.I.

Table 1
Finance Commission Recommended Resource Transfer for Orissa

Finance Commission	*Share in aggregate Transfers to all states*	*Share in Grants-in-aid to all states*
Ninth Finance Commission	5.21%	6.93%
Tenths Finance Commission	4.25%	4.46%
Eleventh Finance Commission	4.77%	2.59%
Twelfth Finance Commission	4.89%	3.70%

Source: Finance Commission Report

From Table 1, it is evident that Orissa percentage share in the form of grants-in-aid was higher in comparison to its share in aggregate transfer including share in central taxes and duties, share in Income tax and share in Union Excise Duties upto the 10th Finance Commission. However, in the 11th and 12th Finance Commissions' award the trend has changed. From the 9th Finance Commission onwards percentage share of Orissa in terms of grants-in-aids has declined. it has slightly increased in the 12th Finance Commission

From Table 2 it is observed that grants, as a percentage of GSDP is less than shared taxes as percentage of GSDP in all the years between 1990-91 to 2005-06.

Table 3 shows Grants to Orissa as percentage of grants to all states smaller in relation to percentage of shared taxes to Orissa in percentage of shared taxes to all states between the periods 1990-91 to 2004-05 except in the year 1997-98 and 1999-2000. Orissa's percentage share of grants in grants to all states is the highest in the year 1999-2000 but lowest in the year 2003-04.

Table 2
Various Transfer to Orissa as a Percentage of GSDP

Year	*Total transfer as Percentage GSDP*	*Shared tax as Percentage GSDP*	*Grants as Percentage of GSDP*
1990-91	11.93	6.37	5.57
1991-92	10.80	5.93	4.88
1992-93	11.65	6.57	5.07
1993-94	10.61	5.86	4.75
1994-95	9.29	5.49	3.80
1995-96	7.87	4.74	3.14
1996-97	9.29	5.91	3.38
1997-98	8.28	4.85	3.43
1998-99	7.05	4.76	2.29
1999-00	8.97	4.53	4.44
2000-01	10.41	6.72	3.69
2001-02	9.24	6.29	2.95
2002-03	10.38	6.32	4.06
2003-04	9.37	6.18	3.19
2004-05	11.93	7.22	4.71
2005-06	12.02	6.56	5.46

Source: Handbook of Statistics on State Government Finances, 2004, RBI.

Table 3
Transfer to Orissa as Percentage of Total Transfer to all States

Year	*Total transfer to Orissa as Total Transfer to all states in percentage*	*Shared tax to Orissa as Percentage of Shared tax to all states*	*Grants to Orissa as Percentage of Grants to all states*
1990-91	4.84	4.87	4.80
1991-92	4.72	4.93	4.49
1992-93	4.60	4.83	4.33
1993-94	4.44	4.77	4.08
1994-95	4.50	4.80	4.12
1995-96	4.27	4.42	4.05
1996-97	4.23	4.47	3.87
1997-98	4.13	3.87	4.57
1998-99	3.97	4.30	3.42

Contd....

Year	*Total transfer to Orissa as Total Transfer to all states in percentage*	*Shared tax to Orissa as Percentage of Shared tax to all states*	*Grants to Orissa as Percentage of Grants to all states*
1999-00	4.63	3.96	5.60
2000-01	4.56	5.13	3.78
2001-02	4.08	5.07	2.88
2002-03	4.50	4.95	3.94
2003-04	4.00	5.10	2.82
2004-05	4.94	5.34	4.44

Source: Handbook of Statistics on State Government Finances, 2004, RBI.

Table 4
Growth Rate of Shared Tax and Grants during 1990-91 to 2005-06

	R^2	*b*	*r* %	*t*	*N*
1.Shared Tax	0.987224	0.050648	12.36	28.037	16
a. Income Tax	0.97224	0.065917	16.39	22.145	16
b. Union Excise Duties	0.94566	0.039607	9.54	15,609	16
2. Grants	0.85259	0.042527	10.20	8.998	16
(a) Plan Grants	0.84451	0.043870	10.63	8.720	16
(i) Central Plan Scheme	0.21228	0.035640	8.55	1.942	16
(ii) State Plan Scheme	0.92019	0.062606	15.5	12.705	16
(iii)Centrally sponsored scheme	0.02455	-.002748	0.63	0.594	16
b. Non-plan Grant	0.35134	0.036793	8.84	2.754	16
Total Transfer	0.97130	0.047453	11.54	21.768	16

Source: Budget at a Glance, Government of Orissa

Table 4, gives growth rate of grants as 10.20% which is less than 12.36% i.e., the growth rate of shared taxes. Growth rate of shared taxes is also higher than the growth rate of total transfer, which is 11.54% between 1990-91 to 2005-06. In the context of grants the growth rate of grants for state plan scheme is the highest i.e. 15. 5% and the growth rate of the grant for the centrally sponsored scheme is 0. 63% the lowest. Growth rate of plan grant is 10.63% and is higher than 8.84%, the growth rate of non-plan grant during the period.

Table 5 proves that plan grant as percentage of total transfer to Orissa is higher than non-plan grant as percentage of total transfer to Orissa except in the year 1999-2000. In 1999-2000. non-plan grant as percentage of total transfer to Orissa was

25.45% the highest but in its preceding year i.e. in 1998-99, it was the lowest i.e. 2.71%. After 1999-2000, the non-plan grant as percentage of total transfer to Orissa is declining up to 2003-04, after that it is now going on increasing. In 2005-06, plan grant, as percentage to total transfer is almost three times that of non-plan grant as percentage to total transfer. In 2004-05 it is almost six times.

Table 5
Plan and Non-plan Grant as a Percentage of Total Transfer to Orissa

Year	*Plan grant as % of total transfer to Orissa*	*Non-plan grant as % of total transfer to Orissa*
1995-96	25.40	14/43
1996-97	26.51	19.91
1997-98	25.52	15.90
1998-99	29.78	2.71
1999-00	24.08	25.45
2000-01	23.82	11.60
2001-02	23.85	8.05
2002-03	30.51	8.58
2003-04	28.76	5.27
2004-05	33.77	5.73
2005-06	33.54	11.88

Source: Orissa Budget at a Glance, Government of Orissa.

Table 6
Shared tax and Grant as Percentage of State's Own Resources

Year	*Shared tax as percentage of state's own resources*	*Grants as percentage of states own resources*
1995-96	38.56	8.77
1996-97	42.45	8.12
1997-98	42.18	4.87
1998-99	43.30	4.45
1999-00	33.56	19.97
2000-01	49.59	6.27
2001-02	42/97	5.79
2002-03	40.14	5.66
2003-04	42.48	1.39
2004-05	45.81	3.34
2005-06	41.00	9.03

From Table 6 it is ascertained that shared tax as percentage of state's own resources is almost six times that of grant as percentage of state's own resources in the average between the period 1995-96 to 2005-06. In the year 1999-2000, grant as a percentage of state's own resources was the highest but in 2003-04 it is the lowest. Average of shared tax as percentage of state's own resources is 45% and average of grants as percentage of state's own resources is 7.5% during the period. On the average shared tax as percentage of state's own resources has increased but that of grants has declined during the period taking the year 1995-96 as the base.

Table 7
Plan and Non-plan Grants

Year	*Plan grant as percentage of Plan Revenue Expenditure*	*Plan grant as percentage of Plan Revenue Receipt*	*Grant from Finance Commission as Percentage Revenue Expenditure*	*Non-plan grant as percentage of Revenue Receipt*
1995-96	47.47	13.74	8.18	7.31
1996-97	42.63	13.44	7.95	5.91
1997-98	42.76	12.51	4.32	1.70
1998-99	38.63	12.96	3.37	1.38
1999-00	36.63	11.38	15.69	14.88
2000-01	42.29	13.03	5.23	4.41
2001-02	37.42	9.64	4.42	1.55
2002-03	85.46	15.91	4.68	3.94
2003-04	81.62	14.21	1.18	0.00
2004-05	111.56	11.74	2.6	2.18
2005-06	107.57	19.63	7.99	6.71

Table 7 proves the percentage share of plan grants in plan revenue expenditure as very high and growing from 2002-03 onwards. It is even more than hundred percent in 2004-05 and 2005-06. However grants from Finance Commission, as percentage of revenue expenditure is very low. It is highest i.e. 15.69% in 1999-2000 and the lowest 1.18% in 2003-04. Percentage of plan grants in revenue receipts is higher than the percentage of non-plan grants in revenue receipts in all the years except

1999-2000. In 2003-04 non-plan grant as the percentage of revenue receipts is nil.

In terms of Gap-filling approach, Finance Commission calculated gap between state revenue receipts and non-plan revenue expenditure and extends non-plan grants to bridge the gap. It is known as fiscal dentistry as Finance Commission acts for filling budgetary cavities of the state.

Balance from current Receipts (BCR)

= State's Own Resource (SOR)

+ Shared taxes from center (STC) – Non-plan Revenue Expenditure (NPRE)

Plan Revenue Expenditure (PRL)

= BCR + Additional Resource Mobilization (ARM) + Central Assistance (CA)

Table 8

BCR and Non-Plan Assistance, Gap-filling Approach

(Rs. In corers)

Year	*State's Current Receipt*	*NPRE*	*BCR*	*Non-plan Assistance (FC)*	*Gap*
	1	2	3(1) · (2)	4	5(2) + (4)
1992-93	2144.8	2300.6	-155.8	150.8	-5.0
1993-94	2348.1	2577.6	-234.5	156.4	-78.1
1994-95	2750.8	3102.7	-351.9	144.3	-207.6
1995-96	3040.3	3593.3	-553.0	308.1	-244.9
1996-97	3389.7	3766.2	-376.5	243.9	-132.6
1997-98	3526.2	3763.0	-236.8	124.5	-112.3
1998-99	3739.1	5170.5	-1431.4	67.06	-1363.5
1999-00	4168.9	6630.7	-2461.8	881.4	-1580.4
2000-01	5473.4	7009.6	-1536.2	467.8	-1068.4
2001-02	5807.3	8061.1	-2253.8	313.1	-1940.7
2002-03	6917.0	9310.7	-2393.7	758.1	-1635.6
2003-04	7723.8	9210.7	-1486.9	169.0	-1317.9
2004-05	8327.3	11661.2	-3333.9	393.9	-2940.0
2005-06	9231.3	11467.7	-2236.4	905.32	-1331.0

Table 8 shows negative BCR in all the years. Due to insufficient non-plan assistance by the Finance Commission through gap-filling approach it attributes towards diversion from plan assistance towards non-plan revenue expenditure. It can be easily verified from Table 9

Table 9
Central Assistance Diversion Towards NPRE

(Rs. In corers)

Year	*BCR+NPA*	*ARM*	*CA(PC)*	*Resource for PRE*	*Actual PRE*	*Shortage of fund for PRE*	*% of CA diverted to NPRE*
1992-93	-5.0	00	768.2	763.2	748.2	-15.0	0.6
1993-94	-78.1	00	864.6	786.5	904.5	118.0	9.0
1994-95	-207.6	00	825.0	617.4	932.6	315.2	25.0
1995-96	244.9	00	850.4	605.5	1104.5	499.0	28.0
1996-97	132.6	00	897.0	764.4	1331.0	586.6	14.0
1997-98	-112.3	00	1105.0	993.5	1773.4	779.4	10.0
1998-99	-1363.5	00	815.3	-548.2	1648.6	2196.8	167.0
1999-00	-1580.4	00	1715.6	135.2	1827.7	1692.5	92.0
2000-01	-1068.4	00	1428.6	360.1	1819.1	1458.9	74.0
2001-02	-1940.7	00	1240.6	-700.1	1816.3	2516.4	156.0
2002-03	-1635.6	00	1800.18	164.5	1505.6	1421.1	103.0
2003-04	-1317.9	00	1716.28	398.3	1643.5	1643.2	105.0
2004-05	-2940.0	00	2568.80	-371.2	-371.2	2404.5	114.0
2005-06	-1331.0	00	3461.72	2130.7	2130.7	185.4	38.0

It is observed that more than 100% of Central assistance given by the Planning Commission has already got diverted towards non-plan revenue expenditure in the year 1998-99, 2002-03, 2003-04 and 2004-05. In 1998-99 it is the highest i.e. 167%. In addition to this from 1993-94 onwards there is also shortage of funds for the plan revenue expenditure after central grants in the form of gap-filling non-plan grants from the Finance Commission and Central assistance from the Planning Commission. The figure is the highest in the year 2001-02 i.e. 2516.4 corers.

Despite the highest Debt-GSDP ratio in the country, Orissa has not gained much from the debt relief recommended by various Finance Commissions. This may be seen from Table-10. The Eleventh Finance Commission did not recommend any debt relief in quantitative terms but recommended "general debt relief" for all states linked to fiscal performance.

Table 10
Debt Relief to Orissa by Different Finance Commission

(Rs. In corers)

Finance Commission	*Total debt Relief for all states*	*Debt Relief for Orissa*	*Orissa's Percentage shares in the total debt relief*
8th 1984-89	2285.39	195.62	8.59
9th 1990-95	975.51	28.69	2.94
10th 1995-2000	210.51	17.50	8.31
11th 20000-2005	Nil	Nil	Nil

It has also been claimed that owing to various reasons-mainly overestimation of tax devolution and under estimation of non-plan deficits central transfers received by Orissa through the Finance Commission recommendations were substantially less than what they ought to have been. These direct losses caused an additional indirect loss to the stat as well. As per the objective of the "Fiscal Reform Policy" recommended by the 11th Finance Commission for Orissa, revenue deficit (RD) as a percentage of revenue receipts (TRR) in the base year 1999-2000 should have been limited to –33.43%. With reduction of 5% in each year, the targets for 2000-01, 2001-02, and 2002-03 were fixed at –28.43%, -23.43%, -18.43% respectively (See, Table 11)

Table 11
TRR, RD and RD/TRR for Orissa if Corrected

(Rs. In corers)

Year	*TRR (Actual)*	*RD (Actual)*	*TRR (If corrected)*	*RD (If corrected)*	*RD/TRR (Actual)*	*RD/TRR (If corrected)*
2000-01	6902.02	-1931.96	8045.57	-788.41	-27.91	-9.79
2001-02	7047.98	-2829.56	9868.57	-8.97	-40.15	-0.09
2002-03	9435.83	1460.48	12250.68	1354.37	-15.47	11.05

Orissa was deprived of the Incentive Fund in 2002-03, as it could not actually fulfill the target of reduction of 5% in the RD/ TRR ratio. Had the ratio been corrected for the direct losses in 2001-02, it would have been only –0.09% and this would have allowed the release of Incentive Fund in 2002-03, which could have improved the ratio of RD/TRR further.

Another indirect loss to the state was in respect of debt relief recommended by the 11th Finance Commission. According to the recommendation of the Commission improvement in fiscal performance is to be measured by comparing the ratio of revenue receipts (including share in central taxes but excluding the grants-in-aid under article 275) to the revenue expenditure in a given year **r** with the average of the corresponding ratio ***r*** of immediately preceding three years. Thus each state is to be considered against its own performance in the past. Debt relief will be calculated as a percentage of repayment falling due in reach year of the period of recommendation, 2000-05. Only these repayments as pertaining to central loans to the state during 1995-96 to 1999-2000 and as outstanding on 31.3.2000 will be covered. The percentage (R) will be five times of (**r**-***r***) defined above. The maximum limit of R has been prescribed as 25%

Table 12
Corrected (r)

(Rs. In corers)

Year	*Net Revenue Receipt (Actual)*	*Net Revenue Receipt (If corrected)*	*Revenue expenditure*	*R (Actual)*	*R (If corrected)*
2000-01	6597.29	6726.49	9558.11	72377	-7304
2001-02	7047.98	7595.92	10133.33	-68588	-7496

Table 13
Debt Relief on Corrected (r-*r*)

Year	*(r-r) (Actual)*	*(r-r)(If corrected)*	*Debt Relief (Actual)*	*Debt Relief (If corrected) %*
2000-01	-.008298	.006	Nil	3
2001-02	-.006003	.053	Nil	26Max:25

It is evident from Table 12 and 13 that Orissa could have been benefited through debt relief of 3% and 25% of repayment of debt to central government falling due in the year 2000-01 and 2001-02 respectively pertaining to central government loan to Orissa during 1995-96 to 1999-2000 in accordance with the provision of 11th Finance Commission.

Table 14
Consolidated debt to TRR Ratio

Year	*Consolidated Debt to Corrected Revenue Receipt (%)*	*2000-03 Average (%)*
2000-01	308.05	
2001-02	299.74	293.82
2002-03	273.67	

Table 14 projects the ratio of consolidated debt to corrected revenue receipt, had there been debt relief from the Center to Orissa during 2000-01 to 2002-03 and derive the average of the ratio in the period 2000-03 at 293.82%.

Debt –TRR ratio for (2000-03) average in actual terms was 378.36% for Orissa. Due to the shortfall of central transfer through shared taxes and non-plan assistance Orissa was deprived of debt relief as mentioned earlier therefore Orissa's claim for debt relief amounts to

Rs (9435.83) X (378.36-300.00)%

=(9435.83) X (78.36) % = 7393.16

Rs 9435.83 corers was the TRR in 2002-03.

It justifies the relevance of central transfer in the form of grants in aid towards improving the state's effort for debt sustainability, the thrust area in the context of state finances at present. In recent years transfer of resources in the form of grants-in-aid by Finance Commissions as well as debt relief for states depend on state's revenue receipt and a major part of it constitutes assistance from the center.

Table 15
Correlation Coefficient

Fiscal Deficit GSDP	Plan Assistance Total Transfer	0.107
Fiscal Deficit GSDP	Non-Plan Assistance Total Transfer	0.277
Debt/GSDP	Plan Assistance Total Transfer	-0.828
Debt/GSDP	Non-Plan Assistance Total Transfer	0.715

During the period 1995-96 to 2005-06 it is found that there is negative correlation between Debt – GSDP ratio with the ratio of plan assistance to total transfer from the center to Orissa. The correlation coefficient is –0.828, seems to be very high. It implies that percentage increase of plan assistance in total transfer of resources from the center to Orissa significantly attribute towards reduction in Debt-GSDP ratio, i.e. enabling to have debt sustainability (Refer, Table 15). Interestingly positive correlation coefficient between Fiscal Deficit –GSDP ratio and ratio of plan assistance to total transfer explains higher percentage of plan assistance to total transfer as the cause for higher ratio of Fiscal Deficit to GSDP ratio even though it is very much insignificant as the value of correlation coefficient is very low that is 0.107. In this context to avoid the confusion it is important to consider the utilization of plan assistance and its leakages towards non-plan expenditure.

There is positive correlation between Debt-GSDP ratio with the proportion of non-plan assistance to total transfer and it is very high as the correlation coefficient is 0.715. Similarly there is positive correlation between Fiscal Deficit- GSDP ratio with the proportion of non-plan assistance to total transfer. In this case the correlation coefficient is 0.277, smaller. However it implies that higher proportion of non-plan assistance to total transfer causes increase in the Debt-GSDP ratio as well as Fiscal deficit-GSDP ratio and it leads towards debt non-sustainability. It explains about the utilization pattern of non-plan assistance for non-plan expenditure which is generally non productive in nature. In the case of expenditure on General Services always the total non-plan revenue expenditure is greater than the plan revenue expenditure. There is an increasing tendency in the percentage of non-plan revenue expenditure on the average plan wise prospectively. It has increased from 34.8% in VI Plan to 43.4%, 45.4%, and 53 % for VII, VIII and IX Plan respectively. In other words unproductive expenditure is increasing plan after plan. In the case of expenditure on Economic Services the plan expenditure is dominating and has registered 41.79% on the average out of total plan revenue expenditure during the last 25 years. However there is a declining tendency of it since IXth plan that is from 1997-98 onwards. In 1997-98 it was 34% but has declined to 18% in 2005-06. It was 47% highest in 2004-05.

Over the plan years plan expenditure have drawn more importance to non-plan expenditure. It is pertinent to note that though there is positive correlation between total non-plan revenue expenditure and on Social and Community Services, correlation coefficient being 0.97, the correlation coefficient between total non-plan revenue expenditure and plan revenue expenditure is negative i.e. (-0.020) very low. It explains the growth of both plan and non-plan expenditure in the Social and Community services with a negligible short fall of plan revenue expenditure due to the expansion of non-plan revenue expenditure in this sector. The social sector has got effected due to inadequate allocation caused by continuing deficit in the revenue account even though in terms of aggregate data the allocation of fund from one plan to another has increased predominance of revenue expenditure on social services in almost all the years. With a lower percentage left for capital expenditure, it creates less permanent infrastructure. A poor capital base results in less efficiency and low productivity of human capital.

CONCLUSION

An analysis of trend and composition of central grants to Orissa rests on the following points to explore the improvement in Orissa State finances towards debt sustainable, deficit stable and maximum growth of the economy. During the period 1990-91 to 2005-06 average annual growth rate of GSDP is calculated as 11.56% for Orissa. In accordance with the norms of FRBM Act, Debt-GSDP ratio be 28% and Fiscal-Deficit-GSDP ratio must converge to 3%. It necessitates a growth rate of 12% for GSDP. Prevailing growth rate of 11.56% approximates to 12%. It directs the Government of Orissa to keep debt-GSDP ratio and Fiscal Deficit-GSDP ratio at 28% and 3% respectively with the prevailing annual growth rate of GSDP approximating to 12% by 2009-10. It requires average annual reduction of Debt-GSDP ratio at the rate of 6.5% and can be possible if the Fiscal deficit to GSDP ratio will be reduced at the rate of 6% annually.

Reduction of Fiscal Deficit, i.e. borrowing further reduce proportion of capital expenditure out of the borrowed funds and thereby the growth rate of GSDP must be adversely effected. It justifies prudent fiscal management by exploring the possibility of resource generation and at the same time expenditure management. Ultimately it highlights reduction in revenue deficits, diversion of larger proportion of borrowed funds towards capital expenditure, interest payment reduction in subsequent years due to lower amount of borrowing, i.e. growing amount of primary expenditure year after year in the form of socio-economic infrastructure development keeping the growth rate of GSDP unaffected negatively.

In a federal set up transfer of resources from the center to state in the context of matching the fiscal needs and capacity of the sub-national government is prominent. The role of grants in aid is very much important for the horizontal equalization apart from central transfer in the form of tax devolution to avoid vertical imbalance between center and states. However now there is the need of evaluating the impact of statutory grants sanctioned by Finance Commissions in comparison to that of plan assistance and particularly plan grants on state finances. In the case of Orissa it is found that plan grants is favourable towards economic growth and debt sustainability in terms of reducing the Debt-GSDP ratio whereas non-plan assistance is the cause for increase in Debt-GSDP ratio. However in the context of inter sate transfers of resources in India it is observed that the Finance Commissions' transfers are the most progressive (negatively co-related with the income level of states). It highlights the utilization pattern of non-plan assistance in Orissa particularly covering the gap filling approach based on in-built diversion of plan assistance towards non-plan expenditure and a deliberate attempt to exaggerate plan revenue expenditure to strengthen for bargaining power of the state for more central assistance.

In the case of Orisssa, which is endowed with vast natural resources, the potentiality of the state for maximum growth can be explored in terms of better infrastructure development, which can lead improvement in the social sector through income generation, linkage for individuals and households. It requires huge amount of plan assistance from the center in the form of grants. Besides this there is the need of non-plan assistance through Finance Commissions, which should be conditional, and for specific purpose in lump sum amount and should complement plan assistance. An effective utilization of central grants both plan and non-plan will favour economic growth, debt-sustainability and horizontal equity with other states. To avoid pervasive incentives to exaggerate non-plan expenditure, which gives, rise to fiscal profligacy, a normative approach for the assessment of filling the budgetary gap up is required based on certain norms. A normative approach based on perfect estimation of fiscal needs and capacity of the state by econometric technique can only keep the state government to assert before the central government justifying its fiscal needs in comparison to fiscal capacity. The composition of central transfer through grants-in-aids can be better dealt with on its demand of resources from the central pool.

NOTES

1. Reader in Economics, Department of Economics, Sambalpur University, Jyoti Vihar 768019, Orissa.

13

DECENTRALIZATION AND DEVOLUTION OF RESOURCES TO LOCAL GOVERNMENTS: CENTRAL FINANCE COMMISSION APPROACH

O.P. Bohra

INTRODUCTION

The phenomenon of decentralization is getting popular across all the developed and the developing countries. The process of strengthening of local governments is welcome step accepted by all sections of the society. The decentralization takes place through devolution of resources and the functional responsibilities to lower level of governance. It is assumed that the local–self governance at the lowest level of decision making powers would offer socio-economic benefits and help in mobilizing more resources and efficient delivery mechanism. The devolution of resources and discharging of the functional responsibilities have assumed great importance in recent past in almost all the countries. In form of two historical amendments India has also initiated the process of decentralization. The Government has implemented the 73rd and 74th Constitutional Amendment Act (CAA) for strengthening the grassroots level of governments in rural as well as urban areas. The following section endeavor a brief discussion on revenue decentralization across the select countries. The section third detailed the important steps initiated in the form of constitutional provisions for devolution of resources from central government to local bodies through central finance commissions (10th, 11th and 12th). A critical review of the criterion adopted by the CFCs for transferring of grants to local bodies constitutes the fourth section. The final section presents the conclusion and the issues for the next (thirteenth) finance commission.

EXTENT OF FISCAL (REVENUE) DECENTRALIZATION-INTERNATIONAL SCENARIO

The following table presents the extent of revenue decentralization across the select countries having federal structure of three levels of governments of central, state/ province and the local. A close look into these figures indicates the prevailing of strong central governments in almost all the countries. The share of revenue mobilized through tax by the central governments varies from less than 50 per cent in Canada, Germany and Switzerland. In these countries the state governments are stronger. On the other hand in the countries of Belgium, South Africa and Colombia, the predominance of the governments at the central level exit. The tax revenue generated by the central governments in these countries goes upto more than 90 per cent of the total tax yield of all the three levels of governments. The revenue mobilized by the state governments through taxes varies from 42 per cent in Canada to lowest figure of less than 5 per cent in the countries of Belgium, Bolivia, Colombia and South Africa. The extent of revenue collected by the lowest level of governments in the total tax income show the level of taxation powers transferred to the local governments. The local government in Switzerland seems to be very strong. The revenue mobilized by the local governments was highest of 21.10 per cent. However, in the countries of Austria, Belgium, Bolivia, Colombia, and Spain, the generated through tax sources were more than the state/ province governments. The governments at the local level in these countries have more taxation powers than the middle level of governance. In India, the lower level of governance have not been allocated adequate taxation powers to generate substantial resources. The GFS doesn't give any figure of revenue collected by local governments in India. These data are not documented by any higher level of governments in any authoritative documents. The C&AG has also not been able to provide any audited figures. In the recent past only Eleventh Finance Commission endeavored to present strong data base of local bodies. As per Rao and Singh (2005)[2] the revenue raised by the local bodies in India is almost negligible.

Table 1

Revenue Decentralization in Select Countries (2000)

Sl. No.	*Country*	*% share in total tax rev.*		
		Central	*State*	*Local*
1.	Australia	77.68	19.26	3.07
2.	Austria	70.92	11.40	17.68
3.	Belgium	90.01	3.82	6.17
4.	Bolivia	76.55	3.75	19.70
5.	Canada	48.28	41.94	9.78
6.	Colombia	83.41	5.48	11.12
7.	Germany	48.80	39.10	12.10
8.	India (1999)	62.65	37.35	na
9.	Mexico	75.62	19.02	5.37
10.	South Africa	92.26	0.70	7.04
11.	Spain	73.47	12.12	14.41
12.	Switzerland	48.81	30.09	21.10
13.	United States	69.27	19.15	11.58

Source: Government Finance Statistics, 2005.

TAX-GDP RATIO AT NATIONAL, STATE AND LOCAL LEVEL

The tax-GDP ratios computed for different level of governments in select countries for different level of governments are discussed in table 2. The total tax GDP ratio varies from highest of over 30 per cent in the countries of Australia, Belgium and Canada. The lower tax-gdp ratio was observed in the countries of Bolivia, Colombia, India and Mexico.

The extent of fiscal (revenue) decentralization is fairly shown in the case of Canada, where the central and state have mobilized about 15 per cent and 13 per cent of GDP respectively. Tax-GDP ratio at central level was more than 20 per cent in the case of Australia, Austria, Belgium, South Africa and United

States. In India it was less than 10 per cent. On the other hand, barring Canada, in most of the countries, the tax-GDP ratio at the state level were less than 10 per cent. In India, it was 5.81 per cent for the year 1999-2000. The resources mobilized through taxation at the lower level of governance as, shown in the table 2, indicates that in the countries of Austria, Belgium, Bolivia, Colombia, South Africa and Spain, the tax-GDP ratios were higher than the state level. However, in almost all the countries it was less than 5 per cent. The local governments in Australia and Mexico, had generated abysmally figure of less than one per cent through local taxation. Apparently, the taxation powers available with the local governments must be very less. The case of India is also not much different. Based on the data provided in the EFC report, the rural local bodies could raise only 1.40 per cent of GDP.[3]

Table 2
Tax- GDP (central, State and Local govt.) Ratio-2000

Sl. No.	*Country*	*Tax-gdp ratio*			
		Total tax	*Central tax*	*State tax*	*Local tax*
1.	Australia	30.20	23.46	5.82	0.93
2.	Austria	27.65	19.61	3.15	4.89
3.	Belgium	30.85	27.77	1.18	1.90
4.	Bolivia	16.12	12.34	0.60	3.18
5.	Canada	31.17	15.05	13.08	3.05
6.	Colombia	16.04	13.38	0.88	1.78
7.	Germany	24.70	12.05	9.66	2.99
8.	India (1999)	15.56	9.75	5.81	na
9.	Mexico	15.43	11.67	2.94	0.83
10.	South Africa	26.95	24.86	0.19	1.90
11.	Spain	22.31	16.39	2.70	3.21
12.	Switzerland	23.05	11.25	6.94	4.86
13.	United States	29.08	20.15	5.57	3.37

Source: Government Finance Statistics, 2005.

NATIONAL PERSPECTIVE

The Constitution through 73rd and 74th Amendments defines 29 subject matters for rural local governments (Panchayati Raj Institutions) and 18 subjects to Urban Local Governments

(Municipalities), though the local governments (bodies) were functioning for long. Presently, it has provided a composite framework delineates fiscal functions among central, state and local governments. The centre-state fiscal relations and its delivery mechanism were in place developed for long but no separate provisions existed for local governments until the recent Constitutional amendments were made. The first generation state level finance Commissions were constituted in all the states and the recommendations were made in view of identifying the resources to carry out the functions enlisted in the 11th and 12th Schedule (of 73rd and 74th Amendments) for PRIs and ULBs. A large number of states have accepted and implemented the most relevant recommendations[4.] Keeping in view the requirements of Article 243 I and Y, most of the States have constituted the Second generation State Finance Commissions and have submitted the reports. The impact of these recent developments of fiscal transfers on the state economy has not been assessed so far. It needs detail investigations of these reports. The issue of fiscal transfers has to be analysed in greater detail and perspective.

Tenth Finance Commission (TFC) Approach

The Center-states relations have been develop in India since long. Under the constitutional provisions the Central Finance Commission was constituted to transfer the funds to the States under various constitutional provisions. Till now this exercise has been carried out for eleven times since independence. With the recent amendments in the constitutional provision the CFC has been assigned another duty to extend this exercise to local governments also. The Article 280(3) has been amended to provide for another mandatory duty to be performed by the Central Finance Commission. At the State level also, these amendments require the constitution of State Finance Commission to recommend the transfers of funds from State to local governments. Since these amendments were introduced at the time of near completion of TFC report, hence the Commission could not work out transfer of funds based on any detail exercise. Therefore, it had made provision of *ad hoc* arrangements and recommended the transfers of funds to the local bodies. The TFC has recommended that this fund would go to PRIs over and above the regular transfer of funds from State to the PRIs· Similarly, for the Urban Local Bodies (ULBs) the funds have been transfers for the maintenance of core civic services provided by CFC.

Eleventh Finance Commission (EFC) Approach

Under the Terms of Reference (ToR) of EFC, for the first time the Presidential Order required a Finance Commission to make recommendations regarding the transfers of fund to the States which further pass on to the local Governments (PRIs and ULBs) for the augment of resources of these bodies. The introduction of these (73rd and 74th) amendments has given a place in the Constitution and recognised them as the institutions of self-governments. These amendments made it mandatory for holding the regular election, obligatory representation of SCs/STs and women, periodic constitution of SFCs for the devolution of financial resources to the sub-national governments at the local level, transfers of functional responsibilities to these bodies, so as to enable them to function as institutions of self-governments. The particular ToR of EFC required it to determine the transfers of resources to the local bodies on the basis of the recommendations of the SFCs. If the SFCs reports were not made available in that case make their own assessment in this regard.

Transfers of Resources to the Local Governments-EFC Approach

For effective functioning of the local governments the process of decentralisation needs to be speeded up. Keeping in view the strengthening of the sub-national governments at the local level the EFC has recommended the transfers of funds for the provision and maintenance of core civic services.

Under the amended constitutional provision the PRIs and the ULBs have to maintain the accounts and get them audited. This would reduce the charges of corruption, generally, leveled against them. Keeping this requirement in view, the EFC has recommended provision of fund to meet needs of the local bodies. Since the exercise of transfeıs of resources to the local governments was carried out for the first time, the EFC has faced the acute problem of database at the local level. To ease out the data problem for the future Commission, the EFC has made provision in this regard also. It has made recommendations and earmarked some fund for maintenance of database at the local level, in the standard format suggested by it.

Grants for the Local Bodies

As a measure of augmenting of Consolidated Fund of States to supplement the resources of local bodies, the EFC has made recommendation considering the availability of resources and the limits prescribed for the overall transfers of funds to these bodies. This would help local governments for provision/ maintenance of core civic services to the local citizens. The EFC has recommended a grant of Rs 1600 crore for the Panchayats and Rs 400 crore for the Municipalities (ULBs) for the period of five years (2000-01 to 2004-05).

Box 1
Principle for Inter se Distribution

The transfers from the national to state governments are generally guided by four basic principles, namely, equity, autonomy, efficiency, and fiscal discipline In the case of local governments the EFC has selected five factors for the distribution of funds to the local governments. These are population, index of decentralisation, distance from highest per capita income, revenue effort and geographical area. In this formula the equity aspect is taken care of by population factor, therefore, the EFC has assigned maximum weightage of 40 per cent to this factor. Next Important factor is that which should speed up the process of decentralisation at the third level of governance. The EFC has worked out an index of decentralisation by taking care of all the important factors envisaged in the provisions made in the recent amendments introduced for decentralisation. The revenue effort made by the local bodies has been assigned 10 per cent weight. The States with low SDP have been duly compensated by the weight of 10 per cent assigned to the factor of distance from highest per capita income. The geographical area has been given the weightage of 10 per cent. This would take care of the differentials in the cost of provision of basic services in the sparsely populated area, where the cost is relatively high.

Source: EFC Report

Box 2
Equity vs. Performance

While estimating the devolution to local bodies the TFC and EFC both have given more importance to the equity aspects. In determination of share of each State the population indicator has played a pivotal role. The TFC has made the allocation on the basis of per capita grants to the PRIs on the basis of 1971 population. For the ULBs the ratio of slum to urban population has been used. We have ranked the states according to their share in the total for PRIs and ULBs and computed the rank correlation. The populous states occupied the higher places in PRIs, and in the case of ULBs the developed states with higher level of urbanization and industrial growth got the high position. The EFC have used the population of 1991 census (rural and urban) for assigning the weights to the different determinants. In addition to the population and geographical criteria, the other determinants such as distance from highest per capita income, revenue efforts of PRIs with respect to own revenue of the state and w.r.t GSDP (primary sector excluding Mining and Quarrying), and the index of decentralization have been used in computation of Composite index for each state's share. The States have been ranked on the basis proportion of each share in the total. On examination of these results, it is noticed that highly populated States got the more share and the high ranks whereas the performing states with less population were deprived of their due shares and ranked at low levels.

Source: EFc Report.

TWELFTH FINANCE COMMISSION'S (TFC) RESOURCE TRANSFERS TO LOCAL BODIES

While making its recommendation for the augmentation of own resources of the local bodies, the TFC has recommended a share of 20 per cent to the local bodies in the urban areas. The factors such as taxable capacity and the need of resources has duly considered in the case of urban local bodies. For the rural local bodies (panchayats) , an amount of Rs 20000 crores (80 per cent of the total grants to local bodies) has been recommended for the period of five years from 2005-06. It was assumed that the level of standard of civic services provided by these local bodies would enhance in future.

GRANTS UTILIZATION

The basic purpose of the devolution of grants to rural local bodies was to improve the level of services in respect of water supply and sanitation. On the other hand, in the case of local bodies in urban areas, the Commission emphasized that there is need to encourage the concept of public–private partnership for improving the mechanism of service delivery wit respect to solid waste management. The ULBs should be assigned the task of collection, segregation and transportation of solid waste. Accordingly, it has recommended that the 50 per cent of the grants allocated for the ULBs should be utilized for the scheme of solid waste management in urban areas.

DATA BASE

The Commission has suggested that the priority areas such as creation of data base and maintenance of accounts due consideration, Therefore, is has recommended that 50 per cent of the grants should be earmarked for this purpose. This would be applicable for both, the RLBs and the ULBs.

CRITERIA OF DEVOLUTION

While making its recommendations for inter-se distribution across the states, the has endorsed almost all the criteria except one. The EFC has stressed on strengthening the aspect of decentralization and recommended 20 per cent weightage. On the other hand the TFC has emphasized on reduction in the disparities with respect to provision of core services of drinking water supply and the sanitation. Accordingly, it has recommended a weightage of 10 per cent assigned to index of deprivation. Besides the equity aspect, there is greater need to push the performance upward. Another important criterion is revenue effort with respect to states' own revenue and the GSDP. This criterion of revenue effort was used by both, EFC and TFC for judging the performance of local bodies across the states. In comparison to EFC, TFC has stressed on revenue effort and assigned 20 per cent weight.

Criterion and Weights Used by EFC and TFC Report for Inter-se Distribution

Sl. No.	*Criteria*	*Weight (per cent)*	
		EFC	*TFC*
1.	Population	40	40
2.	Geographical Areas	10	10
3.	Distance from highest per capita income	20	20
4.	Index of Decentralization/Deprivation	20	10
5.	Revenue Effort	10	20
	(a) With respect to states' own revenue	5	10
	(b) With respect to GSDP	5	10

Source: EFC and TFC Reports.

A COMPARISON OF ALLOCATION OF GRANTS TO LOCAL BODIES THROUGH 10th, 11th AND 12th CFC AND INTER-SE DISTRIBUTION

Tenth Finance Commission

In absolute term, the 10th FC has recommended an amount of Rs. 5380.93 crores for the local bodies. The ULBs' share was Rs. 1000 crore while Panchayats have received larger amount of Rs. 4380.93 crore. The allocation was based on Rs. 100 per capita in rural areas and for ULBs the criteria was ratio of slum population to urban population. The major shares have gone to populous and developed states. The industrialized and urbanized states claimed large chunk in total kitty. The state with less number of people and less developed was the major sufferer. On similar count, the States in north-east region too were deprived required resources. The states are ranked as per their share in total grants. Of the total grants, more than 50 per cent grants have gone to first five states, in both, rural and urban areas. In rural side the states ranked in first five places were: Uttar Pradesh, Bihar, Andhra Pradesh, Madhya Pradesh and Maharashtra. On the urban side two states of Tamil Nadu and West Bengal have replaced Bihar and Madhya Pradesh (see Table 1).

Table 1
Allocation of Grants and Ranks of the States-Tenth Finance Commission

State	*PRIs*			*ULBs*	
	share (%)	*Rank*	*State*	*share (%)*	*Rank*
Uttar Pradesh	17.34	1	Maharashtra	13.3	1
Bihar	11.58	2	Uttar Pradesh	12.12	2
Andhra Pradesh	8.01	3	West Bengal	12.03	3
Madhya Pradesh	7.96	4	Tamil Nadu	11.55	4
Maharashtra	7.92	5	Andhra Pradesh	7.39	5
Total five ststes	52.81		Total five ststes	56.39	

Source: TFC Report.

Eleventh Finance Commission

It has recommended Rs. 8000 crore for PRIs and Rs. 2000 crore for ULBs. The inter-se distribution was made on the basis of criteria such as population (40%), geographical areas (10%), per capita income distance (20%), decentralization (20%) and tax effort. (10%). The states were ranked as per their share in the total allocation for PRIs and ULBs. Similar to 10 FC, the first five states of Uttar Pradesh, Maharashtra, Madhya Pradesh, Bihar and Andhra Pradesh received a little less than 50 per cent of the total grants allocated for the PRIs. In the case of ULBs, the 50% share was accounted for the states of Maharashtra, Tamil Nadu, Uttar Pradesh, Gujarat and West Bengal. They occupied first five places (Table 2).

Twelfth Finance Commission

In absolute term the TFC has recommended more than double the grants allocated by EFC for the local bodies. It has recommended Rs. 20000 crores for the Rural local bodies and

Rs 5000 crore for the local bodies in urban areas. In other words 80 % went to panchayats and 20 per cent to the municipalities for the period of five years beginning 2005-06. The criterion adopted by the TFC was same as used by EFC except the index of deprivation was used in place of index of decentralization. Another minor difference in the weight was done in case of revenue effort. The weight increased from 10 per cent to 20 per cent. More stress was placed on the resource mobilization at the local level. As indicated in the table 3, in case of PRIs, the first five ranks occupied by the states of Uttar Pradesh, Maharashtra, Madhya Pradesh, Bihar and Andhra Pradesh. The scenario was slightly different then the RLBs. Other than Maharashtra and Uttar Pradesh (common states), the states of Tamil Nadu, Gujarat and West Bengal got the place in the band of first five states (see Table 3).

Table 2
Allocation of Grants and Ranks of the States-Eleventh Finance Commission

State	*PRIs*			*ULBs*	
	share (%)	*Rank*	*State*	*share (%)*	*Rank*
Uttar Pradesh	16.489	1	Maharashtra	15.813	1
Bihar	9.813	2	Uttar Pradesh	12.582	2
Andhra Pradesh	9.503	3	West Bengal	9.874	3
Madhya Pradesh	8.943	4	Tamil Nadu	9.668	4
Maharashtra	8.209	5	Andhra Pradesh	8.233	5
First Five States	52.958		First Five States	56.17	

Source: EFC Report.

ALLOCATION OF GRANTS TO LOCAL BODIES- GAIN/LOSS OVER THE PREVIOUS FINANCE COMMISSION

(a) Rural Local Bodies

The state-wise allocation (in per cent term) to the Rural Local Bodies as recommended by the 10Fc, 11Fc and 12FC depicted in the Table 4. The gain or loss (in terms of per cent share) over the previous Commission was computed. A close look into the figures indicate that as many as 11 states incurred losses in their allocation from 10Fc to 11Fc. The 14 states were gainers. On the other hand in the case of 11Fc to 12Fc, more number of states (15 states) have lost in their allocation in comparison to previous Commission. Only 10 states were happy with the more allocation.

Table 3
Allocation of Grants and Ranks of the States-Twelfth Finance Commission

State	*PRIs*			*ULBs*	
	share (%)	*Rank*	*State*	*share (%)*	*Rank*
Uttar Pradesh	14.64	1	Maharashtra	15.82	1
Maharashtra	9.915	2	Tamil Nadu	11.44	2
Madhya Pradesh	8.315	3	Uttar Pradesh	10.34	3
Bihar	8.12	4	Gujarat	8.28	4
Andhra Pradesh	7.935	5	West Bengal	7.86	5
First Five States	48.925		First Five States	53.74	

Source: Twelfth Finance Commission Report.

	11-10fc		12-11fc	
PRIs	loss	11	loss	15
	gain	14	gain	10

(b) Urban Local Bodies

In the case of allocation to ULBs from 10FC to 11FC, the picture is not much different from the Rural Local Bodies. The 12 states incurred losses in their allocation while 13 states received more grants. Whereas in the grants recommended by 11 FC and 12FC, the scenarios was more pleasant for 15 states. Only 10 states contented with low share in allocation in comparison to previous Commission.

	10fc to 11 fc		11fc to 12fc	
ULBs	loss	12	loss	10
	gain	13	gain	15

CONCLUSION

From the above discussions it is difficult to draw any firm conclusion with respect to extent of decentralization initiated during last more than a decade. However, many attempts were made to strengthen the various aspects of decentralization at central as well as state level. The Constitutional provision makes it mandatory for the CFC to recommend measures for the augmentation of resources of the lowest level of governance. The criteria used by CFC for the devolution of grants to local bodies seem to be ineffective. Only five major states (in terms of population and development) claimed the lion share of resources from the CFC allocation, irrespective of any criteria used for the inter-se distribution. For the future CFC a greater need would be to select the criteria very carefully so that an unbiased and balanced devolution should take place.

NOTES

1. See, Rao and Singh (2005), have shown the extent of fiscal decentralization in the case of India for the year 1997-98, based on Eleven the Finance Commission data.
2. As per the estimates of Rao and Singh (2005), the local governments in rural areas could raised only 1.4 per of GDP.
3. See, Action Taken Report Memorandum of all the States.

REFERENCES

Bajaj, J.L. (1995), "Administrative Reforms and Decentra.lization", Report Submitted to Government of Uttar Pradesh.

Bohra, O.P. (1996), State-Local Fiscal Relations in India, Delhi, National Book Shop with Collaboration of Dolphin Publishing House.

Government of India (1994), Report of the Tenth Finance Commission, New Delhi.

———(2000), Report of the Eleventh Finance Commission, New Delhi.

———(2004), Report of the Twelfth Finance Commission Report, New Delhi.

Prud'homme, Remy (1996), "The Economics of Decentralisation in Very Low Income Countries", *Revue Region et Development*, 3.

Rao, M. Govinda (2000), Fiscal Decentralisation in India Federalism", (Bangalore: Institute for Social and Economic Change), Mimeo. September.

Rao, M. Govinda, and Singh, Nirvikar (2005), Political Economy of Federalism in India, Oxford. University Press.

The World Bank (2004), Fiscal Decentralization to Rural Governments in India, Oxford University Press.

Rajaraman, Indira, O.P. Bohra and V.S. Renganathan (1996), "Augmentation of Panchayati Raj Resources", Economic and Political Weekly, XXXI,: 18 May.

Rondinelli, Dennis A. and Others (1983), "Decentralisation in Developing Countries: A Review of Recent Experience, Washington, The World Bank. (World Bank Staff Working Paper No. 581.

Woo, Sik Kee (1975), "Fiscal Decentralisation and Economic Development", Washington: World Bank (World Bank Studies in Domestic Finance No. 10).

14

GRANTS TO PANCHAYATS– TWELFTH FINANCE COMMISSION

*B. Jhansi Lakshmi**

INTRODUCTION

Decentralization promotes better service delivery to the people while ensuring inclusiveness in local governance and accountability. A decentralized decision-making which is an outcome of functioning of local governments can be targeted to combat poverty and also to achieve rural development and social justice. In India, the Panchayat Raj Institutions (PRIs) have been in existence for a long time in several States. But only the 73rd Constitution Amendment made the Rural Local Bodies (RLBs) Constitutionally mandated. As a result 2,32,278 Village level panchayats, 5,905 intermediate level panchayats and 499 district level panchayats[1] have been formed to which lakhs of people have been elected to represent the local governments in the rural areas. It is quit interesting and a surprise world over that in a developing country like India, lakhs of women have been elected for the first time to local bodies. In fact, the 73rd Constitution Amendment Act has provided a new dimension to fiscal federalism by bringing a radical change in the inter-governmental fiscal relations in India[2].

* Member of Parliament, Bobbili Constituency, Andhra Pradesh. Earlier, she was the Chairperson, Zilla Praja Parishad, Vizianagaram District, Andhra Pradesh.

CROSS-COUNTRY COMPARISON:

Decentralization will become realistic and more meaningful only when it is adequately followed by revenue decentralization. This is an important fact to reckon with in view of the past experience of not only our country but also of several developed and developing countries. The following Table reveals such a situation relating to selected countries in the year 2000. Though it is difficult to make generalizations on the basis of such a limited data relating to a few select countries, it reveals how meager the resources are accruing to the local governments in the respective countries.

Table 1
Percentage Share of Local Governments in the Total Tax Revenue in Select Countries

Name of Country	*% Share*
Developed Countries	
Australia	3.06
Canada	9.78
Germany	12.10
Switzerland	21.10
USA	11.58
Developing Countries	
Bolivia	19.70
Mexico	5.37
South Africa	7.04

Sources: Government Finance Statistics, 2005

A perusal of the Table explains that in most of the countries either the Centre or States, predominantly the central governments are financially stronger than the local governments. Only in Switzerland and Bolivia the share of local governments in the total tax revenue seems to be reasonable and it is quite insufficient in the case of other select nations. It may be noted from the Table that the percentage is as low as 3 in the case of Australia and about 5 per cent in Mexico. In India where local governments existed prior to the 73rd Amendment period also, they have not been allocated / delegated adequate tax powers to generate the needed fiscal resources.

GRANTS TO LOCAL BODIES-CENTRAL FINANCE COMMISSIONS:

In due recognition of the above mentioned facts and to fill the void with regard to functional and financial devolution the 73rd Constitution Amendment Act made a provision under which a State Finance Commission is to be constituted in every State for every five years. As per Articles 243(I) and 243(Y) of the Constitution the State Finance Commission has to recommend

(a) The principles that should govern the distribution between the State and local governments of the net proceeds of taxes levied by the State and the inter-se distribution between Panchayat Institution and Municipalities,

(b) The determination of taxes, duties, tolls and fees which may be assigned to or appropriated by the local bodies and grants- in –aid from the consolidated fund of the State to the local bodies. The State Finance Commissions are also required to suggest measures needed to improve the financial position of the local governments. In addition, consequent upon the 73rd and 74th Constitution Amendments and the introduction of sub-clauses (bb) and (c) in clause (3) of Article 280, it has been made obligatory upon the

Central Finance Commission to "recommend measures needed to augment the Consolidated Fund of a State to supplement the resources of the Panchayat Institutions/ Municipalities in the State on the basis of the recommendations made by the Finance Commission of the State."[3] Accordingly the Tenth Finance Commission, in view of its limited time and financial resources, recommended Rs. 4380.93 crores for the period 1996-97 to 1999-2000 as an additionality over and above the regular transfer of funds to Panchayat Raj Institutions (PRIs) from the States. This may be considered as a milestone in the Indian fiscal federalism. The dream of late Shri Rajiv Gandhi, former Prime Minister who was desirous of strengthening the grass-root governments in India to make them self-reliant by channelling funds from the upper layers of government, has been realized.

The Presidential Order dated July 3,1998, for the first time in the history of Indian fiscal federalism, required the Eleventh Finance Commission to make recommendations regarding the transfer of funds to local bodies for augmenting of resources of the local governments. After examining deeply several aspects of augmenting financial resources of the State and local governments, the Commission recommended that an amount of Rs.1600 crore for the Panchayats (Rs.8000crore for five years) and Rs.400 Crore (Rs.2000 crore for five year) to municipalities for each of the five years-2000-2005. Further, the Commission recommended that the total grant amount recommended should be distributed among the States on the basis of following criteria.

Factor	Weightage
(a) Population	40 Per cent
(b) Index of Decentralization	20 Per cent
(c) Distance from highest per capita Income	20 Per cent
(d) Revenue Effort	10 Per cent
(e) Geographical Area	10 Per cent

The Commission unambiguously stated that the fund should be spent for the provision and maintenance of Core civic services, for improving the data base and accounting systems. Such an earmarking of the grants amount would help in abating any diversion of these funds and ensures fiscal discipline. It may be observed that the criteria adopted by the Eleventh Finance Commission is unduly biased in favour of States with larger population and seems to be unfavorable to performing States with less population. This suggests a change in the criteria of inter se distribution of the total grant amount.

GRANTS TO LOCAL BODIES - TWELFTH FINANCE COMMISSION

The Presidential Order dated 1,November,2002 required in its Terms of Reference (TOR) that the Finance Commission shall recommend the "measures needed to augment the Consolidated Fund of a State to supplement the resources of the Panchayats and Municipalities in the State on the basis of the recommendations made by the Finance Commission of the State" [4] Following its immediate predecessors, after considering the views of the State governments, Central Ministries and other stakeholders of local self-governments, the Commission made its recommendations. It recommended an amount of Rs.20000 crore for the Panchayats and Rs.5000 crore for the Municipalities as grant-in –aid to augment the consolidated fund of the States for the period of 2005-10. Doubling, even more, the grant to local bodies by the Twelfth Finance Commission is highly appreciable. It adopted the criteria of the Eleventh Finance Commission for inter se distribution with two important modifications. Following is the criteria used for inter se allocation of grants provided to local bodies.

	Criterion	Weightage (per cent)
(i)	Population	40
(ii)	Geographical Area	10
(iii)	Distance from highest per capita Income	20
(iv)	Index of Deprivation	10
(v)	Revenue Effort of which	20
(a)	with respect to own revenue of States	10
(b)	with respect to GSDP	10

The amount of grant and the States' percentage share as recommended by the Twelfth Finance Commission for the period of 2005-10 for both Panchayats and Municipalities are given in Table 2

It may be observed from the Table that the major 15 States bagged 90 per cent of the total grants given to Panchayats while the same is 93 per cent in the case of grants to Municipalities. Similarly, only five States -A.P,Bihar,Madhya Pradesh, Maharashtra, Uttar Pradesh- have been given 59 per cent of the Panchayati Raj grant while six States bagged more than 60 per cent of the grant given to Municipal bodies. This is mainly due to the undue weightage given to population. The Twelfth Finance Commission also gave 40% weightage to population just like its predecessor. The Commission has discarded the factor of "index of decentralization " in view of its subjectivity and irrelevance and instead adopted a new factor " Index of deprivation" very appropriately. Index of deprivation was measured by the Commission in terms of inter-State disparities

Table 2

Grant and Percentage Share of Major States (2005-10)

Name of the State	*Panchayats*		*Municipalities*	
	Per cent	*Grant (Rs. crore)*	*Per cent*	*Grant (Rs. crore)*
Andhra Pradesh	7.935	1587	7.480	374
Assam	2.630	526	1.100	55
Bihar	8.120	1624	2.840	142
Gujarat	4.655	931	8.280	414
Haryana	1.940	388	1.820	91
Karnataka	4.440	888	6.460	323
Kerala	4.925	985	2.980	149
Madhya Pradesh	8.315	1663	7.220	361
Maharashtra	9.915	1983	15.820	791
Orissa	4.015	803	2.080	104
Punjab	1.620	324	3.420	171
Rajasthan	6.150	1230	4.400	220
Tamil Nadu	4.350	870	11.440	572
Utter Pradesh	14.640	2928	10.340	517
West Bengal	6.355	1271	7.860	393
Major States Total	82.077	18,001	93.540	4677
All States Total	100.00	20,000	100.00	5000

Sources: Finance Commission Report, GOI, 2004, p.157.

of the two core services of drinking water and sanitation in the case of both rural and urban local bodies[5]. This new factor would have given more useful results had it been used with much broader scope by including some more core services. The Commission's suggestions under para 8.19 of the Report would certainly enhance the augmentation of financial resources of the local governments. The recommendations of the Commission with reference to the Constitution, Composition and qualifications of the members, working and submission of the reports and the implementation of the recommendations of the State Finance Commissions are very pertinent. The endorsement of the recommendation of the SFCs regarding raising the Ceiling of Profession Tax would definitely increase the fiscal base of the local governments, if the Centre puts it in practice. While discouraging any delay of channelising the grant amount by the States to local governments, it has categorically recommended a time frame for transferring the funds to the local governments. Though it has recommended that the Centre should not put any additional conditionality over and above the conditions prescribed by the Commission, the Commission itself stipulated a conditionality for utilizing the grant amount. For instance, "of the grants allocated for Panchayats, priority should be given to expenditure on the O&M costs of water supply and sanitation."[6] The Commission felt that such condition would facilitate the Panchayats to take over these schemes and operate them. Similarly, with regard to the grants to Municipal bodies, it puts a condition that " at least 50 per cent of the grants- in aid provided to each State for the urban local bodies should be earmarked for the scheme of solid waste management through public-private partnership." [7] Such a conditionality may ensure avoidance of any diversion of funds, but at the same time curtails the freedom of the governments at the grass root level. Earmarking of grants for utilization of specified services, though core services, may come in conflict with the felt needs of the local people and areas. The local governments need to be given the required freedom in the operation and maintenance of core services. Therefore, what is needed is to identify a shelf of core services and the local governments be given the freedom to choose the services according to the needs of the people and the area. Moreover, the conditionality of utilization of the grant amount only to the specified purposes or services may defeat the very purpose and objective of Gram Sabha, the most important component in the 73rd Constitution Amendment Act to realize the fruits of decentralized governance.

CONCLUSION

The 73rd and 74th Constitution Amendment Acts brought a sea change in the democratic fiscal federalism in India. The goals of decentralization through these Amendment Acts would be realized only when both functional and financial devolution takes place. The grants-in-aid recommended by the Tenth Finance Commission, for the first time in India, and followed by Eleventh and Twelfth Finance Commissions and other recommendations with reference to local bodies would definitely help the local governments, especially the Panchayati Raj Institutions, augmenting more financial resources. However, while awarding grants –in-aid the Central Finance Commissions have been prescribing conditions for their utilization. Such conditions avoid diversion and/or misuse of funds but curtails the freedom of the local governments. It may also defeat the very purpose and objective of Gram Sabha (the Legislature at the lower end). However, the Central Finance Commission can identify the broad purposes for utilizing the grants while giving more freedom to the Gram Panchayat/Municipal body, rather the Gram Sabha, to make decision in accordance with the felt needs of the people.

REFERENCES

Report of the Eleventh F. C, 2000, p.266.

For More Details See, Nirmal Mukarji, "The Third Stratum," *Economic and Political Weekly*, May, 1, 1993, p. 859-621.

Report of the Tenth Finance Commission, GOI, Dec., 1994, p.46.

Report of the Finance Commission, GOI, 2004.

For details see Report of the Finance Commission, GOI, 2004, p.155.

Report, Op. cit, p.160.

Report, Ibid., p. 160.

15

GRANTS TO LOCAL BODIES – A COMPARATIVE ANALYSIS OF TWO FINANCE COMMISSIONS

G. Nanaji Rao & P. Srinivasa Rao

According to Statistical Abstract of India 2003 the term Local Bodies refers to such institutions of Government which carry on the local affairs viz., Panchayat Raj institutions, Corporations, Municipalities etc. In Federal fiscal system, on grounds both of equity and efficiency, resources are generally assigned more to the Central Government where as States together with the local governments have the larger responsibilities. Thus vertical imbalances require transfer of resources from Centre to States.

The additions made to article 280 following the 73rd and 74th Constitutional amendments are to be seen as an implicit recognition of the organic link between the various tiers in India Fiscal Federalism. The Union Finance Commission concerned with macro public finances of the country has a moral and broadly interpreted a constitutional responsibility to review the public finances of the local bodies even without the "restructuring" task. The relevant provision in the constitution relating to the SFCs have been incorporated in Articles 243, 280 (bb) and 280 (c). A perusal of these provisions shows that a heavy responsibility has been cast on the SFCs. The State Finance Commission and Union Finance Commission will have to work in a complementary fashion on several vital issues regarding horizontal equity for any real progress to happen in the country as a whole.

ELEVENTH FINANCE COMMISSION AND LOCAL BODIES

Unlike the other Finance Commission in India, the Eleventh Finance Commission (EFC) following its predecessors took together setout the broad scope of the tasks the Commission has to undertake the sub clause (bb) (c) added to clause 3 of article 280 of the constitution and item 6 and the Para relating to it. The main aim of the EFC is to augmentation of consolidated funds of the states to supplement the resources of the Local Bodies on the basis of SFCs recommendations. However, the 10th Finance Commission has also made recommendations in this regard.

Accordingly Eleventh Finance Commission made Rs. 10,000/- crores for the rural and urban local bodies. The EFC as per the term of reference as to take into account the provisions required to be made for the emoluments and terminal benefits of the employees of local bodies including those of teachers. As Article 280 had been amended before the expiry of its term and the commission felt that it was obliged to deal with the issue in terms of the amended article 280 even though it was not included in its TOR.

Hence, the main tasks of the EFC which includes 73rd and 74th Constitutional Amendments with reference to local bodies were as below:

The 11th Finance Commission reviews the SFCs recommendations with reference to local bodies finances and also with that of State Finances. Basing on these reviews and recommendations the commission evaluate the principals and norms. Since only 19 State Finance Commissions (SFCs) have submitted their reports, this mandate cannot be fully honoured. There is another problem also because the period of recommendations of most of the SFCs covered the period from 1996-1997 to 2000-2001. Where as the EFC covers the period from 2000-2005. Hence the 11th Finance Commission legitimately base its recommendations on the 1st round SFCs and cover the period 2000-2005.

(a) First time the 11th Finance Commission as per its TOR, the measures to augment the consolidated fund of the States to enable them to supplement the resources of the local bodies.

(b) Total transfers from the government to the States (Vertical Transfers) the 11th Finance Commission (EFC) recommended an over all share of 37.5 gross revenue of Centre to State.

(c) The EFC had recommended that the division of the grants in aid should be in the ratio of 80:20 for the panchayats and municipalities respectively.

(d) The EFC allocated Rs. 200 crores for creation of database by local bodies, but only Rs. 90 crores could be utilized. Out of the allocation of Rs. 483 crores for maintenance of accounts, only Rs. 113 crores was utilized.

(e) Regarding horizontal aspects of transfers–relates to their inter-se distribution among States (in per capital terms) cost disabilities arise due to factors that are mainly population hilly areas, rainfall, droughts among States.

As for the inter-se allocation of the grants-in-aid among the states, the EFC had adopted the following factors and weights for working out the inter-se allocation of the grants-in-aid among the states.

Criterion	*Weight (%)*
1. Population	40 (2001 population)
2. Geographical Area	10
3. Per-Capita Income	20
4. Index of Decentralization	20
5. Revenue Effort	10

The term of reference of the EFC have taken note of the fact that there are several SFCs that have not submitted their reports and that EFC will have to take measures to accommodate these categories. This make the task of EFC slightly more complicated. The constitutional mandates and TOR define the tasks of EFC taking a broad view which includes the letter and spirit of the 73rd and the 74th amendments, the tasks of the EFC with reference to local bodies are to promote minimum standards of basic services throughout the country or promote any other national objective involving local bodies.

THE TWELFTH FINANCE COMMISSION AND LOCAL BODIES

The Presidential Order constituting the Twelfth Finance Commission (TFC) dated November, 1, 2002 mentions that the commission will make recommendations, interalia on measures needed to augment the consolidated fund of a state to supplement the resources of the panchayats and municipalities in the state on the basis of the recommendations made by the Finance Commission of the state" The wording of this clause is similar to that of sub clauses (bb) (c) of article 280 of the constitution.

The term of reference (TOR) interpreted "Restricting of Public Finance" with reference to restoring budgetary balance, equitable growth and so on cannot ignore local bodies. This note is a main approach and recommendations of the Twelfth Finance Commission with reference to the rural and urban local bodies. The Twelfth Finance Commission well aware of the role of the local bodies in the Indian Federal Policy but did not think it important enough to be made a part of the restructuring plan. Although the primary responsibility regarding States, Sub-State level transfer arrangements rests with State Finance Commission. The Union Finance Commission has a constitutional responsibility to review the public finances of the local bodies. Hence the SFCs and EFCs will have to work in a complementary fashion on several vital issues regarding horizontal equity for any real progress to happen in the country as a whole.

The Twelfth Finance Commission had an opportunity to going through two sets of State Finance Commissions reports. It is an advantage because substantial literature would be available to the TFC to rely upon. But the advantage is its contents are too confusing and disarranged to make over all macro projection. The Commission had laid emphasis on strengthening the local bodies in keeping with the constitutional mandate for effective and autonomous local self governance, recognizing that local bodies must be supported by a scheme of transfers that encourages decentralization and own effort for raising revenues.

(a) The recommended transfers for the local bodies constitute about 1.24 per cent of the sharable taxes and 0.9% of Centers gross revenue receipts.

(b) TFC used the indicators for determining the horizontal transfers which was used by the Eleventh Finance Commission.

(c) The commission shall review the fiscal reforms facility introduced by the Central Government on the basis of the recommendations of the 11th Finance Commission of India and suggest measures for effective achievement of its objectives.

(d) One important area is building a reliable database. The Twelfth Finance Commission on its part also made efforts to build the local finance data base.

(e) The TFC has recommended a very generous grants-in-aid of Rs. 25,000/- Crores. 20,000 Crores (80%) for panchayat Raj institutions and Rs. 5,000/- crores (20%) for urban local bodies for the period of 2005 to 2010.

(f) Out of the grants allocated for the Panchayats, priority should be given to expenditure on the costs of water supply and sanitation.

(g) Atleast 50% grants provided to each state for the urban local bodies for the scheme of solid waste management through public and private partnership.

(h) State Government should not take more than 15 days in transferring the grants to local bodies after these are released by the Central Government. The centre should take a serious view of any undue delay on the part of the State.

(i) The TFC has contributed significantly towards healthy fiscal federalism for inter-state allocation of grants to local bodies. It follows population, geographical area and per capita income as the allocation criteria but dropped the decentralization index, besides modifying the revenue effort factor.

These are the basic recommendations of Twelfth Finance Commission regarding local bodies in India. Data contained in

TFC report for 2002-2003 shows the total expenditure of local bodies as percentage of the combined expenditure of the Union, States and Local bodies works out only to about 4.7%. It shows how negligible has been local finance in the fiscal structure of India. As a percentage of GDP, the tax revenue of local bodies is only 0.26 per cent. But the Twelfth Finance Commission (TFC) recommends GDP ratio is set at 17.6 per cent.

To conclude the TFC has contributed significantly towards healthy fiscal federalism. The available local data are very poor quality and need drastic improvement. The future Union Finance Commissions and State Finance Commissions play more important role to make fiscal decentralization in India.

A COMPARISON OF BOTH THE COMMISSIONS

The TFC is free to take an independent view on the issues on which the EFC gave certain narrow opinions. The EFC made recommendations on the basis of SFCs recommendations. But the TFC lay down some common firm principles and guidelines to be followed by the SFCs in future. The Eleventh Finance Commission ventured to published a set of state wise data on revenue and expenditure of each tier of rural and urban local bodies for a period of 8 years from 1990-1991 to 1997-1998. But unfortunately the data found unrealistic and came out with spurious conclusions. The reason is that the quality of the data at the grass roots level is poor. Most states do not have accurate information on the finances of their local bodies. A proper accounting system has to be put in place at the grass roots level to facilitate realistic assessment of the needs of the panchayats and municipalities for basic civic and developmental functions. Though the Comptroller and Auditor General prepared budget and accounting formats for Panchayat Raj institutions and Urban Local Bodies with a view to rationalizing them, only six states have issued formal orders to implement them.

The TFC on its part also made efforts to build the local finance data base. Data were collected through a format prepared by it. Covering the five years from 1998-1999 through 2002-2003 a period after the new decentralized governance was well underway. The data thus obtained in the TFC report may be more reliable than that reported by the Eleventh Finance Commission. Even so, there are some general comments were there on it i.e. the data provided in the TFC report show heavy budgetary deficits.

Now we can observe the difference between the percentage share of grants-in-aid to Local bodies as per the TFC and EFC allocations.

Table 1

No.	State	PRIs		ULBs	
		TFC	EFC	TFC	EFC
1.	Andhra Pradesh	7.935	9.503	7.480	8.233
2.	Arunachal Pradesh	0.340	0.348	0.060	0.034
3.	Assam	2.630	2.918	1.100	1.077
4.	Bihar	8.120	9.813	2.840	4.695
5.	Chattishgarh	3.075	Nil	1.760	Nil
6.	Goa	0.090	0.116	0.240	0.232
7.	Gujarat	4.655	4.351	8.280	6.626
8.	Haryana	1.940	1.839	1.820	1.832
9.	Himachal Pradesh	0.735	0.821	0.160	0.195
10.	Jammu and Kashmir	1.405	0.930	0.760	0.783
11.	Jharkhand	2.410	Nil	1.960	Nil
12.	Karnataka	4.440	4.926	6.460	6.241
13.	Kerala	4.925	4.120	2.980	3.762
14.	Madhya Pradesh	8.315	8.943	7.220	7.801
15.	Maharashtra	9.915	8.209	15.820	15.813
16.	Manipur	0.230	0.235	0.180	0.220
17.	Meghalaya	0.250	0.320	0.160	0.135
18.	Mizoram	0.100	0.098	0.200	0.192
19.	Nagaland	0.200	0.161	0.120	0.089
20.	Orissa	4.015	4.320	2.080	1.998
21.	Punjab	1.620	1.933	3.420	2.736
22.	Rajastan	6.150	6.137	4.400	4.971
23.	Sikkim	0.065	0.066	0.020	0.010
24.	Tamil Nadu	4.350	5.826	11.440	9.668
25.	Tripura	0.285	0.356	0.160	0.201
26.	Uttar Pradesh	14.640	16.489	10.340	12.582
27.	Uttaranchal	0.810	Nil	0.680	Nil
28.	West Bengal	6.355	7.222	7.860	9.874
	Total	100.000	100.000	100.000	100.000

Compared to the Eleventh Finance Commission, the Twelfth Finance Commission has recommended a very generous grant-in-aid of Rs. 25,000 crore, with a break up of Rs. 20,000 crore (80%) for PRIs and Rs. 5,000 crore (20%) for Urban Local Bodies for the period 2005-2010. Table 1 gives the percentage share of grants-in-aid to local bodies as per TFC compared with EFC allocations. Whereas the 11th Finance Commission recommended 10,000 crores for the Rural and Urban Local Bodies. Excluding Chattisgarh, Jharkhand and Uttaranchal (New States). The percentage allocation of TFC grants to PRIs in 8 States and ULB in 13 States (Table 1) were higher than those made by the Eleventh Finance Commission.

According to Table 1, Haryana, Gujarat and Maharashtra admittedly richer states, accounts for 16.5% of the total allocation made by the TFC to PRIs. They get 2.11% which is more than the corresponding EFC Awards. However, the rural population share of these states is only 13.8%. The share to ULBs, Gujarat and Maharastra got 1.66% which is more compared to the EFC award. It is clear that horizontal equity des not seem to have been scrupulously honoured.

The Twelfth Finance Commission followed for inter-se states allocation of grants to local bodies of the three criteria followed by EFC i.e. Population, geographical area, distance from the highest per capita income with the same weights, but dropped the decentralization index besides modifying the revenue effort factor. Hence the Twelfth Finance Commission does not use an index of decentralization unlike the EFC but substituting it with the index of deprivation. The only implicit criteria of decentralization followed by the TFC is 5% weightage given to own revenue as a percentage of States own revenue. Here a better criterion would have been the percentage of own tax revenue and that of local bodies. The TFC was probably not correct in abandoning the decentralization index especially because the States, generally have a poor record of fiscal decentralization and administrative autonomy to local bodies.

The Twelfth Finance Commission had noticed that States have often been not prompt enough to constitute the State Finance Commission with required regularity. In many cases, after the recommendations are received, decisions have been kept pending. Even grants recommended and earmarked for the local bodies by the earlier finance commission, having been received into the consolidated fund of the State, have not been passed on to the local bodies in certain cases.

CONCLUSION

To conclude the TFC has contributed significantly towards healthy fiscal federalism. But local bodies are yet to be put prominently on the public finance map of India. This is needed to facilitate an inclusive and equitable economic growth and to secure better horizontal equity.

The task of achieving greater equality does not depend on Finance Commission transfer alone. Transfers by the Planning Commission and those by other Central Ministries need to play a complementary role that would help reduce these disparities. It is only when interstate and intra-state disparities are reduced, that the federal fiscal system would become stable.

REFERENCES

"Twelfth Finance Commission and Panchayat Finances" by D. Bandhopadhyaya, Economic & Political Weekly, 2003.

Inaugural Address by Dr. C. Rangarajan in the Annual Conference of the State Finance Secretaries (RBI).

"Eleventh Finance Commission and Local Bodies" by M.A. Oommen, Economic and Political Weekly, 1998.

India: Fiscal Decentralization to Rural Government by M.A. Oommen (2004).

Fiscal decentralization for Rural Governments in India by Geeta, Sethi (2004).

World Bank Report on State Fiscal Reform in India (McMillan 2004).

A review of the transfer system in Canada and Australia and Relevant Comparison with India by Sri C. Rangarajan, D.K. Srivastava.

16

FINANCING OF CALAMITY RELIEF EXPENDITURE OF THE STATES AND RECOMMENDATIONS OF THE TWELFTH FINANCE COMMISSION

*M. Mageswara Rao**, *R. Sudarsana Rao***
& *Radha Pushpavathi****

INTRODUCTION

The suffering due to floods, cyclones and droughts in one state or the other has become an annual feature causing lot of hardships to both the public as well as the State governments concerned. Though financing of relief expenditure is the responsibility of the states, the center cannot be a silent spectator of the suffering of the people affected by natural calamites due to the principle and the spirit of a federation. Moreover, the damages caused by the natural calamities are very huge in magnitude that no single state can afford to face the challenge on its own and without the financial assistance from the Centre. The damage caused and the economic losses sustained by Andhra Pradesh during 1993-94 to 2001-02 have been presented in Table 1. A perusal of the table reveals the precarious situation experienced by Andhra Pradesh due to natural calamities. In fact, State governments in India often face similar situations whenever natural calamities occur for reasons more than one.

* Assistant Prof. in Economics, PG Courses, MR. College Vizianagaram.

** Prof., Department of Economics, Andhra University, Visakhapatam.

*** Senior Lecturer, SKDBM Kalasala, Tamaku, West Godawari District.

Firstly, the state finances are thrown out of gear due to the sudden nature of calamity.

Table 1
Damages due to Natural Calamities in Andhra Pradesh: 1993-94 to 2001-02

Type of Damage	*Extent of loss / damage / affected*
Population affected in lakhs	1148.1
Human Deaths	2752
Live stock loss	59863
Houses damaged	1483375
Crop area damage (in lakh hectares)	58.15
Estimated loss (Rs. in crores)	13525.06

**Source:* Compiled from Memorandum submitted to Twelfth Finance Commission, Government of Andhra Pradesh

Secondly, the sates often are unable to meet the huge relief expenditure that arises due to calamities without depending upon Central government for financial assistance. Thirdly, the delayed process of estimation and the release of assistance by the Central Government and the scrutiny there upon even in the case of a calamity of national scale. As relief operations required huge amounts of funds that no state government can afford to spend sufficiently on its own. The center has to necessarily extend its helping hand to bail out the state concerned.[1] In fact the central government has been assisting the states in meeting the relief expenditure that arise due to the natural calamities in the states for the last several decades. The scheme of assistance of the central government has been based onthe recommendations of the successive finance commissions.

An attempt has been made in this paper to analyze the scheme of financial assistance by the center as recommended by the successive Finance commissions in general, and the recommendations of the Twelfth Finance Commission (TFC) in particular. Central assistance recommended by the successive Finance Commissions right from the Second Finance Commission recommended specified sum, ranging from Rs.I0 lakh to Rs.I00 lakh as a margin money scheme for relief expenditure under 64 Famine Relief to meet the expenditure on natural calamities. This margin money scheme was first termed by the Second Finance Commission. This arrangement was endorsed by the Third, Fourth, Fifth, Sixth and Seventh Finance Commissions.[2] Later the Finance Commission continued this arrangement up to the Eighth Finance Commission. The President of India recommended the Sixth Finance Commission to review the policy and arrangements made in this regard to financing of relief expenditure by the states. It also stressed on the development of drought and flood-prone areas through plan programmes.

DISTINCTION BETWEEN DROUGHT AND CYCLONES

The Seventh Finance Commission made a distinction between drought on the one hand and cyclone, flood and earthquake on the other, on the basis of suddenness and severity. It recommended that the centre should provide assistance to the affected State as advance plan assistance. In case the expenditure exceeds 5% of the states plan outlay the excess amount should be provided to the state by the Centre as grant cum loan (50:50). Regarding the relief and restoration to cyclone, flood and other calamities which are of sudden nature, the Seventh Finance Commission while suggesting norms and limits for share in the expenditure of the states in respect of droughts on the one hand and cyclones, floods on the other. The Seventh Finance Commission recommended that 75% of the expenditure incurred by the State, in excess of the margin should be provided by the Centre as non-plan grant and the balance 25% can be met by the State in order to discourage the wasteful expenditure. The Eighth Finance Commission recommended that the Centre should contribute 50% of the margin money for each state. It also recommended that the unspent balance of the margin money contributed by the state as well as the centre need not be invested in any other securities but should be carried forward to the subsequent years to be released during the need. There was an enormous increase in the size of the margin money provided by the States which covered RS.6.15 crore per annum by the Second Finance Commission to Rs.240.75 crare per annum by the Eighth Finance Commission.

CALAMITY RELIEF FUND (CRF)

The Ninth Finance Commission (NFC) made fundamental change by recommending for the establishment of Calamity Relief Fund (CRF) for each state wherein the Centre and the state has to contribute a ratio of 75:25. The total amount of CRF for all states was worked out at Rs.804 crore per year during its period. The NFC further recommended that the CRF should be separated to general revenues of the State and should be kept in a nationalized bank administered by a Committee headed by the Chief Secretary of the state. The NFC did not recommend any norms or guidelines for classifying a natural calamity as one of rare severity. It also did not recommend any additional fund for this purpose. Consequently, the Government of India did not release any special fund during 1990~95 to any state to meet the calamities of rare severity, though some of the states had faced such situations. The examples that can be cited in this context are the earthquakes in Latur in Maharashtra, Kandla in Gujarat, Jabalpur in Madhya Pradesh, the devastating cyclone in Andhra Pradesh etc.

NATIONAL FUND FOR CALAMITY RELIEF (NFCR)

The Tenth Finance Commission recommended that a National Fund for Calamity Relief (NFCR) should be established to which the centre and states contribute in the ratio of 3:1. This fund should be managed by National Calamity Relief Committee (NCRC) chaired by Union Minister of Agriculture, the Members being the Deputy Chairman of Planning Commission and State Chief Ministers.4 The TFC felt the need to assess the calamity of rare severity on the basis of intensity and magnitude of it. The State should have the capacity to tackle the problem, the alternative and flexibility available with the plans to provide relief etc.,

The Ministry of Agriculture sought to lay down broad guidelines for declaring a natural calamity as one of the rare severity. They have projected that the States in the past presented any calamities as cases of rare severity and whenever the corpus of CRF got exhausted the states sought additional assistance from NFCR. As a result 70 memoranda were received by the central government from 23 states during 1995-98 seeking an assistance of RS.24000 crore from NFCR, while the corpus of NFCR for the five year period was only RS.700 crore. In many cases it was found that the funds released from NFCR were not spent even in an year after the date of release. Therefore, Ministry of Agriculture recommended a time limit for utilization of funds given from the NFCR and the unspent amount should either be returned to the NFCR or adjusted against the contribution of centre in the CRF. By and large NFCR continued funding the states by presenting clear guidelines to identify calamities of rare severity.

The TFC's recommendations for additional funds from NFCR to a state in case of inadequacy of funds in CRF on a request basis is really appreciable. But in this process states felt a long drawn procedure, delays etc. However, the existence of NFCR was short-lived.

THE NATIONAL CALAMITY CONTINGENCY FUND (NCCF)

The Eleventh Finance Commission pointed out that the NFCR is not adequate in view of huge expenditure commitments from the states. It got exhausted in the first three years and had to be supplemented. The Commission was of the view that in the case of occurrence of calamity of rare severity the centre and other states have to come forward to provide relief to an affected state. Therefore, EFC felt the need to develop a system in which the Central Government to assess the damage and extend the relief required without waiting for any memorandum from the state government. Accordingly, the Commission has recommended for the establishment of National Calamity Contingency Fund.

NATIONAL CENTRE FOR CALAMITY MANAGEMENT (NCCM)

A National Centre for Calamity Management (NCCM) under

the Ministry of Home Affairs has been established to monitor National Calamities relating to cyclones, droughts, earthquakes, fire, floods and hailstorms. It expected to monitor such mishap on a regular basis and assess the severity and check whether the state is in a position to provide relief from the CRF and its own resources. It should then make recommendations of the Central government on the severity of the situation and is liable to get assistance from the central government and the state governments. The Commission made a remarkable recommendation that the central government levies a special surcharge on central taxes, the proceeds would accrue to the NCCF and be available for providing assistance to State government. The balance in the National Fund at the end of the financial year will be presented as a source for the next plan.

The Eleventh Finance Commission's recommendation to establish a National Calamity Contingency Fund and the National Centre for Calamity Management of Finance relief expenditure that arise due to natural calamities of severity, their monitoring and the impact assessment respectively can be considered as a milestone as far as the scheme of relief operations are concerned. Moreover, the recommendations gave scope for assisting the affected States adequately and on a continuous basis. The NCCM is expected to playa greater role not only by providing training to carryout the relief operations but also in designing appropriate strategies of preparedness.

THE TWELFTH FINANCE COMMISSION

Under para 10 of the Terms of Reference,6 the TFC requires to review the existing arrangements with regard to financing of disaster management with reference to National Calamity Contingency Fund and the Calamity Relief Fund (CRF) and to make its recommendations. The Commission after thoroughly examining the existing arrangements as recommended by its predecessors, considered the views of the States and the Union government. It felt that the existing scheme of Calamity Relief Fund has fulfilled the objective of meeting the immediate relief needs of the States.

Accordingly, it recommended the continuance of the Calamity Relief Fund (CRF) with a size of Rs.21333.33 crore for the award period (2005-10). The year-wise amount of fund and the respective shares of Centre and States for the award period as recommended by the commission is presented in Table 2.

Table 2
Calamity Relief Fund and Share of Centre and States-Twelfth Finance Commission

Year	*Total Amount of Fund (2005-10)*	*Central Grant*	*States' Contribution*
(1)	*(2)*	*(3)*	*(4)*
2005-06	3944.42	2958.32	986.10
2006-07	4097.79	3073.34	1024.44
2007-08	4258.85	3194.14	1064.68
2008-09	4427.97	3320.97	1107.02
2009-10	4604.31	3453.23	1151.09
TOTAL	21333.33	16000.00	5333.33

*Source: Report of the Twelfth Finance Commission

The Commission recommended an amount of Rs.1901 crores of Calamity Relief Fund for the five year period to Andhra Pradesh as may be seen in Table 3.

Table 3
Calamity Relief Fund to Andhra Pradesh-Twelfth Finance Commission

Year	*Total Amount of Rs. Crores*	*Central Rs. Crores*	*State Rs. Crores*
2005-06	344.08	258.06	86.02
2006-07	361.28	270.96	90.32
2007-08	379.35	284.51	94.84
2008-09	398.31	298.73	99.58
2009-10	418.23	313.67	104.56
Grand Total	1901.24	1425.93	475.32

*Source: Report of the Twelfth Finance Commission

In spite of the request made by several states including Andhra Pradesh, the Commission has not changed in the method of determining the size of the Calamity Relief Fund, nor the composition of sharing of the fund between the Centre and States. In fact, several states demanded either the states' share be reduced or the commission should take into account due allowance for inflation during the period of the award. The states demand for increased size of CRF and the central share merits consideration in view of the hiatus between the central grant and the states actual expenditure for Calamity Relief Operation. The Central grant and the actual expenditure incurred by the state of Andhra Pradesh and all states for undertaking relief operations on account of natural calamities for the period 2000-01 to 2004-05 is presented in Table A.

Table 4
Expenditure Incurred by Government of Andhra Pradesh for Calamity Relief Operations

	Expenditure incurred (Rs.Crs)		*Grant provided by the Centre (Rs.Crs)*		*Col. 2 as % of Col A*	*Col. 3 as % of Col.5*
Year	*Andhra Pradesh*	*All States*	*Andhra Pradesh*	*All States*	*Andhra Pradesh*	*All States*
(1)	*(2)*	*(3)*	*(4)*	*(5)*	*(6)*	*(7)*
2000-01	315	3878	149	1494	47.30	38.53
2001-02	293	5012	156	1569	53.24	31. 30
2002-03	461	4169	163	1647	35.36	39.51
2003-04	377	4542	172	1730	45.62	38.09
2004-05	509	5390	181	1816	35.56	33.69

* *Source:* Compiled from report of CMIE, 2006 Reserve Bahk of India.

A perusal of the table reveals that the Central grant recommended by the Eleventh Finance Commission accounts for less than 50 percent of actual expenditure incurred by the government of Andhra Pradesh except in the year 2001-02. It may be observed from the table that the Central grant as recommended by the Finance Commission accounts only around 40% with regard to actual relief expenditure of all states. This explains the need for not only an increased size of CRF but also an increased share of Central grant as requested by several states to the Twelfth Finance Commission.

The commission also, more or less, followed the methodology by its predecessors in determining the size of the CRF by taking the relief expenditure incurred by the States during the year 1993-94 to 2002-03 by setting aside suggestions made by several states. But it is necessary to take into account the proneness of a state to natural calamities by an objective pre-determined criteria to determine the size of the CRF instead of the average expenditure method. This is mainly because of the possible over or lower estimation of the Relief expenditure and thus the Calamity Relief Fund. However, the inclusion of calamities that result due to landslides, avalanches, cloud burst and pest attacks to the existing list of natural calamities would provide greater scope forrelief to some states which are prone to these disasters. The recommendations relating to more disaster preparedness and mitigation are appreciable.

CONCLUSION

The Twelfth Finance Commission, more or less accorded the recommendations of its predecessor with regard to scheme of financing relief expenditure. It also expanded the coverage of calamities by adding some more to the existing list. It may be suggested that the states may be allowed to spend a fixed percentage, say 10 percent from the unspent balances of CRF towards developing some programmes of preparedness and mitigation of natural calamities in the vulnerable areas. Such a measure will help to mitigate future disasters thus saving expenditure that necessitates due to relief expenditure in future. In view of the huge amount of relief expenditure due to natural calamities the state may also allow to levy a surcharge a kin to that of the Centre to mobilize the financial resources for the specific purposes of relief operations. It may be pertinent to note that eventhough the successive Finance Commissions, especially, the last three Commissions, have dwelt upon much with regard to mitigation and preparedness of disasters through National Centre for Calamity Management. (NCCM), the outcome appears to be substantially less than the outlays. This calls for more initiatives by the NCCM with long term objectives in future.

REFERENCES

Sudarsana Rao R: "Federal Fiscal Transfers in India A.P.H. Publishing Corporation, New Delhi, 1996. P.59.

B.P.R. Vithal and M.L. Sastry; Fiscal Federalism in India, Oxford University, New Delhi. 2001, P.180

Sudarsana Rao R, op. cit; P.

Report of the Eleventh Finance Commission 2000-2005, Govt. of India, p.90.

Ibid - p.91.

Report of the Twelfth Finance Commission.

17

WOMEN IN TWELFTH FINANCE COMMISSION

B. Ratna Kumari & A. Rajani

The Twelfth Finance Commission has broken new ground in several key areas and made recommendations which, if fully implemented, will have a far-reaching impact on the finances and functioning of government in the country at all levels. The basic function of the Finance Commission as envisaged in the Constitution has been to help redress the twin imbalances-vertical and horizontal – that all federations face, determining the percentage of shareable union taxes to be devolved to the states (Article 280) and if that did not suffice, to indicate the amounts to be provided to the states in need of assistance as grants-in-aid (Article 275). Since such determination has to make in the context of the emerging economic and fiscal situation, the FC has to focus its attention towards women's perspective under the Vision 2020 in order to gain women empowerment in our country by devolving gender budget. Of course our honorable Finance Minster had already initiated Gender budgeting for the first time, even than many women groups felt that more needed to be done. So there is a greater need to emphasis the importance of women in the Finance Commission by allocating special directions to the states in the federal structure. The present study has made an attempt to whether the 12th finance commission has made any specifications about women's issues or not for their empowerment.

OBJECTIVES

The objectives of the study are:

- To define gender budgeting and analyze various states of India,
- To study the women component in various programes in the budget and
- To suggest the measures to be added in the 12th Finance Commission towards women's empowerment through gender budgeting.

In India, gender perspective on public expenditure had been gaining ground since the publication of the report of the Committee on the Status of Women in 1974. The Eighth Five Year Plan (1992-97) highlighted for the first time the need to ensure a definite flow of funds from the general developmental sectors to women. The Plan document made an express statement that "*...the benefits of development from different sectors should not by pass women and special programmes on women should complement the general development programmes. The latter, in turn, should reflect greater gender sensitivity*". This approach, however, could not make much dent in ensuring adequate flow of funds and benefits to women, especially in the 12th finance Commission.

The Ninth Five Year Plan (19972-2002), while reaffirming the earlier commitment adopted Women Component Plan (WCP) as one of the major strategies and directed both the Central and the State Governments to ensure "*not less than 30 per cent of the funds/benefits are earmarked in all the women's related sectors*". It also directed that a special vigil be kept on the flow of the earmarked funds/benefits through an effective mechanism to ensure that the proposed strategy brings forth a holistic approach towards empowering women.

Gender Budgeting is not a separate budget for women; rather it is a dissection of the government budget to establish its gender-differential impacts and to translate gender commitments into budgetary commitments. The main objective of a gender-sensitive budget is to improve the analysis of incidence of budgets, attain more effective targeting of public expenditure and offset any undesirable gender-specific consequences of previous budgetary measures.

In India, gender perspective on public expenditure had been gaining ground since the publication of the report of the Committee on the Status of Women in 1974. The Eighth Five Year Plan (1992-97) highlighted for the first time the need to ensure a definite flow of funds from the general developmental sectors to women. The Plan document made an express statement that "*...the benefits of development from different sectors should not by pass women and special programmes on women should complement the general development programmes. The latter, in turn, should reflect greater gender sensitivity*". This approach, however, could not make much dent in ensuring adequate flow of funds and benefits to women.

The Ninth Five Year Plan (19972-2002), while reaffirming the earlier commitment adopted Women Component Plan as one of the major strategies and directed both the Central and the State Governments to ensure "*not less than 30 per cent of the funds/benefits are earmarked in all the women's related sectors*". It also directed that a special vigil be kept on the flow of the earmarked funds/benefits through an effective mechanism to ensure that the proposed strategy brings forth a holistic approach towards empowering women.

Gender Budgeting is not a separate budget for women; rather it is a dissection of the government budget to establish its gender-differential impacts and to translate gender commitments into budgetary commitments. The main objective of a gender-sensitive budget is to improve the analysis of incidence of budgets, attain more effective targeting of public expenditure and offset any undesirable gender-specific consequences of previous budgetary measures.

Gender budgeting is gaining increasing acceptance as a tool for engendering macro economic policy-making. The Fourth World Conference of Women held in Beijing in September 1995 and the Platform for Action that it adopted called for a gender perspective in all macroeconomic policies and their budgetary dimensions. The Outcome Document of the UN General Assembly Special Session on Women held in June 2000, also called upon all the Nations to mainstream a gender perspective into key macroeconomic and social development policies and national development programmes. Emphasis on gender budgeting was also placed by the Sixth Conference of Commonwealth Ministers of Women's Affairs held in New Delhi in April 2000.

Preliminary results of gender analysis of State budgets pertaining to the year 2001-02 have been received from some of the institutions/social scientists, but due to wide variations in nomenclature of schemes and programmes across States and wide discrepancies in data which require further validation, immediate collation of results and comparative analysis is difficult at this stage.

Initial reports received from 10 states have been compiled and tabulated below. The results are only indicative and would need to be further validated.

GENDER ANALYSIS OF THE UNION BUDGET 2002-2003 - A FIRST GLANCE

Taking existing studies as a base, the present study has carried out an analysis of the Union Budget 2002-2003 in a gender perspective, which reveals the following pattern:

- Allocation on Women Specific Schemes has increased from Rs. 3260 crores in 2001-2002 to Rs. 3358 crores in the Budget for 2002-2003, an improvement of three per cent.
- Allocations on most of the women specific schemes have been enhanced. The only scheme where allocation has been reduced is the Reproductive and Child Health Programme of the Department of Family Welfare, which is attributable to the revamping of the scheme due to which some of the components of the programme are now covered under the Immunization Programme. Two schemes have been transferred to the States (Balika Samridhi Yojana, Post Partum Programmes) and a few schemes have been dropped (Mahila Samridhi Yojana, Socio Economic Programme, Women's Empowerment Year.)

- Budgetary allocations on Pro Women Allocation has increased from Rs. 10596.37 crores in 2001-2002 to Rs 13036.01 crores in 2002-2003 reflecting a percentage increase of 23%. The Department of Family Welfare, which is attributable to the revamping of the scheme due to which some of the components of the programme are now covered under the Immunization Programm,which accounting for 70 per cent of its toal budget for women. Two schemes have been transferred to the States (Balika Samridhi Yojana, Post Partum Programmes) and a few schemes have been dropped.
- Budgetary allocations on Pro Women Allocation has increased from Rs. 10596.37 crores in 2001-2002 to Rs. 13036.01 crores in 2002-2003 reflecting a percentage increase of 23%.

However the review has highlighted the fact that the WCP has created considerable awareness and sensitization amongst the planners, policy-makers and administrators to ensure that the funds/benefits from other development sectors do not by-pass women. Under WCP funds were earmarked for schemes, which target women and girls and those with a significant women's empowerment. The following tables 1and 2 gives an inference that the difference between the budget allocation of the department of women and child development and department of social welfare after the Beijing commitment.

Table 1
Budget allocations of the Dept of Women and child Development
Annual plan (Rs. in Millions)

1997-98	9000.00
1998-99	12250.95
1999-00	13200.00
2000-01	14600.00
2001-02	16500.00
2002-03	22000.00
2003-04	26000.00
2004-05	24000.00
2005-06	39000.00

Source: Government of India's II AND III PERIODIC Report on the CEDAW.

Table 2
Budget Allocation for Social Welfare Programme after the Beijing Commitment. Plan Expenditure under Social Services

Year	*% Distribution*
1997-98	20.7
1998-99	25.6
1999-00	23.9
2000-01	22.0
2001-02	24.9
2002-03	27.1
2003-2004	27.3
2004-05	23.3

Source: Government of India's II AND III PERIODIC Report on the CEDAW.

GENDER BUDGETING TO BE DONE BY MINISTRIES

Taking forward the gender budgeting exercise started last year, Finance Minister P. Chidambaram on Tuesday announced that 30 per cent of the allocations of some major ministries would be focused on programmes for women. Presenting the budget for 2006-07 fiscal in Parliament, Chidambaram said so far 32 ministries have set up gender budgeting cells.He said it is proposed to have 30 per cent allocation of some of the key ministries focusing on programme for women. This would see an allocation of Rs. 28,737 crore for gender budgeting. So far 23 ministries have placed specific demands for grants for programmes with focus on improving the health, education and other facilities catering to the needs of women and children, he said.

WHAT KIND OF BUDGET- WE REQUIRE PRO WOMEN OR ANTI WOMEN?

Planning and budgetary process are considered to be instruments towards eradication of poverty, by providing the minimum basic needs of literacy, health and housing, employment and social justice to all the people. If production growth and creation of wealth are accomplished without equitable of distribution of benefits, it will not only widen the gap between the rich and the poor, but it will make the lives of the poor more miserable with galloping price-rise and fall in living standards. The budget for poverty alleviation is itself in a poor state of health, limping and disabled. The budget for removal of poverty will be effective only after removal of poverty of the budget itself with respective of women empowerment. Therefore the state and central government should strictly follow the gender budget process in order to remove the poverty in our country, because most of the women folk belongs to below the poverty line.In this contest the finance commission must be cautious in devolving the powers to the states, which have to take care of the women's development through their participation. Let us examine the gender budget process in our state. Andhra Pradesh has got good reputation in implementation of women empowerment policy through self help group approach.

AN ANALYSIS OF GENDER BUDGET IN ANDHRA PRADESH THROUGH WOMEN AND CHILD WELFARE BOARD

The objectives of this board are to mobile voluntary efforts in AP for mobile voluntary organizations by rendering them financial assistance. Institutions which provides residential care for women and children welfare of handicapped and for the aged are eligible for financial assistance. During the year 2002-2003 the budget allocated is Rs. 24,22,000. The budget provision for the year 2003-04 is Rs. 27,12,000.

INTEGRATED CHILD DEVELOPMENT SERVICES

The ICDS Scheme is Centrally Sponsored Scheme, covering 351 blocks in the states. The scheme gives six crucial services to the children and women. These services are delivered at the village level through AWCs.

Table 3

Physical Achievements under ICDS

Year	*Projects*	*No. of Angan wadi centers*	*Beneficiaries*	
			Women	*Children*
2001-02	251	37425	739466	3143654
2002-03	351	54133	1900068	672319
2003-04	351	54133	1900068	6723319

Source: Women Development & Child Welfare.

PRADHAN MANTRI GRAMODYA YOJANA (PMGY)

Eradicating Mal Nutrition amongst under 3 year children by additional nutritional coverage of supplementary feeding of these children through the ICDS SCHEME. In the ICDS as per existing guide lines the feeding is supplemental to meet calorie/ protein gap of 300 k.cal an 8-10 gms. Of protein for the grade– I and Grade- II children and double the amount for Grade- III and IV children.

Adolesent Girls Scheme:

Aims:

To reduce nutritional anemia

To reduce gender inequality

Provide supportive environment for self development

No. of ICDS blocks implementing the activity: 250

Action Plan for 2003-04:

For the year 2003-04 exclusive budget of Rs. 1.00 crore is sanctioned for capacity building of mothers committee under Women Empowerment. The following are the activities proposed for the budget sanctioned.

Imparted 2 days training to all 8 members of Mothers of Mothers Committees in 100 new ICDS Projects with an outlay of Rs. 93.58/- lakhs. The focus of the training was on other roles and responsibilities in implementation of ICDS.

Women Component Plan: This has been adopted to ensure that the benfits from other developmental sectors do not by-pass women and not less than 30 per cent of funds/benfits flow to them from all the women–related sectors implemented during Ninth Plan. The strategy through a multi- sectoral approach enables holistic development and advancement of women. Substantial amount of funds are flowing to women through both women- specific and women related schemes, which are implemented by fifteen Central Ministries/ Departments.

The financial allocations for the Tenth Plan period for these programmes have been stepped up considerably. As against a total expenditure of Rs. 358660 million in the Ninth Plan, the allocation for the Tenth Plan period has been increased to Rs. 567480 million. So there is no use of sanctioning financial allocation of budget under women component plan, unless we have to follow the gender development indices.

GENDER DEVELOPMENT INDICES:

"In order to support better planning and programme formulation and adequate allocation of resources, Gender Development Indices (GDI) will be developed by networking with specialized agencies. Gender auditing and development of evaluation mechanisms will also be undertaken along side. Collection of gender disaggregated data by all primary data collecting agencies of the Central and State Governments as well as research and academic institutions in the Public and Private Sectors will be undertaken. Data and information gaps in vital areas reflecting the status of women will be sought to be filled in. All Ministries/Corporations/Banks and financial institutions etc. will be advised to collect, collate, disseminate data related to programmes and benefits on a gender-disaggregated basis. This will help in meaningful planning and evaluation of policies." (GOI: National Policy for Empowerment of Women 2001):

Tasks Ahead

The gender budget initiative of the Department has opened new vistas of research and analysis of public expenditure in the country and opened serious methodological debates for carrying out such analysis. This has also highlighted the urgency of sharpening the methodological tools for monitoring the progress of Women's Component Plan introduced in the Ninth Five Year Plan.

The most difficult task in the gender analysis of budget is to compile gender segregated data on allocation and expenditure on pro- women and gender neutral schemes which are not generated from the existing formats and schedules of budgetary procedures and reporting systems. Again, mere expenditure analysis does not give any true picture about the actual impact of such expenditure on women. This certainly calls for more in depth analysis on sectoral issues over a larger than annual time frame. It is also necessary to formulate uniform guidelines and procedures so that valid comparisons and inferences can be made at the regional and national level.

Therefore, initiatives of the Department, in the coming year, in the direction of a comprehensive assessment of gender impact of Government Budgets would be to:

- Organize workshops and studies on refining methodology for gender analysis of budgets;
- Formulate and disseminate uniform guidelines on gender budgeting and analysis to States and develop appropriate software for such analysis;
- Pursue formulation and adoption of schedules and formats for working out women's share in all public expenditure at center, state and district levels;
- Extend the nature and scope of gender analysis of budgets to include benefit incidence analysis in specific geographical and sectoral areas and over a larger time frame;
- Promote capacity-building of research organizations for such analysis.
- Specific Instructions towards the women empowerment must be guided and included by the finance commission of our country.

CONCLUSIONS

The above analysis of gender budgeting shows that the Finance Commission has to give direction and guidance to the federal structure in a way that the all departments of both centre and state should focus their attention towards women empowerment process by maintaining the women component plan. Of course the government undertaken various measures, through law, policies, and programmes in the last ten years to address gender inequality and to eliminate discrimination against women and girl children. Even though there are significant improvements on various indicators the gender discrimination continues to be a daunting challenge and the government is supposed to eliminate the bias against women and to translate the dejure rights into defacto enjoyment of rights and equal results through gender budgeting tool.

REFERENCES

Amaresh Bagchi (2005), Symposium on Report of Twelfth Finance Commission:Introduction and Overview: Economic and Political Weekly, July 30th August 5th.

Government of India's II and III Periodic Report on the Convention on the Elimination of All Forms of Discrimination Against Women (CEDAW) 1997-2005, Department of Women and Child Development, Ministry of Human Resource Development, Government of India 2005.

Oomen M.A. (2005), Twelfth Finance Commission and Local Bodies: Economic and Political Weekly, May 14th.

Standing at the Crossroads: A Situational Analysis of Indian Women: National Institute of Public Cooperation & Child Development, New Delhi.

18

12th FINANCE COMMISSION RECOMMENDATIONS ON PANCHAYATS AND MUNICIPALITIES

Shamshuddin Shaik & Khadar Baba Shaik

INTRODUCTION

Finance is very easy to spell and pronounce but equally difficult to practice in real life as an individual. This is not even exception for the organizations or Governments at any point of administration. So one of the important area in the Indian government administration is Financial administration i.e Ministry for Finance which plays a dominant role in the Indian development of Economic growth is concerned. The 12th Finance Commission has given an importance to develop the Panchayats as per revenue and capacity utilization etc. The Twelfth Finance Commission (TFC) was required to make recommendations on the measures needed to augment the Consolidated Funds of the States to supplement the resources of the Panchayats and Municipalities on the basis of the recommendations of the State Finance Commissions (SFCs). TFC has given recommendations on this term of reference, which have been accepted by the Union Government. The Twelfth Finance Commission (TFC) was required to make recommendations on the measures needed to augment the Consolidated Funds of the States to supplement the resources of the Panchayats and Municipalities on the basis of the recommendations of the State Finance Commissions (SFCs). TFC has given recommendations on this term of reference, which have been accepted by the Union Government. The Twelfth Finance Commission (TFC) was required to make recommendations on the measures needed to augment the Consolidated Funds of the States to supplement the resources of the Panchayats and Municipalities on the basis of the recommendations of the State Finance Commissions (SFCs). TFC has given recommendations on this term of reference, which have been accepted by the Union Government.

OBJECTIVES OF THE PAPER

1. To Study the importance of the Panchayat and Municipalities in Indian Administration.
2. To understand the role of Government to develop the Panchayat and Municipalities.
3. To study and analyze the recommendations of TFC (12th Finance Commission Recommendations on Panchayat and Munisipalities.

RESEARCH METHODOLOGY

The data mostly collected from the Books, Magazines, Journals, News Papers, Internet, Reports etc.

PANCHYAT RAJ AND MUNICIPALITIES

As our Father of Nation Mahathma Gandhi revealed that unless Panchayats are developed independently the nation can not be called a developed nation and we may not have experience of full freedom of the national growth and development.

Twelfth Finance Commission's Recommendations of Local Body Grants and Inter-state Distribution

1.1 Criterion	Weight (per cent)
(i) Population	40
(ii) Geographical area	10
(iii) Distance from highest per capita income	20
(iv) Index of deprivation	10

(v) Revenue effort of which 20

(a) with respect to own revenue of states 10

(b) with respect to GSDP 10

The States would make the allocation amongst various Municipalities and Panchayati Raj Institutions and also autonomous councils in excluded areas.

SHARES OF STATES IN ALLOCATION (2005-2010)

Sl. No.	*State*	*Panchayats*		*Municipalities*	
		Per cent	*(Rs. Crore)*	*Per cent*	*(Rs. Crore)*
1.	Andhra Pradesh	7.935	1587.00	7.480	374.00
2.	Arunachal Pradesh	0.340	68.00	0.60	3.00
3.	Assam	2.630	526.00	1.100	55.00
4.	Bihar	8.120	1624.00	2.840	142.00
5.	Chhatisgarh	1.075	615.00	1.760	88.00
6.	Goa	0.090	18.00	0.240	12.00
7.	Gujarat	1.655	911.00	8.280	414.00
8.	Haryana	1.940	188.00	1.820	91.00
9.	Himachal Pradesh	0.735	147.00	0.160	8.00
10.	Jammu & Kashmir	1.405	281.00	0.760	38.00
11.	Jharkhand	2.410	482.00	1.960	98.00
12.	Karnataka	4.440	888.00	6.460	323.00
13.	Kerala	4.925	985.00	2.980	149.00
14.	Madhya Pradesh	8.315	1663.00	7.220	361.00
15.	Maharashtra	9.915	1983.00	15.820	791.00
16.	Manipur	0.230	46.00	0.180	9.00
17.	Meghalaya	0.250	50.00	0.160	8.00
18.	Mizoram	0.100	20.00	0.200	10.00
19.	Nagaland	0.200	40.00	0.120	6.00
20.	Orissa	4.015	803.00	2.080	104.00
21.	Punjab	1.620	324.00	3.420	171.00
22.	Rajasthan	6.150	1230.00	4.400	220.00
23.	Sikkim	0.065	13.00	0.020	1.00
24.	Tamil Nadu	4.350	870.00	11.440	572.00
25.	Tripura	0.285	57.00	0.160	8.00
26.	Uttar Pradesh	14.640	2928.00	10.340	517.00
27.	Uttaranchal	0.810	162.00	0.680	34.00
28.	West Bengal	6.355	1271.00	7.860	393.00
	Total	100.000	20000.00	100.000	5000.00

MONITORING AGENCIES

Every State shall constitute a High Level Committee (HLC) to ensure proper utilization of Local Bodies Grants. This HLC shall be headed by the Chief Secretary to the State Government and will include Finance Secretary and Secretaries of the concerned Departments as members.

HLC SHALL BE RESPONSIBLE FOR THE FOLLOWING

(a) Approval of the projects at the beginning of every year to be undertaken in each sector, quantify the targets, both in physical and financial terms and lay down a time-table for achievement of specific milestones;

(b) Monitoring both physical and financial targets and ensuring adherence to the specific conditionalities in respect of each grant, wherever applicable;

HLC shall meet at least once in every quarter to review the utilization of grants and to issue directions for mid-course correction, if considered necessary. Minutes of HLC meetings shall be provided to the Department of Expenditure (Finance Commission Division), Ministry of Finance, Government of India for information.

A Central Review Committee will be constituted in the Government of India, headed by Secretary to Government of India, Ministry of Finance, Department of Expenditure to review the releases and utilization of grants. The Committee will include representatives from the Ministry of Panchayati Raj, Ministry of Urban Development and Poverty Alleviation, Ministry of Home Affairs and Ministry of Finance (Department of Expenditure). The Committee shall meet at least once in a year.

MODE OF RELEASE OF LOCAL BODY GRANTS TO STATES

Local bodies grants will be released in two equal installments in July and January every year. States have to mandatory transfer the grants released by the Centre to the PRIs and ULBs within 15 days of the same being credited to the States' account.

ELECTED PANCHYATS AS PER THE PROVISIONS OF THE CONSTITUTION

Two sets of details, one on allocation of funds and another on release of funds, will be reported by the State Government in the format prescribed at Annexure II for the purpose prior to the release of each installment by the Government of India. However, the first six monthly installment for 2005-06 shall be released to a State after receiving only the details (in the above said format) of the allocation of these funds to the PRIs and ULBs in that State. All subsequent installments shall be released after receiving both sets of details–the certificate of the release of funds to the PRIs and ULBs for the previous installment and the information about allocation of funds for the subsequent installment. For the first installment for 2005-06, information on allocation upto district level alone need to be sent by the State. For the subsequent releases, the break up of the allocation to each PRI and ULB at the three levels should be provided. The States are advised to inform Government of India about allocated share of each PRI and ULB at all levels before October 31, 2005. State Finance Secretary would be required to provide a certificate within 15 days of the release of each installment by Government of India under his signature certifying the dates and amounts of local grants received by the State from the Government of India, and the dates and amounts of grants released to the PRIs and ULBs. This certification and information will be in the above mentioned format.

State Finance Secretary would also be required to provide a certificate every year of the percentage of grants spent by the ULBs on schemes of solid waste management and on schemes of water supply and sanitation by the PRIs. States would also be required to provide details of recurring O&M cost recoverable by the PRIs on schemes of water supply.

The second installment of local bodies grants for the year 2005-06 shall be released upon receipt of the release certificate for the previous installment and allocation information for the subsequent installment referred to in para 6.2. In case of delayed transfer to PRIs/ULBs beyond the specified period of 15 days, the State Government shall transfer to PRI/ULB amount of interest at the rate equal to the RBI Bank rate along with such delayed transfer of grants.

The second installment from the year 2006-07 would be released on receipt of the certificate referred to in para 6.1 in addition to the release certificate and allocation information referred to in para 6.2. Government of India will hold the amount short spent on the schemes of solid waste management by the ULBs and on schemes of water supply and sanitation by the PRIs. The withheld amount will be subsequently reimbursed upon confirmation that the short spending has been compensated in the subsequent period.

AUDIT BY THE COMPTROLLER AND AUDITOR GENERAL OF INDIA

Comptroller and Auditor General of India would be expected to audit the release and use of the local bodies grants within the time and for the purposes mentioned by the TFC, reproduced above. Government of India may take appropriate decision about withholding grants of a State if the Comptroller and Auditor General of India reports that the State has either not transferred the grants to the local bodies or has allowed the grants to be used for purposes other than for which these are being provided or that local bodies have not been able to give priority to spend on the O&M of water supply and sanitation for the rural areas and on schemes of solid waste management in the urban areas.

The States should avoid delays in the constitution of the SFCs, their constitution in phases, frequent reconstitution, submission of reports and tabling of the ATR in the legislature. It is desirable that SFCs are constituted at least two years before the required date of submission of their recommendations, and the deadline should be so decided as to allow the state government at least three months' time for tabling the ATR, preferably along with the budget for the ensuing financial year.

The SFC reports should be readily available to the Central Finance Commission, when the latter is constituted so that the Central Finance Commission on the basis of uniform principles could make an assessment of the state's need. This requires that these reports should not be too dated. As the periodicity of constitution of the Central Finance Commission is predictable, the States should time the constitution of their SFCs suitably.

SFCs must be constituted with people of eminence and competence with qualification and experience in the relevant fields.

The convention established at the national level of accepting the principal recommendations of the Finance Commission without modification should be followed at the State level in respect of SFC reports.

The SFCs must clearly identify the issues which require action on the part of the central government to augment the consolidated fund of the State and list them out in a separate chapter for the consideration of the Central Finance Commission.

The suggestions made by SFCs regarding raising the ceiling on professional tax is endorsed for action by Central Government.

It is desirable that the SFCs follow the procedure adopted by the Central Finance Commission for transfer of resources from the Centre to the States in respect of resources transfers from State Governments to local bodies. The SFC reports should contain an estimation and analysis of the finances of the State government as well as the local bodies at the pre and post transfer stages along with a qualification of the revenues that could be generated additionally by the local bodies by adopting the measures recommended therein. The gaps that may still remain would then constitute the basis for the measures to be recommended by the Central Finance Commission.

While estimating the resources of the local bodies, the SFCs should follow a normative approach in the assessment of revenues and expenditure rather than made forecasts based on historical trends.

A permanent SFC cell may be created in the finance department of State governments as the collection and collation of data would need to be done constantly and data would need to be made available to the SFC as and when it is constituted.

A sum of Rs. 20,000 crore for the Pnachayats and Rs.5000 crore for the Municipalities may be provided as grants-in-aid to augment the consolidated fund of the States for the period 2005-10 to be distributed with inter-se shares as indicated in table 8.1 of the report. (Annex-I).

The PRIs should be encouraged to take over the assets relating to water supply and sanitation and utilize the grants for repairs/rejuvenation as also the O&M costs. The PRIs should, however, recover at least 50 per cent of the recurring costs in the form of user charges.

Of the grants allocated for Panchayats, priority should be given to expenditure on the O&M costs of water supply and sanitation. This will facilitate Panchayats to take over the schemes and operate them.

At least 50 per cent of the grants-in-aid provided to each State for the urban local bodies should be earmarked for the scheme of solid waste management through public-private partnership. The Municipalities should concentrate on collection, segregation and transportation of solid waste. The cost of these activities whether carried out in house or out sourced could be met from the grants. Most States do not have credible information on the finances of their local bodies. Local bodies would continue to need funding support for building data base and maintenance of accounts. States may assess the requirement of each local body in this regard and earmark funds accordingly out of the total allocation recommended by us.

Separate grants-in-aid for the normal and the excluded areas are not proposed. It is for the State concerned to distribute the grants recommended for the State among the local bodies including those in the excluded areas in a fair and just manner.

No conditionality over and above these recommended by us need be imposed by the Central Government for releasing the grants-in-aid.

RECOMMENDATIONS OF THE TFC

The summary of the recommendations of the TFC is reproduced below:

The best practices listed in para 8.19 of the report (included in para 4 of these guidelines) may be considered for adoption by States to improve the resources of the panchayats.

The States should avoid delays in the constitution of the SFCs, their constitution in phases, frequent reconstitution, submission of reports and tabling of the ATR in the legislature. It is desirable that SFCs are constituted at least two years before the required date of submission of their recommendations, and the deadline should be so decided as to allow the state government at least three months' time for tabling the ATR, preferably along with the budget for the ensuing financial year.

The SFC reports should be readily available to the Central Finance Commission, when the latter is constituted so that an assessment of the state's need could be made by the Central Finance Commission on the basis of uniform principles. This requires that thehse reports should not be too dated. As the periodicity of constitution of the Central Finance Commission is predictable, the States should time the constitution of their SFCs suitably.

SFCs must be constituted with people of eminence and competence with qualification and experience in the relevant fields.

The convention established at the national level of accepting the principal recommendations of the Finance Commission without modification should be followed at the State level in respect of SFC reports.

The SFCs must clearly identify the issues which require action on the part of the central government to augment the consolidated fund of the State and list them out in a separate chapter for the consideration of the Central Finance Commission.

The suggestions made by SFCs regarding raising the ceiling on professional tax is endorsed for action by Central Government.

It is desirable that the SFCs follow the procedure adopted by the Central Finance Commission for transfer of resources from the Centre to the States in respect of resources transfers from State Governments to local bodies. The SFC reports should contain an estimation and analysis of the finances of the State government as well as the local bodies at the pre and post transfer stages along with a qualification of the revenues that could be generated additionally by the local bodies by adopting the measures recommended therein.

The gaps that may still remain would then constitute the basis for the measures to be recommended by the Central Finance Commission. While estimating the resources of the local bodies, the SFCs should follow a normative approach in the assessment of revenues and expenditure rather than made forecasts based on historical trends.

A permanent SFC cell may be created in the finance department of State governments as the collection and collation of data would need to be done constantly and data would need to be made available to the SFC as and when it is constituted.

A sum of Rs.20,000 crore for the Pnachayats and Rs.5000 crore for the Municipalities may be provided as grants-in-aid to augment the consolidated fund of the States for the period 2005-10 to be distributed with inter-se shares as indicated in table 8.1 of the report. (Annex-I).

The PRIs should be encouraged to take over the assets relating to water supply and sanitation and utilize the grants for repairs/rejuvenation as also the O&M costs. The PRIs should, however, recover at least 50 per cent of the recurring costs in the form of user charges.

Of the grants allocated for Panchayats, priority should be given to expenditure on the O&M costs of water supply and sanitation. This will facilitate Panchayats to take over the schemes and operate them.

At least 50 per cent of the grants-in-aid provided to each State for the urban local bodies should be earmarked for the scheme of solid waste management through public-private partnership. The Municipalities should concentrate on collection, segregation and transportation of solid waste. The cost of these activities whether carried out in house or out sourced could be met from the grants.

Most States do not have credible information on the finances of their local bodies. Local bodies would continue to need funding support for building data base and maintenance of accounts. States may assess the requirement of each local body in this regard and earmark funds accordingly out of the total allocation recommended by us.

Separate grants-in-aid for the normal and the excluded areas are not proposed. It is for the State concerned to distribute the grants recommended for the State among the local bodies including those in the excluded areas in a fair and just manner.

No conditionality over and above these recommended by us need be imposed by the Central Government for releasing the grants-in-aid.

RECOMMENDATIONS OF THE TFC

The summary of the recommendations of the TFC is reproduced below:

The SFCs must clearly identify the issues which require action on the part of the central government to augment the consolidated fund of the State and list them out in a separate chapter for the consideration of the Central Finance Commission.

The suggestions made by SFCs regarding raising the ceiling on professional tax is endorsed for action by Central Government.

It is desirable that the SFCs follow the procedure adopted by the Central Finance Commission for transfer of resources from the Centre to the States in respect of resources transfers from State Governments to local bodies. The SFC reports should contain an estimation and analysis of the finances of the State government as well as the local bodies at the pre and post transfer stages along with a qualification of the revenues that could be generated additionally by the local bodies by adopting the measures recommended therein. The gaps that may still remain would then constitute the basis for the measures to be recommended by the Central Finance Commission.

While estimating the resources of the local bodies, the SFCs should follow a normative approach in the assessment of revenues and expenditure rather than made forecasts based on historical trends.

A permanent SFC cell may be created in the finance department of State governments as the collection and collation of data would need to be done constantly and data would need to be made available to the SFC as and when it is constituted.

A sum of Rs.20,000 crore for the Panachayats and Rs.5000 crore for the Municipalities may be provided as grants-in-aid to augment the consolidated fund of the States for the period 2005-10 to be distributed with inter-se shares as indicated in table 8.1 of the report. (Annex-I).

The PRIs should be encouraged to take over the assets relating to water supply and sanitation and utilize the grants for repairs/rejuvenation as also the O&M costs. The PRIs should, however, recover at least 50 per cent of the recurring costs in the form of user charges.

Of the grants allocated for Panchayats, priority should be given to expenditure on the O&M costs of water supply and sanitation. This will facilitate Panchayats to take over the schemes and operate them. At least 50 per cent of the grants-in-aid provided to each State for the urban local bodies should be earmarked for the scheme of solid waste management through public-private partnership. The Municipalities should concentrate on collection, segregation and transportation of solid waste. The cost of these activities whether carried out in house or out sourced could be met from the grants.

Most States do not have credible information on the finances of their local bodies. Local bodies would continue to need funding support for building data base and maintenance of accounts. States may assess the requirement of each local body in this regard and earmark funds accordingly out of the total allocation recommended by us.

Separate grants-in-aid for the normal and the excluded areas are not proposed. It is for the State concerned to distribute the grants recommended for the State among the local bodies including those in the excluded areas in a fair and just manner. No conditionality over and above these recommended by us need be imposed by the Central Government for releasing the grants-in-aid.

CONCLUSION

The best practices listed in the report may be considered for adoption by States to improve the resources of the panchayats. The States should avoid delays in the constitution of the SFCs, their constitution in phases, frequent reconstitution, submission of reports and tabling of the ATR in the legislature. It is desirable that SFCs are constituted at least two years before the required date of submission of their recommendations, and the deadline should be so decided as to allow the state government at least three months' time for tabling the ATR, preferably along with the budget for the ensuing financial year. The SFC reports should be readily available to the Central Finance Commission, when the latter is constituted so that an assessment of the state's need could be made by the Central Finance Commission on the basis of uniform principles. This requires that these reports should not be out dated. As the periodicity of constitution of the Central Finance Commission is predictable, the States should time the constitution of their SFCs suitably. SFCs must be constituted with people of eminence and competence with qualification and experience in the relevant fields. The convention established at the national level of accepting the principal recommendations of the Finance Commission without modification should be followed at the State level in respect of SFC reports.

REFERENCES

The Hindu; Times of India; The New Indian Express, Deccan Chronicle News Paper; India Today; Business Line.

19

TWELFTH FINANCE COMMISSION FOR FISCAL DEMOCRACY

A. Ranga Reddy

The Paper highlights the pertinent issues of Twelfth Finance Commission for bringing fiscal Democracy.

The Finance Commission (FC) mandated by the Constitution to be appointed by the President periodically to mediate revenue sharing between Centre and States is a key pillar of India's federal structure. Transfers mediated by the FC, and its recommendations in responses to matters additionally referred to it have a profound impact on the budget, of all States and Union. Article 280 of the Constitution, which specifies the functions of the Finance Commission, stipulates that the Commission should make recommendations to the president on: (a) the shares of the Centre and the States of the taxes that are to (b) Principle which should governs the grants-in-aid to be given to the States in need of assistance. Late Guhan felt that Finance Commission can only bark at the Centre but bite the States.[1]

The Eleventh Finance Commission (FFC) has recommended an overall share of 37.5 per cent of the Centres gross revenue receipts as transfers to States, fiscal transfers to the States, through all channels. As percentage of the gross revenue receipts of the Centre increased from an average of 31.4 per cent in the period of the Sixth Finance Commission to 38.1 per cent for the Seventh Finance commission. It further increased further to 40.3 per cent for the period covered by the Ninth commission.

The two principal modes of fiscal transfers viz., tax devolution and grants have certain distinguishing features. Tax devolution has a built-in-flexibility as it can increase automatically if the Central taxes are more buoyant. Grants-in-aid are mainly targeted towards achieving a degree of equalization. That is why many of the better- off states assessed to be in revenue surplus do not get article 275 grants[2]. Prior to the 80th Constitutional amendment, two main central taxes are found other than corporation tax and the union excise duties. With the 88th amendment of constitution, article 268A, provides that "Taxes of services shall be levied by the Govt. of India and the States......" It also further specifics that the principles of collection and appropriation will be determined by parliament.

GOOD GOVERNANCE AND STATES

The better-off states have represented that their share has steadily fallen in the overall concern.

The plan assistance is given to the States as consisting of grants and loans. The grants-loan ratio for the States in general is 30:70 whereas for the special category States, this ratio is 90:10. In normal Central assistance, 30 per cent is earmarked for the special category states.

The Mastricht Treaty role of 3% of GDP as the fiscal deficit target and 60 per cent as the desired debt-GDP ratio are well known. In U.K. a 'golden rule' of limiting borrowing only to finance capital expenditure has been followed since 1997 as a sustainable investment rule.

To strengthen the basic idea of promoting a fiscal domain for the local bodies as being the key to effective local self-governance. The provision of local goods requires that the link between local service and the responsibility of financing it by the potential beneficiaries is appreciated.

GADGIL-MUKERJEE FORMULA

Distribution of plan assistance to States is governed by the Gadgil Mukerjee formula. According to the formula, 60% weightage is given to population of a state-the state with large share. States which have been successful in birth control have been complaining that they are being penalised for better performance. Under the Gadgil-Mukerjee formula, performance criteria, such as per capita income of a State get (25%) weightage. Other criteria are tax efforts (2.5%), fiscal management (2%), population control (1%), female literacy (1%) completion of on going externally aided projects (0.5%) and land reforms (0.5%). Quantum of assistance also depends on special performance of a particular state (7.5%) experts opine that there is an urgent need to change this formula.

Very recently, National Advisory Council (NAC) chairperson Sonia Gandhi has called a meeting of experts to redefine Central fund allocations to states by reducing population weightage from 60% to 25%. States under attack are U.P. Bihar and Madhya Pradesh.[3]

FISCAL RESPONSIBILITY AND BUDGET MANAGEMENT ACT, (FRBM) 2003

The FRBM Act marks a watershed in fiscal reforms. The Act provides an institutional framework binding the government to purpose a prudent fiscal policy. The Act casts responsibility on the Central government to ensure inter-generation equality in fiscal management and long term macro-economic stability by achieving sufficient revenue surplus, removal of fiscal impediments in the effective conduct of monetary policy and prudential debt management through limits on borrowings and deficits. (a) The main features are to take appropriate measures to reduce fiscal deficit and revenue deficit so as to eliminate revenue deficit by March 31, 2008, and there after build up adequate revenue surplus. (b) Rules are to be made to specify the annual targets for reduction of fiscal deficit and revenue deficit. (c) The revenue deficit and fiscal deficit may exceed the targets specified in the rules only on grounds of national security or national calamity or such other exceptional grounds. (d) The Central government shall not borrow from the Reserve Bank of India except by way of advances to meet temporary excess of cash disbursements over cash receipts. (e) Reserve Bank of India not to be subscribed to the primary issues of the Central government securities from the year 2006-07. (f) Central government to take suitable measures to ensure greater transparency in its fiscal operations. (g) Central government to lay in each financial year before both houses of parliament three statements Viz., medium term fiscal policy statement, fiscal policy strategy statement and macroeconomic framework statement along with the Annual financial statement and Demands for grants. (h) Finance Minster to make a quarterly review of trends in receipts and expenditure in relation to the Budget and place the review before both houses of parliament[4] The award of 11th and 12th Finance commissions have shown relative differences in the values of variables over time. The States are classified into three groups-gainers, losers and no change. Debt written of scheme has the right set of incentives in some ways it is more stringent.

FINANCE OF STATE GOVERNMENTS

The deterioration in the finances of State governments has been sharper than that of the Central government. All the major fiscal indicators reveal a worsening of the fiscal situation as compared with the position obtaining in 1990-91. Fiscal deficit of states as a proposition of GDP increased from 3.3 per cent in 1990-91 to 4.7 per cent in the revised estimates for 2002-03. Revenue deficit witnessed a sharper deterioration from 0.9 per cent of GDP to 2.5 per cent of GDP in the same period. The factors responsible for such a deterioration include growing burden of interest payments, pension liabilities and administrative expenditure. Losses of State owned public enterprises, in appropriate user charges and deceleration in central transfers compounded the problem. In recent years, the need for state level fiscal reforms has been well recognized. The problem of fiscal consolidation cannot be addressed unless reforms encompass both the Centre and States. With the worsening of the fiscal situation, particularly since 1998-99, a number of states have taken up fiscal reforms in right earnest.

Finance commission transfers have in recent years accounted for between and 60 per cent of total transfer to states from the Centre. The remainder was transferred through the Planning Commission through assistance for state plans[5].

TAX DEVOLUTION AND GRANTS UNDER TWELFTH FINANCE COMMISSION

The notable departures made by the Twelfth Finance Commission (TFC) in the scheme of Tax devolution and grants from that of its predecessor, the eleventh finance Commission (FFC) are:

- Enhancing the share of the States in the net proceeds of the shareable Central taxes of 30.5 per cent from 29.5 per cent.
- Raising the limit of the revenue transfers to the States to 38 per cent of the Centre's gross revenue receipts from 37.5 per cent.
- Changing the formula for tax devolution in the re-allocation weights in favour of population and efficiency factors.
- Application of norms in the assessment of non- plan revenue gap for determining the amount of grants – in – aid to States.
- Applying the equalization principle to provide grants for education and health to States which are relatively deficient in their revenue capacity, provided they maintain their normal expenditure on these heads at the current level.
- Providing grants for maintenance of roads and bridges, heritage conservation, state specific needs local bodies an calamity relief on a larger scale.
- Enlarging the grants to local bodies substantially and modifying the, formula for their allocation among States, to take account of deprivation in the provision of drinking water and sanitation, the index of decentralization which was used by EFC as one of the criteria has been dropped[6].

Chelliah argues for a new an scientific approach to federal financial relations in which the States should be treated as autonomous units and should be asked to determine for themselves the levels of revenue and expenditures. A key point is to keep the States' share in Union taxes, once fixed, unchanged for a larger period at least 15 years, unless there is a clear shift in their responsibilities.

To cure these deficiencies, a composite Index of fiscal performance (FPI) made up of three major components,. Viz., deficit index own revenue effort index and expenditure and debt repayment index. These are derived by combining eight indicators reflecting various aspects of fiscal performance. By using the data of 1990-99 years, Gujarat and Maharastra improve dramatically and those of Bihar, Madhya Pradesh and Uttar Pradesh worsen if the proposed indices are used instead of the TFCs.

Finances of even some of the better-of states turned alarming, with payments on salary, pension and interest accounting for 75 per cent of their revenue receipts, crossing 100 percent in some states and the outstanding debt doubling, every five years beginning 1995 reaching nearly Rs. 9,00,000 crores in 2005 (Contingent liabilities accounting for another Rs. 2,00,000 Crore) clearly the debt situation of the states cried out for relief.

The urge to control fiscal policies in order to please international capital markets must not lead to strategies that undermine economic democracy and social cohesion, especially in counties that are as heterogeneous and federal as India.

Rakshit questions the TFC focus on saving as the engine of growth. In a demand deficient economy, he argues, it is investment which drives sowing and not the other way round. Even in a full employment economy, creation of investment opportunities through fiscal policy, such as investment infrastructure helps to raise savings by inducing investors to plough back a large share of their income/profits.

Investment in human development and environmental improvement considered as composition of government expenditure, which certainly changes shape of economy positively.

LOAN COUNCIL

TFC also stresses the need to have an independent body like loan council to decide the borrowing limits to the states and oversee their implementation. Union government is not much concern over it. However, Finance Ministry has constituted a

"Central Monitoring Committee" consisting of officials to consider the details of the States' fiscal correction paths, examine their waiver. Claims from the States and recommend the quantum of the waiver. The task of fixing caps on the States' borrowing also rests with the Ministry of Finance. Clearly these go against the spirit of the TFC's recommendations. In the interest of federalism, sooner the transition is made to market based discipline the better. The Centre should help the disadvantaged State's if they find it difficult to access the market, as the TFC has suggested.

Chelliah was cautious that fiscal consolidation cannot be sustained unless some of the root causes of the states' fiscal distress are addressed. In particular, it is necessary to review the planning process and do away with the plan/non-plan dichotomy as the TFC has urged.

The future of federalism in India will depend very much on how the transfer system reconciles equality with efficiently while respecting the fiscal anatomy of the State.

The virtuous cycle of reforms, robust government finances, and an equlising system of fiscal transfers, should help establish a sound federal fiscal system in India[7].

GOVERNMENT. EMPLOYMENT POLICY AND PAY COMMISSIONS

In federal structure, a state government has to formulate its policies on government employment, levels of employee's remuneration, the relative size of the government sector. Keeping its own economic conditions in view, State had to decide the numbers to be employed. The federal government cannot underwrite equal salary levels in the government sector across the country. Equalization grant given to a State would strengthen its capacity to pay wages. The Central government in India has no systematic policy of controlling or regulating the size of its work force. But it follows the policy to rising upward, periodically, the real wages and pensions of its employees. This is done on the basis of the recommendations of a pay commission appointed at intervals of 10 to 15 years. By all means, the real wages of government employees have to be increased with the growth of the economy and the rise in per capital income. Generally, senior civil servants in *"ad hoc"* way increase the salaries in *lump sum*. Substantially, Central government raises the salary bill by Trade unions pressure and its impact fall on State governments, which approaches Finance Commission to support the gap by grant. The revision of salaries of employees could be linked to the rise in real per capital income of the Centre and also individual States. This can be done within three or four years.

The states should be treated as autonomous units and be asked to determine for themselves the levels of revenues and expenditure[8]. The Twelfth Commission recommended performance budgeting, doing away with the distinction between plan and non-plan expenditure, and transparency including elimination of hidden subsidies[9].

CONCLUSION

Finance Commission (FC) mandated by the Constitution to be appointed by the President of India periodically to mediate revenue sharing between Centre and States is a key pillar of India's federal democracy.

In course of time, good governance States' lost their share from Finance Commission devolution of resources. The grants-loan ratio for the states, in general is 30:70, Currently, National Advisory Council's Chairman has interested to reduce the population weightage from 60% to 25%. The FRBM Act 2003 has made the States have made the States to eliminate fiscal deficit as on March 31, 2008. State level fiscal reforms are highly needed. Enlargement of grants to local bodies for drinkable water, sanitation etc was considered as top priority. States should not mould the fiscal policies to please international capita and undermine economic democracy.

Sooner or later, the federal structure is to be made to market based discipline. The Centre should help the disadvantaged States, if they find it difficult to access the market. Chelliah suggested that the revision of salaries and pensions of employees could be linked to the rise in real per capital income of Centre and individual States.

NOTES AND REFERENCES

1 M. Govinda Rao, Pratap R. Jena (2005), Balancing Stability Equality & Efficiency Economic & Political Weekly, July 30, p. 3405.

2. Govt. of India (2005), Reports of the Finance Commission of India Academic foundation, New Delhi, p. 13.

3. Rajeev Jayaswal (2006), For Sonia, Big Aim't Beautiful: calling for slashing population weight in central fund allocation, The Economic Times Feb. 17, 2006, p. 1.

4. Govt. of India (2004), Economic survey 2003-04, p. 36.

5. Indira Rajaraman, D. Majundar (2005), Equity and Consistency Properties of TFC Recommendations EPW, July, 30, p. 3419.

6. (Amaresh Begchi (2005), for Sonia Big Aint' Beautiful: calling for slashing population weight in central fund allocation, The Economic Times Feb. 17, 2006, p. 1).

7. C. Rangarajan (2005), Approach and Recommendations, *Economic and Poli weekly*, July 30, p. 3398.

8. Raja J. Chellaiah (2005), Malady of continuing fiscal Imbalance, Economic and Political Weekely, July 30, 3403.

9. Mihir Rakshit (2005), Some Analystics and Empirics of fiscal Restructuring in India, *Economic and Political weekly*, July 30, p. 3448.

20

CENTRE-STATE FINANCIAL RELATIONS IN INDIA- A COMMENT

M. Prasada Rao & T. Koteswara Rao

The issue of Centre-state financial relations has assumed much significance since long back. The problem came to more focus only after 1967 with the formation of non-Congress Governments in nine states. This is a multi-dimensional subject, of which the financial aspect is the key element and consequently it became the burning issue of the day.

Before discussing the issue in detail, one should think over the rationality behind the argument of some of the non-Congress State Governments. Their argument is as follows:

The States need more funds to fulfill their expenditure commitments in respect of such vital sectors as health, education, agriculture and rural development. But the present system of resource allocation to the states is not adequately catering to their requirements. People seek more help from the state government. rather than the centre because the governments in states are within their reach.

Hence there is a need to reform the present arrangements in this regard. In formulating the new guidelines, our aim is to create strong states as well as a strong Centre. It is a well known fact that the healthy and strong states can alone ensure a strong centre, which can meet the external and internal contingencies effectively, and at the same time the unity and integrity of our Nation need to be kept in mind.

The main thrust of this paper is to identify the areas which need thorough revision and reformation according to our present requirements.

The Central Government determines the volume of State Plans through the Planning Commission which is not a Constitutional Body and which is completely under the control of the centre. Around 60 per cent of the funds allotted to the states are in accordance with the recommendations of the Planning Commission and Central Government Departments. The remaining 40 percent is left to the recommendations of the Finance Commission.

This simple fact itself proves the deprivation of the states from their legitimate rights. Moreover, the National Development Council, which is also not a constitutional body finally approves the plan document without any serious discussion and involvement of the states. Therefore, it is necessary to provide constitutional status to both the Planning Commission and the NDC. The states should be given due representation and active involvement in the Planning Commission. Decentralization of our Planning process is also needed in view of the regional economic variations. The state planning boards should be strengthened. There should be proper coordination between Planning Commission and State Planning Boards. The NDC should have the opportunity of expressing its opinion on the matters of national importance. The NDC should also act as a coordinating body between Centre and States on planned development activities. But it needs to be more effective.

It may be seen in Table 1 that the total receipts of the Central Govt. increased from Rs5506 corers in 1970-71 to Rs.526529 corers in 2004-2005.Of the total receipts an amount of Rs. 2395 corers was transferred to the states and UTS in 1970-71 which increased to about Rs.128239 corers in 2002-03. Though there is a phenomenal increase in absolute gross transfers the percentage of net transfers from Center to States has been showing a declining trend. For instance, it may be seen in Table-1 that the Net Transfers in absolute terms to states increased from Rs1737 crores in 1970-71 to 144853 crores in 2004-05.However, Net transfers to states as a percent to total receipts of central Govt. have declined gradually from 31.5percent in 1970-71 to 27. 5 percent in 2004-05. This is mainly due to the

Table 1

Fiscal Transfers from Centre tothe States (1970-71 to 2004-05)

Year	*Receipts of the Central Government*				*Resources transferred to the States*						
	Revenue receipts Including States share in taexs	*Capital receipts (exclude) repayment of loans*	*Budgetary deficit/ draw down of cash balance of Central Govt.*	*Total receipts Central Govt.*	*Share of states in Central taxes*	*Grants from the Centre to States & UTs*	*Loans (gross) from the Centre to States & UTs*	*Repay-ment of loans by States & UTs*	*Gross transfers to States (2+3+4)*	*Net Transfers to States (2+3+4+5)*	*Col. 7 as % of 1*
				1	2	3	4	5	6	7	8
1970-71	4097	1124	285	5506	755	612	1028	658	2395	1737	31.5
1980-81	16621	6309	2577	25507	3792	2796	3146	917	9734	8817	34.6
1990-91	71408	34542	11347	117297	14535	13293	14522	4653	42350	37697	32.1
1995-96	143062	54428	9807	207297	29285	21577	19627	4790	70489	65699	31.7
1996-97	165532	54004	13154	232690	35061	23545	24031	6459	82637	76178	32.7
1997-98	190223	7828	66288	264339	43548	30452	14729	7125	88729	81604	30.9
1998-99	201503	101536	-144	302895	39145	25844	15935	9475	80924	71449	23.6
1999-2000	242527	121944	-13817	350654	43481	29837	21462	9791	94780	84989	24.2
2000-01	256859	113359	6911	377129	51945	37684	20490	11691	110119	98428	26.1
2001-02	274018	82078	62923	419019	53528	42489	24528	14002	120545	106543	25.4
2002-03	307940	124918	10095	442953	56841	43167	28231	30303	128239	97936	22.1
2003-04 (R.E.)	355033	114814	-14147	455700	67384	47871	25672	59789	140927	81138	17.8
2004-05 (R.E.)	410469	128471	-12411	526529	83827	57518	29356	25848	170701	144853	27.5

Sources: RBI Bulletins, Various Issues

Note:
1. Figures in brackets represent the ratios after adding the loans given to the States for cleaning their overdrafts/deficits with the R.B.I. to the total receipts of the Central Government as well as to the gross transfer to the states.
2. Article 270 of the constitution was retrospectively amended with effect from 1st April, 1996. Under the provision of the Constitution (80th Amendment) Act, 2000, prescribed share of States in the net proceeds of Central taxes and duties does not form part of the Consolidated Fund of India.

huge amount of repayments of loans by the States, and UTs to the central Govt. Unless the states' indebtedness is reduced by a kind of debt relief measures, the advantage of increased fiscal transference cannot be enjoyed by the states. So what is needed is a systematic approach to reduce the ever growing borrowing and the huge amount of outstanding public debt of the states. The debt swap scheme introduced by the center in recent years is appreciable as the states would be benefited by reducing their cost of borrowing. More over, several states have been benefited under the Fiscal Reform Facility as recommended by the eleventh Finance commission. The grants-in-aid sanctioned by the Centre to the states are of temporary nature and they made the states depend on the centre for financial resources. Article 275 and 282 of the Constitution provide the sanction of grants to the states. The grants sanctioned under article 275 are compulsory and the centre has no option in this regard. But the grants sanctioned under article 282 are conditional grants and the willingness of the centre determines these grants. Hence it is argued that the conditional grants are harmful to the freedom of the states. All plan grants are conditional grants and the Finance Commission recommends only on non-plan grants. Hence, this dichotomy awarding grants should be rectified. All grants-in-Aid from center to state should be given on the recommendation by the Finance Commission.

Table 2
Revenue Centralisation in the Indian Federations 1984-2004

Year	*States own Revenue*	*States Total Revenue*	*Combined Revenevues of the Center & States*	*Col.(2) as % age of Col. (4)*	*Col.(3) as% age of Col.(4)*
(1)	(2)	(3)	(4)	(5)	(6)
1984-85	16810	27425	45296	37.11	37.11
1994-95	73020	118174	178012	41.02	66.39
2000-01	148336	221791	349979	42.38	63.37
2001-02	176025	248501	379371	46.40	65.50
2002-03	193446	263561	423008	45.73	62.31
2003-04	230977	325453	512833	45.04	63.46
2004-05	269142	368168	590533	45.58	62.35

Source: Indiàn Public Finance Statistics, Ministry of Finance, Govt. of India, 2001-02, 2004-05

Another important issue is the sharing process of the tax revenue between the centre and the states. The Administrative Reforms Committee (ARC) Study Team on Centre-State Relations has observed that the outstanding feature of the financial relationship between the Centre and the States is that the former is the given and the receiver. The State resources on their own have not been enough to meet all non-plan expenditure and there is thus a heavy financial dependence on the centre. At this juncture, we should consider the transfer of more elastic taxes to the states list.

This shows a decline in the revenue centralization But it may be observed that the proportion of states' Own revenue in all the years was less than 46 per cent, which suggests fiscal dominance of the Center over the states.

In this context, mention may be made of the recommendations of the Sarkaria Commission. This reviewed various aspects of the Centre-State relations within the frame-work of the Constitution, and recommended that a fresh look is needed with reference to the sharing of both tax power as well as tax revenue between the Center and State.

Fallowing are important suggestions which may help in strengthening the Center State fiscal relations in India.

(1) The tax share from the central divisible pool as recommended by the successive Finance Commitions is quite inadequate. Hence, there is a need to increase the states' Share.

(2) The Center may consider of giving a share from its non-tax revenues like profits from public Sector undertaking dividends, interest receipts and other receipts, at least to the backward States.

(3) All key industries, major Irrigation and Power projects involving two or more states Should be declared as national projects like Bhakra-Nangal.The cost-of construction of these projects needs to be borne by the Centre

(4) An Inter-state Council was to be set up to co-ordinate the relation between the Centre and States as per our Constitution. This needs to be activised.

(5) The Inter-state Council is required to formulate appropriate guidelines with regard to Several important aspects of economic development including planning and execution.

(6) A National Expenditure Council should be set up to regulate the ever increasing non- development revenue expenditure of the Centre and the States.

(7) A comprehensive and coordinated national policy is required to determine the size and nature of borrowings that the Centre and States have to raise.

(8) Above all, the tax collection system needs to be further rationalized to mobilize more resources.

In order to mobilize more financial resources, it is necessary that both the Centre and the States should adopt stringent measures to avoid tax evasion, smuggling, black money, hoarding etc.

In view of the above observations and suggestions, if necessary, relevant Articles in the Constitution should be amended so as to provide a stable and rational financial relations between the States and the Centre in India.

21

ANDHRA PRADESH AND TWELFTH FINANCE COMMISSION

M.L. Kantha Rao

Twelfth Finance Commission (TFC) had recommended total transfers amounting to Rs. 50,353.26 crores to A.P. for the award period 2005-06 to 2009-10. Out of this amount, Rs. 5214.58 crores pertain to Grants-in-Aid for maintenance of Roads & Bridges, maintenance of Public Buildings, Heritage conservation, maintenance of Forests, state specific needs, local bodies and calamity relief and the residual amount pertains to state's share in central taxes and duties.

Apart from the above, the state stands to benefit to an extent of Rs. 2683.74 crores as interest relief on account of consolidation of central loans and reduction in the rate of interest to 7.5%, consequent to the recommendations of TFC. Further, based on the fiscal performance of the Government in terms of reduction of revenue deficit, incentive for total debt relief amounting to Rs. 3834.29 crores during the TFC award period of 2005-10 is also available and this incentive can be availed at the rate of Rs. 766.86 crores per year, if we reduce our revenue deficit in each successive year and reach revenue surplus by 2008-09.

The following table shows the quantum of AP's share in the divisible pool of Taxes and Duties levied by the Union Government both before and after the implementation of the Recommendations of the TFC.

From the fore going table it is clear that the share of Central taxes in the Revenue Receipts of AP was 21.07% in 2004-05.

Andhra Pradesh Budget-2006-07 -rs In Lakhs

		2004-05- ACCTS	2005-06 BE	2005-06 RE	2006-07 BE
II	Revenue Receipts	28749,50. (100)	35976,52 (100)	36270,72.34 (100)	44331,16 (100)
1.	Share of Central Taxes	6058,51 (21.07)	6688,15 (18.50)	6990,29 (19.30)	8038,83 (18.13)
2.	Tax Revenue	16254,49 (56.54)	19980,79 (55.53)	20233,35 (55.88)	23867,92 (53.84)
3.	Non Tax Revenue	3755,56 (13.06)	4403,47 (12.23)	4570,72 (12.62)	5240,05 (11.82)
4.	Grants-in-aid	2680,92 (9.32)	4904,10 (13.63)	4476,36 (13.16)	7184,35 (16.21)

Source: AP Budget 2006-07-presented on 20-02-2006.

However the RE of the same for 2005-06 is19.3% and the BE for 2006-07 is at18.13%.

LET US NOTE A FEW OTHER TRENDS

1. Share of AP in the total devolution has been coming down. Decline between 10th and 12th Finance Commission reports is by 17 per cent. The following table vividly shows the same.

Rs. in crores

	Item 10th FC	*11th FC*	*12th FC*	
1.	Share of AP in total Taxes And duties	16,326	28,980	45,139
2.	Total for all states under Taxes & Duties	2,06,343	3, 76,318	6,13,112
3.	Percentage of AP's share that is (%) row 1 to row 2	7.91	7.70	7.36
4.	Share of AP in Grants in Aid	1,756	2,031	5,215
5.	Total of Grants in Aid for All States	20,300	58,587	1,42,640
6.	Percentage of AP's share i.e. row 4 to row 5	8.65	3.47	3.66
7.	Share of AP in total Transfers	18,082	31,011	50,353
8.	Total Transfers–Taxes & Duties +Grants to all States	2,26,643	4,34,905	7,55,752
9.	AP's share in the aggregate transfers Index Number	7.98(100)	7.13(89)	6.66(83)

10th FC Report — Page-53
11th FC Report — Pages-98-99
12th FC Report — Page-197

The annual average Tax -GSDP ratio of AP for the period 1999-2002 was7.27, as against the all states average of 6.54%

Mahesh Purohit in his study compares relative tax effort and taxable capacity of the central government in India with the average tax effort of other similar countries. The study also compares the tax effort and taxable capacity of the state governments with the average tax effort of all the states in India. Various determinants of tax bases have been selected to estimate the average rate and taxable effort as well as the taxable capacity of the states. The results indicate that during the period 2000 to 2003 Gujarat ranked first in this regard, with West Bengal and Andhra Pradesh in the second and third places respectively. EPW 25-02-06.(Mahesh C. Purohit)

But the aggregate share of AP in total devolution has come down to 6.66%- From 7.98 in the tenth FC report

2. Frequent changes in the Weight ages assigned to different indictors by successive Finance commissions-particularly decline in the relative importance of factors favorable to AP- adversely affected the relative share of AP.

Indicator	*Weight given by the Tenth FC*	*Weight given by the Eleventh FC*	*Weight given by the Twelfth FC*
Area	05	7.5	10
Population	20	10	25
Distance with reference to Per capita income	60	62.5	50
Tax effort	10	05	07.5
Fiscal Discipline		07.5	07.5
Infrastructure	05	07.5	-
Total	100	100	100

3. The deceleration in the growth of central revenues and the decline in the TAX -GDP ratio also affected the quantum of AP's share.

The tax-GDP ratio of the Centre has suffered steady deterioration from more than 10 per cent in the late 1980s to just about 9 per cent by the end of the 1990s. The drag on revenue collection was also reflected in the deceleıation in tax buoyancy. Between the Eighth and Ninth Plan periods, the buoyancy of Central taxes decreased from 0.9 to 0.8; while the buoyancy in direct tax collection was maintained at 1.3 between these periods, the buoyancy in indirect taxes declined from 0.7 to 0.6. This is reflective of the steady deterioration in revenue collections from the major indirect taxes, such as excise duties and customs duties during the 1990s. The buoyancy observed earlier in direct taxes had stagnated in subsequent years and had not been compensated adequately for the proportionate fall in indirect taxes.

4. The one factor that adversely affected the share of AP in the Taxes and Duties component is the level of per capita income attributed to AP.

Comparable Estimates of Per capita SDP as furnished by the 12th Finance Commissions indicate that the per capita income of AP was higher than the national average by 11%.

Finance Commission	*Per capita Income of AP Annual average*	*Per capita Income of All States' Average*	*Index Number of col. 2 to 3*
Tenth FC	1987-1990 Rs. 3455 (95.4)	1987-1990 Rs. 3621 (100)	95.4
Eleventh FC	1994-97 Rs.11366	Not Furnished by EFC	–
Twelfth FC	1999-2002 Rs. 18869 (111)	1999-2002 Rs. 16978 (100)	111

Tenth FC - Page - 131
Eleventh FC - Page - 218
Twelfth FC - Page - 41

The Real Per capita income of AP in 1990 rupees was Rs. 2567 in1961 as against Rs. 2857 for All India that is-90% of the Nation's average.

The corresponding figures for 1991 were Rs. 4728 and 4934 respectively that is 96% of the Nation's average.

PER CAPITA INCOME OF AP & INDIA

(Position as on 23-02-2006)

Per capita NSDP, by States at current prices (1993-94 base year series), 1993-94 onwards

Per capita NSDP, by States at constant (1993-94) prices, 1993-94 onwards

	Year	*CONSPRI*	*TANTCES*	*Index of Col4 to 5*	*CURPRI*	*RENTCES*	*Index of Col.7. to 8*	
		AP	*India*		*AP*	*India*		
1	2	3	4	5	6	7	8	9
1.	1993-94	7416	7690	96	7416	7690	96.4	1
2.	1994-95	7711	8070	96	8732	8857	98.6	2
3.	1995-96	8071	8489	95	9999	10149	98.5	3
4.	1996-97	8514	9007	95	11202	11564	96.9	4
5.	1997-98	8191	9244	89	11650	12707	91.7	5
6.	1998-1999	9144	9650	95	13965	14396	97.0	6
7.	1999-2000	9445	10071	94	15049	15625	96.3	7
8.	2000-2001	10195	10308	99	16708	16555	100.9	8
9.	2001-2002	10609	10754	99	17932	17823	100.6	9
10.	2002-2003	10875	11013	99	19087	19040	100.2	10
11.	2003-2004	11756	11799	99.6	21372	20989	101.8	11
12.	2004-2005	12352	12416	99.2	23153	23241	99.6	12
13.	2005-06	13135	20813@	@25526	@25788			13
14.	ACGR-FOR 1993-2005	4.754	4.1999		10.522	10.044		

Source: Directorate of Economics & Statistics of respective State Governments, and CSO for All-India

@New Base-1999-2000.

Rs. 16563 was the average annual per capita income of A.P. for the period 1999-2002 according to Table 1.8 Per Capita Net State Domestic Product At Current Prices-Economic Survey 2005-06.

However according to the Twelfth FC Report Andhra Pradesh with Rs18, 869 of annual average per capita income for the period 1999-2002 occupied the 14th rank among the 28 States of India.

But even the publication entitled Golden Jubilee of AP-50 years-Department of Economics and Statistics of AP. 2005 stated-During the years 1960-61 to 2004-05.

The per capita income of AP was always lower than the per capita income of All India except in the year 2000-01.

At constant prices AP has been always behind the per capita income of All India-including 2000-01(p. 9).

This inflated crucial variable has naturally eliminated the economic distance of AP–a factor that adversely affected the relative share of AP in devolution.

Even the latest releases of the CSO are as follows.

AP's Average for 1999-2002 works out to Rs. 16563 only (99.4% of India) as against Rs. 16668 for All India.

Another Study of the Planning Commission also corroborates the fact that the per capita income of AP was less than that of the national average during 1997 and 2000 by about 8%.

ECONOMIC REFORMS AND REGIONAL DISPARITIES IN ECONOMIC AND SOCIAL DEVELOPMENT IN INDIA

(Report of a Research Project funded by the SER Division of the Planning Commission of the Government of India)

N.J. Kurian in his work Regional Disparities in India Stated

All States in the forward group, except Andhra Pradesh, have literacy rates above the national average. Their rates vary from 90.9 per cent in Kerala to 67.0 per cent in Karnataka. The level of literacy in Andhra Pradesh is only 61.1 -28 the rank.

Per capita gross state domestic product (GSDP) as a percentage of per capita GDP of the country at four time periods since 1980-81 for forward and backward group of States are presented in the table below:

State Relatives of Per Capita NSDP at constant (1993-94) Prices for the Post-reform period*. (Table 2)

S. No.	*State*	*State Relatives in*		*% change*
		1991-92 to 1993-94	*1997-98 to 1999-2000*	
(1)	(2)	(3)	(4)	(5)
1.	Bihar	51.20	41.93	-18.11
2.	Orissa	62.23	53.65	-13.78
3.	Uttar Pradesh	69.30	56.78	-18.07
4.	Assam	74.84	59.55	-20.42
5.	Madhya Pradesh	81.33	75.85	-6.74
6.	Rajasthan	85.01	89.03	4.73
7.	West Bengal	86.34	90.58	4.92
8.	Andhra Pradesh	94.01	91.50	-2.67
9.	Kerala	97.19	98.50	1.34
10.	Karnataka	100.14	105.88	5.73
11.	Himachal Pradesh	101.52	103.29	1.74
12.	Tamil Nadu	111.64	120.87	8.27
13.	Gujarat	123.63	134.78	9.02
14.	Haryana	146.21	133.95	-8.38
15.	Maharashtra	147.12	146.20	-0.63
16.	Punjab	164.06	146.78	-10.54

Note: *States are arranged in ascending order of the value of the state relative in the initial period, which refers to 1991-92 to 1993-94 . The terminal period refers to 1997-98 to 1999-2000.

Source: Calculated from Economic and Political Weekly Research Foundation (EPWRF) (2002): Domestic Product of States of India 1960-61 to 2000-01.

The foregoing tables indicate the relative backwardness of AP in respect of per capita income among the advanced States of India.

The table sharply focuses the differential growth in per capita incomes of the two groups of States over the last two decades, especially during the last decade. Per capita incomes of four out of eight States in the group were below the national average in the eighties. But by late nineties, all except Andhra Pradesh have gone above the national average.

Table 3
Three-year average of per capita incomes at current prices centered on the year with national average per capita as 100
(Three-year average of incomes at current prices centered on)

States	*1981-82*	*1985-86*	*1990-91*	*1997-98*
Forward group				
Andhra Pradesh	**87.4**	**82.4**	**92.5**	**92.9**
Gujarat	125.3	124.4	118.8	137.4
Haryana	146.5	139.9	146.6	139.4
Karnataka	92.8	93.7	95.4	107.2
Kerala	90.5	90.9	87.8	116.4
Maharashtra	143.0	134.7	144.7	167.5
Punjab	168.6	165.0	169.7	146.5
Tamil Nadu	92.8	97.0	100.0	119.5
Backward group				
Assam	83.6	92.1	83.1	62.2
Bihar	58.8	60.6	53.5	44.2
Madhya Pradesh	80.8	74.8	78.1	73.5
Orissa	75.0	74.7	66.9	61.8
Rajasthan	76.6	74.0	79.3	81.1
Uttar Pradesh	75.8	71.9	70.6	64.4
West Bengal	103.3	102.9	91.7	85.1
All India	100	100	100	100

Kurian-This table is based on table 2 in Saumitra Chaudhuri.

5. CSO stated—Comparable estimates of Gross and Net State Domestic Product (GSDP/NSDP) and corresponding per capita estimates by industry of use for each State were prepared after detailed discussions with the representatives of State Directorates of Economics & Statistics. These estimates were sent to Finance Commission and Planning Commission for their use.

For AP the Per Capita figures furnished to the Finance Commissions were however higher than those prepared by the AP Directorate of Economics& Statistics for the period cited. Distance with reference to Per capita income of a State was given a weight age of 62.5 % and 50% by the EFC and TFC respectively. Since the per capita figures to be considered by the Finance Commission are crucial variables, there should not be scope for ambiguity or distortion of any type. There should be redoubled effort for reconciliation of facts/estimates to infuse confidence among all those concerned with these matters. Horizontal equity is as important as vertical equity. If it can be however shown that the per capita figures adopted by the TFC are closer to reality and reflect inter state comparability beyond doubt then all other records, particularly post 2004 figures at least, that show A.P. as lagging behind should be amended to avoid confusion.

But look at the stakes involved

For 2006-07, Rs. 1,13,448 cores is the estimated States' Share in the Gross Tax Revenue of the centre. In this AP's share has been reduced from 7.70 in the EFC to 7.36 in the TFC. Even 0.5% difference in the share would work out to Rs. 567.24 crores for this year alone.

Hence this disparity in per capita income is a cause of concern. For 2006-07, Rs. 1,13,448 cores is the estimated States' Share in the Gross Tax Revenue of the centre. In this AP's share has been reduced from 7.70 in the EFC to 7.36 in the TFC. Even 0.5% difference in the share would work out to Rs. 567.24 crores for this year alone. Is it not therefore necessary to re examine whether AP's share in Taxes and Duties got reduced because of the inflated average per capita income attributed to it? GoAP should seriously consider this matter and take up the issue in an appropriate forum.

The Finance Minister of AP in his budget Speech for 2006-07 in a complacent mood however claimed

Our Government has passed the Fiscal Responsibility and Budget Management (FRBM) Act 2005, to ensure prudence in fiscal management and fiscal stability through progressive reduction in fiscal deficit and elimination of revenue deficit as well as the conduct of fiscal policy in a Medium Term Fiscal Framework (MTFF). In fact the moment we took over the governance, we have been making efforts to reduce revenue deficit. The revenue deficit of Rs. 2961.64 crores during 2003-04 has been reduced to Rs. 2557.83 crores in 2004-05. As percentage to GSDP the Revenue Deficit decreased from 1.61 % in 2003-04 to 1.26 % in 2004-05.

As part of the States' Debt Consolidation and Relief Facility (DCRF), the state Government needs to develop its own Fiscal Correction Path for the TFC period i.e., 2005-06 to 2009-10. Accordingly, we have drawn up our Fiscal Correction Path, which entails reduction of fiscal deficit from 3.6% in 2005-06 to 2.6% in 2008-09 and reaching revenue surplus by that year.

The state Government has effectively managed its cash balances, which is reflected by comfortable cash position during the year, and as evidenced by the fact that the state had not resorted to any "Ways & Means" advances during the past two years. The State Government's efficient fiscal management is recognized in the financial markets, as reflected by the successful mobilization of funds through RBI at very low rates of interest, which is a mark of strength of state Government's sound financial position.

Further, fiscal accountability has been strengthened with respect to various accountability norms and timely preparation of accounts and quick response to audit.

The final accounts of 2004-05 show a revenue deficit of Rs. 2557.83 crores. After taking into account the transactions on capital as well as public debt and public account, the year closed with a positive balance of Rs. 286.15 crores.

Revised Estimates 2005-06 102. Transactions as per the revised estimates of 2005-06 indicate a revenue deficit of Rs. 1117.95 crores against the budgeted revenue deficit of Rs. 1401.38 crores.

BUDGET ESTIMATES 2006-07

During the financial year 2006-07, an expenditure of Rs. 40,624.24 crores under non-plan and Rs. 22,903.50 crores under Plan are proposed. This will result in a revenue deficit of Rs. 995.84 crores, which would be 0.40 per cent of GSDP. The fiscal deficit is estimated to be Rs. 8147.20 crores, which would be 3.25 per cent of GSDP.

22

TWELFTH FINANCE COMMISSION –GRANTS FOR EDUCATION AND HEALTH–THE CASE OF ANDHRA PRADESH

K. Ranigopal, R. Sudarsana Rao and B. Sailaja Kumari

The constitution provides for the Division of financial powers and financial responsibilities between the centre and the state. But the revenue raising power of the states is limited comparatively. As we are all aware, with the passage of time the expenditure needs of the states increased considerably, while the income could not cope up with this trend. In this context, the role of successive finance commissions is of great importance, in the sense that not only it makes recommendations for transferring shared tax revenue and gap filling grants but also often recommends grant-in-aid for the upgradation of select essential social and administrative services.

An attempt has been made in this paper to focus on the share of Andhra Pradesh in upgradation grants during the period covered by the recommendations of the sixth Finance Commission to Twelfth Finance Commission i.e. during 1975-80 to 2005-2010 and to present a case for grants to Andhra Pradesh in view of its low human development.

The Finance Commission laid down five basic principles. In addition to the first three, relating to the examination of state budgets on a uniform basis, assessing genuine deficits of individual states, the extra vacancies in state budgets and the provision for abnormal conditions faced by a state, two more principles were added. They are "where standard of social services in any state are significantly lower than in others, it should qualify for special assistance", and "grants may be made to certain states for the furtherance of broad purposes of national importance, such as primary education, in respect of which they may be backward". Following these principles, the first Finance Commission began by formulating special assistance to states, to start with, for the expansion of primary education. But by the time the second Finance Commission was set up, the Planning commission was already established and therefore Finance Commission took the view that it is the function of the Planning Commission and the National Development Council to ensure the equalisation, of the standard of essential social services in the various states of the union as far as practicable. Unfortunately, the Planning Commission and the National Development Council have not been able to provide adequate assistance for providing the basic minimum needs of the people in such matters as primary education, primary health services, and provision of protected drinking water.[1]

Recognising the role of human capital formation and the need for social spending and the importance of growth with equity, the sixth Finance Commission made a departure by recommending provision to states which were unable to provide a national minimum of certain administrative and social services by the way of "upgradation grants". The Finance Commission identified certain administrative and social services like land revenue, general administration, administration of justice, jails, police, education, medical & public health and welfare of the SC, ST and other backward classes.[2]

The following tables (Table 1 & Table 2) reveals that Uttar Pradesh, Madhya Pradesh and West Bengal are the major states which received biggest amount of upgradation grants from the sixth Finance Commission to Twelfth Finance Commission due to their backwardness of social services. Least amounts are allotted to Kerala and Maharashtra and Himachal Pradesh because of their development in social services. Andhra's rank has varied from 5th position to 7th position during the period because of is medium level of development index.

Table 1
Grants-in-aid for Upgradation of Essential Administrative and Social Services During VI to XII Finance Commission

(Rs. in crores)

State	*Finance Commission*						
	VI	*VII*	*VIII*	*IX*	*X*	*XI*	*XII*
Andhra Pradesh	52.62 (5)	19.60 (8)	80.49 (5)	31.19 (7)	88.88 (6)	225.23 (7)	500.00
Assam	18.02	21.70	63.35	11.96	146.86 (3)	102.54	130.00
Bihar	166.79 (2)	63.02 (3)	130.27 (2)	65.08	183.13 (1)	341.60 (3)	400.00
Gujarat	9.19	-	-	-	-	184.85	200.00
Haryana	21.45	-	-	24.88	-	82.65	100.00
Himachal Pradesh	-	7.79	16.26	13.63	30.03	46.16 (least)	50.00
Karnataka	26.45	-	-	12.64	-	256.53	600.00
Kerala	6.53	4.18 (least)	16.81 (least)	2.11 (least)	29.83 (least)	79.14	500.00
Madhya Pradesh	50.34	63.58 (2)	157.69 (1)	41.78	146.37	434.52 (2)	500.00
Maharashtra	3.63 (least)	-	-	50.00	-	271.97	300.00
Orissa	57.06	32.26	74.84	28.80	86.79	155.05	170.00
Punjab	13.94	-	20.00	89.01 (2)	81.31	80.01	96.00
Rajasthan	27.43	19.29	53.48	29.43	79.87	239.85	450.00
Tamilnadu	-	27.21	-	25.00	40.85	202.86	300.00
Uttar Pradesh	290.16 (1)	112.02 (1)	108.18	88.05 (3)	167.54 (2)	609.91 (1)	800.00
West Bengal	72.23 (3)	24.51	126.37 (3)	91.47 (1)	114.17	179.45	890.00
Total	838.43	436.80	967.33	605.03	1195.63	3492.32	7100.00

Source: Reports of various Finance Commissions, Government of India.

Table 2
Proportionate share of upgradation grants of Essential Administrative and Social Services during VI to XI Finance Commissions (1975-1980 to 2000-2005)

Name of the state	*VI Finance Commission grants (Rs. in crores)*	%	*XI Finance Commission grants (Rs. in crores)*	%
Andhra Pradesh	52.62 (5)	6.3	225.23(7)	6.5
Assam	18.02	2.4	102.54	2.9
Bihar	166.79(2)	19.9	341.60(3)	9.8
Gujarat	9.19	1.1	184.85	5.3
Haryana	21.45	2.6	82.65	2.4
Himachal Pradesh	-	-	46.16 (least)	1.3
Karnataka	26.45	3.2	256.53	7.3
Kerala	6.53	0.8	79.14	2.3
Madhya Pradesh	50.34	6.0	434.52 (2)	12.4
Maharashtra	3.63 (least)	0.4	271.97	7.8
Orissa	57.06	6.8	155.05 (1)	4.4
Punjab	13.94	1.7	80.01	2.3
Rajasthan	27.4	3.3	239.85	6.9
Tamil Nadu	-	-	202.86	5.8
Uttar Pradesh	290.16	34.6	609.91 (1)	17.5
West Bengal	72.23 (3)	8.6	179.45	5.1
Total	838.43		3492.32	

Table 3
Andhra Pradesh's Share in Upgradation Grants During VI to XII Finance Commissions

Finance Commission	*Grant-in-aid (Rupees in crores)*
VI	52.62
VII	19.60
VIII	80.49
IX	31.19
X	88.88
XI	225.23
XII	500.00

Twelfth Finance Commission has recommended Rs. 10,171 crores of grant to eight states for education and Rs. 5,887 crores to seven states for health over its award period 2005-2010 because of their 'low' performance in providing education and health services.

Table 4
States received Upgradation Grants for Health & Education under Twelfth Finance Commission

(Rupees in crores)

State	*Health*	*Education*
Assam	966.02	1107.37
Bihar	1819.69	2683.76
Jharkhand	360.98	651.73
Madhya Pradesh	181.64	459.56
Orissa	196.37	323.30
Rajasthan	-	100.00
Uttar Pradesh	2312.38	4454.07
Uttaranchal	50.00	-
West Bengal	-	391.86
Total	5887.08	10171.65

Source: Twelfth Finance Commission Report (2005-2010).

According to the recommendations of Twelfth Finance Commission, Andhra Pradesh did not receive upgradation grants for social services i.e. Health and Education, although it received a specific grant of Rs. 500 crores.

Basing on the analysis by Prof. A.S. Rao, in the paper entitled "Inter-State Disparities in the Development of Tertiary Sector in India", published in the Indian Journal of Regional Science, Vol. XXXVI, No. 2, 2004, page No. 103 & 104, we can state that Andhra Pradesh has got a genuine need for grants-in-aid which is clearly indicated by the fall in the Human Development Index rank of the state (HDI value 0.377 with Rank 9th in 1991 to 0.416 with 10th Rank in 2001[3]) and also the decline in the Development Index regarding to Health Sector from (11th to 12th rank). Though there is a favourable shift in the Development Index pertaining to Education Sector, but still these are lower levels of literacy in comparison with major states. Literacy rates in half of the 8 states which received education upgradation grants as per the recommendations of Twelfth Finance Commission i.e. Assam (64.28%), Madhya Pradesh (64.11%), Orissa (63.61%), West Bengal (69.22%) are above the literacy rate of Andhra Pradesh (61.11% in 2001).

Moreover, classification of states on the basis of Development Index (tertiary sector) clearly reveals that the position of Andhra Pradesh in the category of "Developing" remained the same through out ie. 1971 to 2001.[4]

Indeed the two pillars of human development are Health and Education. The above analysis provides abundant justification for providing grant-in-aid for the upgradation of social services in Andhra Pradesh, so as to enable, particularly the lower strata of the population, to actively participate in the process of development.

NOTES

1. Nilakanta Rath (2004), "Twelfth Finance Commission and Minimum Needs", Economic and Political Weekly, Vol. XXXIX, No. 26, June, pg. 2668.
2. R. Sudarsana Rao (1996), "Federal Fiscal Transfers APH. Pub., in India", pg. 37.
3. National Human Development Report of India, 2001, Oxford.
4. Indian Journal of Regional Science, Vol. XXXVI, No. 2, 2004, p.103, 104.

ANNEXURE TABLES

Table 1
Development Index – Education Sector

State	*1971*	*Rank*	*1991*	*Rank*	*2001*	*Rank*
Andhra Pradesh	84.41	13	163.98	15	290.83	10
Assam	104.13	8	247.53	4	395.31	4
Bihar	84.92	11	170.84	14	251.21	17
Gujarat	110.25	7	210.22	10	293.12	9
Haryana	116.86	6	225.04	9	385.36	5
Himachal Pradesh	74.80	16	240.59	5	428.65	2
Jammu & Kashmir	84.82	12	235.93	7	292.15	11
Karnataka	91.69	9	179.35	12	272.89	15
Kerala	223.34	1	348.28	1	494.60	1
Madhya Pradesh	69.97	17	148.00	17	252.77	16
Orissa	79.76	14	191.76	11	284.84	12
Punjab	124.10	5	251.56	3	404.56	3
Rajasthan	75.38	15	157.45	16	278.54	14
Tamil Nadu	139.33	2	235.96	6	383.02	6
Uttar Pradesh	88.42	10	174.45	13	282.22	13
West Bengal	138.59	3	270.02	2	354.90	8
India	100.00		190.58		328.13	
C.V.	34.08		23.15		19.72	

Table 2
Development Index – Health Sector

State	*1971*	*Rank*	*1991*	*Rank*	*2001*	*Rank*
Andhra Pradesh	97.89	10	160.99	11	217.97	12
Assam	92.02	12	156.84	12	233.94	11
Bihar	59.38	16	100.72	15	180.43	16
Gujarat	97.60	11	225.12	8	381.36	6
Haryana	146.39	4	209.50	9	291.57	10
Himachal Pradesh	188.34	1	280.21	4	468.90	3
Jammu & Kashmir	117.82	8	306.71	3	396.24	4
Karnataka	110.18	9	252.99	5	363.69	8
Kerala	123.54	7	333.71	1	592.39	1
Madhya Pradesh	59.97	15	99.85	17	185.62	15
Orissa	75.30	14	136.24	14	197.65	14
Punjab	184.93	2	308.38	2	492.91	2
Rajasthan	90.25	13	137.90	13	216.70	13
Tamil Nadu	126.44	6	239.27	7	385.83	5
Uttar Pradesh	58.63	17	99.89	16	155.06	17
West Bengal	151.98	3	188.07	10	294.32	9
India	100.00		173.61		262.31	
C.V.	34.65		36.59		39.31	

Table 3
Classification of States on the basis of Development Index
(Tertiary Sector)

Year	*Relatively Developed*	*Developing*	*Relatively Backward*
1971	Gujarat	Andhra Pradesh	Assam
	Haryana	Himachal Pradesh	Bihar
	Kerala	Karnataka	Jammu & Kashmir
	Maharashtra		Madhya Pradesh
	Punjab		Orissa
	Tamil Nadu		Rajasthan
	West Bengal		Uttar Pradesh
1981	Gujarat	Andhra Pradesh	Assam
	Haryana	Jammu & Kashmir	Bihar
	Himachal Pradesh	Karnataka	Madhya Pradesh
	Kerala	Uttar Pradesh	Orissa
	Maharashtra		Rajasthan
	Punjab		
	Tamil Nadu		
	West Bengal		
1991	Gujarat	Andhra Pradesh	Assam
	Haryana	Himachal Pradesh	Bihar
	Kerala	Jammu & Kashmir	Madhya Pradesh
	Maharashtra	Karnataka	Orissa
	Punjab	West Bengal	Rajasthan
	Tamil Nadu		Uttar Pradesh
2001	Gujarat	Andhra Pradesh	Assam
	Haryana	Himachal Pradesh	Bihar
	Kerala	Karnataka	Jammu & Kashmir
	Maharashtra	West Bengal	Madhya Pradesh
	Punjab		Rajasthan
	Tamil Nadu		Uttar Pradesh

Source: A.S. Rao–"Inter-state Disparities in the Development of Tertiary Sector in India", Vol. XXXVI, No. 2, 2004, Indian Journal of Regional Science.

23

NEED FOR EDUCATION GRANT TO ANDHRA PRADESH

P. Tara Kumari

Education is widely recognized as a powerful instrument of economic development and it also brings important changes in the attitudes and institutional set up. Often education competes with other public goods such as defence, transportation etc., for its resources. But, education should be given importance in allocating resources as the expenditure on education brings social justice and removal of poverty through increasing equal opportunity, reduction of dependency and economic growth for the 21st Century, in the context of rapid globalization. Unfortunately in countries like India, illiteracy and dropout rates at the primary educational level (72.37% in 2003-04) are high and primary education has been neglected. It is evident that the total expenditure on education reveals a disturbing downward trend between 2000-01 to 2004-05 as the percentage of total expenditure is declining from 11.3% to 9.4% and formal education is becoming increasingly expensive. It is, therefore, necessary to analyze the educational system in India from three points of view.

1. Need for horizontal expansion at all levels of education by auguementing the total resources available, with special attention to primary education and post-graduate education and research as priority areas;
2. Utmost economy should be observed in the use of resources; and

3. Improvement in the quality of education at all levels by appropriate reforms and reconstruction, which again involves considerable investment of resources;

Andhra Pradesh is one of the major states of India and it has been lagging behind on educational front. The literacy levels are far less than the national average and one of the lowest among the major states in the country. The gross enrolment ratio for primary schooling is also lower and the drop-out ratio is higher than several other states including the southern states in India. The government expenditure on education was not only low but also declining with regard to the physical status of education at primary and upper primary levels in India and Andhra Pradesh.

In the light of this background the present paper addresses to the following objectives:

1. To analyze the growth of physical educational facilities in Andhra Pradesh; and
2. To examine the need for grants–in–aid to upgrade the educational standards in Andhra Pradesh.

The paper is based on the secondary data, and is taken from selected educational statistics, published by Commission and director of school education, Andhra Pradesh and Economic Survey 2004-05, Government of Andhra Pradesh.

INDICATORS OF EDUCATION IN ANDHRA PRADESH

The physical indicators of education in Andhra Pradesh from 2000 to 2001 are shown in Table 1.

The number of pre-primary schools has declined from 27 in 2000 to 25 in 2001. The number of primary schools has increased from 55,901 in 2000 to 58,249 in 2001. Similarly the number of upper-primary and high schools were also increased. The number of upper-primary schools increased from 9,804 in 2000 to 14,472 in 2001 and high schools increased from 10,277 in 2000 to 11,464 in 2001. The total number higher secondary schools and oriental education registered a decline from 82 to 73 and 175 schools to 163 schools respectively during 2000-2001. The enrolments in pre-primary, primary, higher secondary schools and oriental education have registered a decline. The number of teachers in the pre-primary, primary, higher secondary and oriental education schools in the state also declined.

Table 1
Select Indicators of Education in Andhra Pradesh 2001

Sl. No.	*Physical Indicators*	*As on 30.9.2000*	*As on 30.9.2001*
1.	Pre-Primary Schools		
	(i) Number	27	25
	(ii) Enrolment of Total	1,484	1,272
	(iii) No.of Teachers Total	30	28
2.	Primary Schools		
	(i) Number	55,901	58,249
	(ii) Enrolment of Total	60,60,394	52,30,748
	(iii) No.of Teachers Total	1,33,546	1,27,313
3.	Upper Primary Schools		
	(i) Number	9,804	14,472
	(ii) Enrolment of Total	26,28,185	33,22,826
	(iii) No.of Teachers Total	69,265	85,263
4.	High Schools		
	(i) Number	10,277	11,464
	(ii) Enrolment of Total	45,37,791	49,63,392
	(iii) No.of Teachers Total	45,37,791	1,45,246
5.	Higher secondary schools		
	(i) Number	82	73
	(ii) Enrolment of Total	84,675	74,765
	(iii) No.of Teachers total	4,018	3,498
6.	Schools for special education		
	Number	63	80
	Enrolment of Total	6,583	7,042
	No.of Teachers Total	634	650
7.	Oriental education (Hindi vidyalayas and Sanskrit pathasalas)		
	Number	175	163
	Enrolment of Total	47,768	44,304
	No.of Teachers Total	1,615	1,535

Source: 1. Economic survey 2004-2005 Government of India Ministry of Finance Economic division.

2. Directory of School Education Andhra Pradesh.

3. Economic –Survey 2004-2005 Government of Andhra Pradesh Planning Department Andhra Pradesh, Secretariat, Hyderabad.

TEACHER PUPIL RATIO IN THE SCHOOLS

Teacher is the most important human resource in the school system. Teacher acts as a facilitator for learning by the pupils. Teacher is instrumental in developing knowledge, skills, attitudes and values among children at any stage of education. Hence, it is of interest to examine the teacher pupil ratio in the school at Andhra Pradesh. The teacher pupil ratio in schools in Andhra Pradesh during 1999-2000 to 2003-2004 is presented in Table 2.

Table 2
Teracher Pupil Ratio in Schools in Andhra Pradesh-1999 to-2004

Year	*Primary*	*Upperprimary*	*Highschool*
1999-00	47	38	34
2000-01	45	38	34
2001-2002	41	39	34
2002-2003	37	33	29
2003-2004	35	31	31

Source: 1. Economic survey 2004-2005 Government of India Ministry of Finance Economic division.
2. Directory of School Education Andhra Pradesh.
3. Economic–Survey 2004-2005 Government of Andhra Pradesh Planning Department Andhra Pradesh, Secretariat, Hyderabad.

The Teacher pupil ratio at primary stages is more than optimum ratio (i.e. 1:40,which is determined by the SCERT and other commissions and committees on elementary education) up to 2002. If we look at the Teacher-pupil ratio at upper primary and high school stages, it is quite different. The Teacher-pupil ratio at upper primary and high school stages is below the optimum ratio.

EDUCATIONAL FACILITIES AT HIGHER, SECONDARY LEVEL

The educational facilities based on no. of schools and teachers at higher secondary level in Andhra Pradesh during 1999-2000 to 2003-04 are shown in Table 3.

It is evident from the above table that, the number of higher secondary schools in the state has declined from 88 in 1999-

2000 to 79 in 2002-03, but slightly increased to 82 in 2002-03. The statistical figures relating to enrolment and teachers also indicate a declining trend.

Table 3
Educational Facilities at Higher Secondary Level in Andhra Pradesh 1999 to 04

Year	No. of schools	Enrolment total	Teacher total
1999-2K	88	92292	4154
2000-01	82	82227	3847
2001-02	73	74765	3498
2002-03	79	78336	3628
2003-04	82	82033	3305

Source: 1. Economic survey 2004-2005 Government of India Ministry of Finance Economic division.
2. Directory of School Education Andhra Pradesh.
3. Economic–Survey 2004-2005 Government of Andhra Pradesh Planning Department Andhra Pradesh, Secretariat, Hyderabad.

DROPOUT RATIOS IN SCHOOL EDUCATION

The drop out rate is defined as a percentage of the number of children to total enrolment dropping out of the educational system in particular year. The ratio does not take into account repeaters and children who enter the system after class 1. The statistical data relating to dropout ratios in school education for selected years are presented in Table 4.

The dropout ratio, at primary stage (classes I-V) is 42.61, while the drop-out ratio in upper primary stage (classes IV-VII) is 54.27 and in secondary schools, it is 66.70 during 2003-04. The dropout rates during 1971-72 are 70.65 in case of primary stage, 81.59 in case of upper primary stage and 90.56 in case of secondary stage. But it is interesting to note that the declining dropout ratios at all the primary, upper primary and secondary stages during the period under consideration augurs well for the state of Andhra Pradesh.

GRANTS-IN-AID FOR EDUCATION SECTOR

In the process of developing the education sector in the states, grants-in-aid play an important role.

Table 4
Dropout Ratios In School Education in Andhra Pradesh
1971 to 2004

Year	*Primary*	*Upper primary*	*Secondary*
	I-V	*I-VII*	*I-X*
	Total	*Total*	*Total*
1971-72	70.65	81.59	90.56
1981-82	60.31	67.98	81.35
1991-92	54.28	64.65	75.54
2001-02	34.54	53.78	72.37
2002-03	32.39	51.52	69.12
2003-04	42.61	54.27	66.70

Source: 1. Economic survey 2004-2005 Government of India Ministry of Finance Economic division.
2. Directory of School Education Andhra Pradesh.
3. Economic–Survey 2004-2005 Government of Andhra Pradesh Planning Department Andhra Pradesh, Secretariat, Hyderabad.

The Twelfth Finance Commission has recommended that the following eight states be given grants in-aid of Rs. 10171.65 cores over the award period 2005-10 for the educational sector with a minimum of Rs. 20 cores in a year for any eligible state. The details of grants-in-aid for education sector were shown in Table 5.

Table5
Grants-in-aid For Education Sector (Major Head 2202)

State	*2005-06*	*2006-07*	*2007-08*	*2008-09*	*2009-10*	*2005-10*
1	2	3	4	5	6	7
Assam	183.20	200.60	219.66	240.53	263.38	1107.37
Bihar	443.99	486.17	523.36	582.93	638.31	2683.76
Jharkhand	107.82	118.06	129.28	141.56	155.01	651.73
Madhya Pradesh	76.03	83.25	91.16	99.82	109.30	459.56
Orissa	53.49	58.57	64.13	90.22	76.89	323.30
Rajasthan	20.00	20.00	20.00	20.00	20.00	100.00
Uttar Pradesh	736.87	806.87	883.52	967.45	1059.36	4454.07
West Bengal	64.83	90.99	77.73	85.11	93.20	391.86
Total States	1686.23	1844.51	2017.84	2207.62	2415.45	10171.65

Source: The reports of the twelfth finance commission, Government of India 2004.

The commission did not recommend grants for education to Andhra Pradesh, though Andhra Pradesh has the lowest literacy rate among the major states in the country. Grants-in-aid are required for Andhra Pradesh to improve the physical status of literacy in the state in the coming five years.

CONCLUDING REMARKS

1. Since formation of Andhra Pradesh, state recorded a phenomenal growth in respect of educational institutions, enrolment of children, and teachers in different stages of education particularly from primary to higher secondary education stage.
2. Andhra Pradesh was one of the states that was re-organized on linguistic lines in 1956. The State claims rank 5th in area and 7th interms of volume of the state domestic Product in the country. But this state is backward in the provision of education and takes the rank 22nd in the levels of literacy in the Indian union of 28 states. The drop out rate in the primary education is about 42.6%, 54.21% in upper primary and 66.70% in secondary stage in 2003-04. The Teacher pupil ratio in the primary education works out to be 1:35, 1:31 in upper primary, and in secondary stage.
3. The government has also launched mid-day meal programme to provide nutritional support to the school children and to improve the retention in the schools and also to achieve total literacy in the state. Under this scheme an amount of rupees 250 cores has been provided during 2003-2004.covering 69.47 lakhs of children . For the first time in the country the Government of Andhra Pradesh has enacted "community participation Act 1998" to involve the community in school management.
4. The scheme of computer education is also being introduced in 1000 government and Zillah perished schools having classes 6th to 10th during 2002. District primary education programme (DPEP) is a major intervention in state for the improvement of primary education in all aspects so as to realize the national goal of universal primary education. In

an effort to universalize elementary education Sarva Shiksha Abhiyan (SSA) has been introduced during 2001-2002. It aims to provide useful and relevant elementary education for all children in 6 to14 age group by 2010. To provide minimum basic facilities to schools, such as construction of school building , providing accommodation furniture, lab and library equipment etc. various schemes have been taken up. In ordered to encourage primary education among specific social groups and discourage drop outs , the government implemented programmes like 'back to school.

5. It is observed through empirical evidence that Andhra Pradesh deserves up gradation grants-in-aid for education. It would have been better had the Twelfth Finance Commission considered Andhra Pradesh for upgradation grants for education, as the Government has been putting in all possible efforts to improve its lower literacy rates among the major states in the country.

In short, this paper suggests that there is immense need for educational grant to Andhra Pradesh.

REFERENCES

Baljit Singh (Ed.) (1967), "Economics of Indian Education", Meenakshi Prakash, Meerut.

Basu, A.N. (1946), "Primary Education in India and its future", Calcutta: Indian Association Publishing Company.

Tilak, J.B.G. (1987), "The Economics of Inequality in Education", Sagar Publishers, New Delhi.

World Bank, "Indian Primary Education Achievements", South Asia Department-2, 1996.

Economic Survey 2004-2005 Government of India Ministry of Finance Economic Division.

Directory of School Education Andhra Pradesh.

Economic–Survey 2004-2005 Government of India Andhra Pradesh Planning Department Andhra Pradesh, Secretariat, Hyderabad.

The Reports of the Twelfth Finance Commission, Government of India 2004.

24

DEVOLUTION OF FUNDS TO LOCAL BODIES IN A.P.

Lilly Grace Bodapati & Addai Biddiki

A key pillar of India's Federal Structure, the Finance Commission, appointed by the President periodically to mediate revenue sharing between the Centre and the States. The President of India appointed the Twelfth Finance Commission on 1st November, 2002 under the Chairmanship of Dr.C.Rangarajan, the then Governor of Andhra Pradesh. Article 280 of the Constitution describes the duties of the finance commission, the core of which relates to sharing of central taxes under article 270 and determination of grants for the states as provided for under article 275. With the 73rd and 74th Constitutional Amendments, the needs of the States arising from the requirement of the local bodies (Panchayats and Municipalities) are also required to be taken into account.

In the present paper an attempt is made to explain the issues covered under participatory development approach and to examine how far the powers, both functional and financial, devolved to local bodies (Panchayat Raj Institutions {PRIs}) during the period of Post 73rd Amendment. It is mainly descriptive to present the status of decentralization experience in Andhra Pradesh and is based on secondary sources and published literature.

The Royal Commission report of 1909 laid emphasis on the desirability of keeping Panchayats, as far as possible, away from the other administrative bodies. They emphasised the complete popular control in local bodies and the largest possible independence for them. So the provincial government was forced to enact the local Boards Act and the village Panchayat Act of 1920. This Act gave an independent status to each class of local boards and increased not only their strength but also the proportion of elected members, their resources and their powers. The Taxation powers of all the three categories of local boards were enlarged. They were given a free hand in framing their budgets. Provision was made for the appointment of a District Board Engineer and a District Health Officer. The local boards became more or less autonomous and the Collector and the Government were empowered to interfere only in cases of emergency and malnutrition[1].

Andhra State was a part of composite Madras State upto 30-9-1953. Therefore, the Madras Local Act continued to be in force in Andhra State and Andhra Pradesh State, till new Acts were enacted. The Madras Village Panchayat Act of 1950 was enacted conferring large powers on Panchayats, vesting the inspector of Municipal Councils and Local Boards with control of District Collectors to certain emergency powers. This Act was brought into force on 1st April 1951. The fundamental objective of this Act was to make Panchayats Dynamic nurseries of democracies.

This Act was in effect for the implementation of the Article 40 of the Constitution, which says that "the State shall take steps to organise village Panchayats and endow them with such powers and authority as may be necessary to enable them to function as units of self Government."[2]

The State of Andhra Pradesh has a good record of Panchayat Raj Institutions (PRIs) compared to almost all States in the Indian Union. It was one of the first States to implement many of the recommendations of the Balwant Rai Committee report of the year 1957, which resulted in the advent of the three-tier Panchayat Raj System in 1959. Though, most parts of India witnessed decadence of the PRIs during 1969-77, Andhra Pradesh did not suffer it. The phase of reconstitution and revitalisation of PRIs in Andhra Pradesh started much earlier to the 73rd Constitutional Amendment of 1992.

In order to enable the PRIs as Institution of self-government, as per Article 243 G and 243 W of the Indian Constitution, the

State Government have enacted the Andhra Pradesh Panchayat Raj Act in 1994, which has come into force with effect from 30th May 1994.

According to Human Development report, 1993 where decentralisation has taken place, it has been successful in encouraging local participation, increasing accountability of local officials, reducing the costs and increasing the efficiency. Decentralisation can help to mobilize the resources, introduce locally and regionally diverse solutions and promote equitable growth by bringing the poor into the mainstream of development[3].

Keeping the main objectives of 73rd Amendment Act, the Government of Andhra Pradesh has passed the A.P. Panchayat Raj Act 1994. The main features of the Act are:

(a) It aims at promoting Participatory Approach of development.

(b) It seeks to ensure regular elections to the PRIs for a period of 5 years and prevent scandalous suppression of the local bodies.

(c) It aims to create institutions of self-government at the Panchayat level by endowing them with the needed powers, authority and finances. It provides for revenue raising powers for the Panchayats.

(d) It specifically mandates the creation of an independent State Finance Commission (SFC) for the purpose of ensuring financial transfers to the PR bodies.

(e) Finally, it seeks to promote bottom-up planning process.

THE ROLE OF LOCAL BODIES AND VISION 2020

In its vision 2020 Government of Andhra Pradesh envisages the development process by providing growth conducive deregulated policy environment. Decentralisation will be the norm. Local bodies encouraged and empowered to participate in administration. By involving public in the Governance the A.P government will remain transparent, effective and responsive to the people. For which decentralisation is an essential part of the programme. Therefore, the State determined to strengthen its administration by PRIs and Community Organisations. To this end, it will enable local management devolving administrative and economic powers and responsibilities.

As the 73rd Amendment emphasised the local empowerment the State Government will devolve the administration of Government services mentioned in the 73rd to the appropriate PRIs. It also will provide Gram Panchayats control over services like sanitation and primary schools and to Mandals and Zilla Parishads control over secondary schools and colleges. The people can play a major role in managing education, health and infrastructure services through Community Based Organisatons (CBOs) such as School Committees, or Development of Women and Children in Rural Areas (DWCRA)[4].

POWERS AND FUNCTIONS

In the sphere of devolution of powers on local level governance, some important principles should be kept in view such as:

1. The subsidiary principle which postulates any function can be performed by a lower tier should be handled by that alone and not by any higher tier of PRI.
2. The State Government should not unilaterally withdraw the responsibility and powers already granted to the Panchayat without adequate justification and prior consultation with the latter.
3. Responsibilities, authorities and power granted to the panchayats should be extremely specific, clear and simple in order to be comprehended by the panchayats.
4. Whenever functions and responsibilities are transferred to the panchayats it should be ensured that the necessary funds, functionaries and freedom of decision making also accompany such transfer[5].

PRIs IN ANDHRA PRADESH

The extent of devolution required should be adequate to perform the functions enlisted in the Act. In Andhra Pradesh when actual devolution has taken place the ground reality is not satisfactory. To become an institution of self-government, it is required to bring the various development departments under the control of PR bodies to enable them to discharge functions listed in 11th Schedule (29 items). The real position of Andhra Pradesh is that majority of the departments listed are separately existed and are not under the control of PR bodies. A separate 'Panchayat Raj Cadre' has not been created. Besides District Rural Development Agency (DRDA), there are a few other development corporations like AP Scheduled Caste Corporation, AP Backward Caste Corporation, AP Women Development Corporation, which work independently of PR bodies in the State. It is very difficult to call PR bodies as institutions of self-government unless these bodies brought under the purview of PR bodies.

Government of Andhra Pradesh constituted an expert committee to study the pattern of devolution of powers and functions. Based on the committee recommendations the State government has decided to transfer 16 out of 29 subjects of the PRIs and actually orders were issued for only 14 subjects for transfer.

Table 1 shows the status of devolution/Subjects with functions, funds and functionaries to PRIs in a few important States. It is clear from the Table that in Karnataka all the 29 subjects/departments have been transferred to panchayats with functions, funds and functionaries. Next Kerala followed by Madhya Pradesh and Andhra Pradesh.

It is pertinent to mention here that even though the State of Andhra Pradesh stood first in implementing many of the recommendations of the Balwant Rai Committee report of the year 1957, which resulted in the advent of the three-tier Panchayat Raj System in 1959, it could not transfer all its functions, funds and functionaries listed in 11th Schedule to the Panchayats.

In Andhra Pradesh the Gram Panchayats and the Mandal Parishads are not required to plan for 'economic Development and social justice'. All the tiers of panchayats have been assigned with large number of functions. But none of them has financial or administrative sources under their control to execute them. The Mandal Parishad do not have control over the staff of the Development Blocks and Zilla Parishads do not have control over the DRDA, which controls large funds under various poverty alleviation programmes[6].

Table 1
The Status of Devolution/Subjects to PRIs in A Few Important States

State	*No. of Departments/ subjects transferred to Panchayats with*			*No. of Departments/subjects yet to be transferred to Panchayats with*		
	Fun-ctions	*Funds*	*Functio-naries*	*Fun-ctions*	*Funds*	*Functio-naries*
Andhra Pradesh	16	05	02	13	24	27
Karnataka	29	29	29	-	-	-
Kerala	29	15	15	-	14	14
West Bengal	29	12	12	-	17	17
Madhya Pradesh	23	10	09	06	19	20

Source: Ministry of Rural Development.

FINANCIAL DEVOLUTION

The present situation of Andhra Pradesh tells that inadequate unsound financial base has impaired the working of the local bodies. In AP by and large, the income of ZPs, MPs and GPs derive in the form of grants from the State Government and Central Government. The other sources of revenue are negligible. The grants from the State government to MPs are mostly tied in nature. Another important feature of mandal level finances is that they have to deposit 15 per cent of their grants exclusively for the housing programmes implemented by the State Housing Corporation.

The revenue of Zilla Parishads raised from their own non-tax avenues; from assigned duties such as land cess, mineral cess, stamp duty etc., tied grants from the State and Centre and also other grants. Table 2 shows the sources of revenue of ZPs in A.P from 1993-94 to 2001-02. It is clear from the Table that the proportion of grants is much higher than other sources of income. It is observed from the Table that the percentage share of Grants-in-Aid to Zilla Parishads in Andhra Pradesh increased from 87.66 per cent in 1993-94 to 90.54 per cent in 1999-2000 and again there is a decline in the year 2000-01 and 2001-02. The percentage change over the previous year shows many fluctuations during the study period. There is no stability in the annual growth of finances.

The data shown in the Table 2 visualises the over dependence of the Zilla Parishads for their funds on the State and central Government Grants. They do not have any other noticeable source of income other than this. It is pertinent to refer to the three-tier PR system, only GPs are empowered to levy taxes while the other two tiers are permitted to impose surcharge on the taxes levied by the panchayats. Mandals and Zilla Parishads are not utilised the said facility[7].

The revenue base of the ZPs in Andhra Pradesh consists of four categories, such as (a) mobilize revenue through non-tax avenues, (b) assigned duties such as land cess, mineral cess, stamp duty etc; (c) tied grants from the State and Centre towards social sectors like education, drinking water supply and rural supply and rural roads and (d) the grants.

Table 2
Revenue Receipts of Zilla Parishads in Andhra Pradesh 1993-94 to 2001-02

(Rs. in Crores)

Year	*Tax Revenue*	*Grants-in-Aid*	*Other Receipts*	*Total Receipts*	*% Change over previous year*
1993-94	33.21	365.47	18.25	416.93	
	(7.97)	(87.66)	(4.38)	(100.0)	
1994-95	26.47	390.05	24.09	440.61	5.68
	(6.01)	(88.52)	(5.47)	(100.0)	
1995-96	21.22	449.05	35.29	505.56	14.74
	(4.20)	(88.82)	(7.0)	(100.0)	
1996-97	23.83	500.10	30.02	553.95	9.57
	(4.30)	(90.28)	(5.42)	(100.0)	
1997-98	22.24	613.97	32.63	668.84	20.74
	(3.33)	(91.80)	(4.89)	(100.0)	
1998-99	31.17	705.61	47.60	784.38	17.27
	(3.97)	(89.96)	(6.07)	(100.0)	

Contd...

Year	*Tax Revenue*	*Grants-in-Aid*	*Other Receipts*	*Total Receipts*	*% Change over previous year*
1999-00	35.80 (4.23)	765.53 (90.54)	44.16 (5.22)	845.49 (100.0)	7.79
2000-01	55.33 (5.24)	915.94 (86.79)	84.14 (7.9)	1055.41 (100.0)	24.83
2001-02	48.00 (5.92)	681.09 (84.01)	81.68 (10.7)	810.77 (100.0)	-23.18

Source: Government of Andhra Pradesh, Finances of Zilla Parishads, Directorate of Economics and Statistics, Hyderabad.
Note: Figures in brackets indicate percentages to the total revenue.

In case of Gram Panchayats (GPs) sources of revenue are large in number and are more diversified. They derive income from grants, tax and non-tax sources and property and others. The revenue of GPs in AP is shown in the Table 3. The important tax powers of GPs in the State are house tax, vehicles tax, land cess, surcharge on stamp duty etc. it is observed from the Table that the tax revenue of Gram Panchayats are higher than the grants in the initial period of the study but this position shows a reversal at the end of the study period especially in the last two years i.e. 2001-02 and 2002-03.

Table 3
Revenue Receipts of Gram Panchayats in Andhra Pradesh 1993-94 to 2002-03

(Rs. in Crores)

Year	*Tax Revenue*	*Grants-in-Aid*	*Other Receipts*	*Total Receipts*	*% Change over previous year*
1993-94	59.24 (41.64)	35.55 (24.99)	47.49 (33.38)	142.28 (100.0)	
1994-95	59.10 (39.17)	36.16 (23.97)	55.66 (36.86)	150.87 (100.0)	6.04
1995-96	55.35 (27.89)	72.05 (36.31)	71.02 (35.79)	198.42 (100.0)	31.52
1996-97	61.02 (28.06)	71.53 (32.90)	84.9 (39.04)	217.45 (100.0)	9.59
1997-98	69.67 (27.74)	81.40 (32.42)	100.06 (39.84)	251.13 (100.0)	15.49

Year	*Tax Revenue*	*Grants-in-Aid*	*Other Receipts*	*Total Receipts*	*% Change over previous year*
1998-99	94.87 (37.40)	80.53 (31.75)	78.26 (30.85)	253.66 (100.0)	1.01
1999-00	110.42 (37.61)	90.42 (30.79)	92.78 (31.60)	293.62 (100.0)	15.75
2000-01	105.49 (31.77)	103.38 (31.13)	123.2 (37.10)	332.07 (100.0)	13.10
2001-02	131.77 (32.24)	186.87 (45.73)	90.0 (22.02)	408.64 (100.0)	23.06
2002-03	156.40 (34.74)	191.96 (42.64)	101.78 (22.61)	450.14 (100.0)	10.16

Source: Government of Andhra Pradesh, Finances of Gram Panchayats, Directorate of Economics and Statistics, Hyderabad.

Note: Figures in brackets shows the percentage of item wise receipts to total receipts.

The gram panchayats are financially weak not because of the absence of the tax bases in the APPR Act, but it is the attitude of the GPs not to tax for the benefit of the GPs, due to the fear that imposition of tax would estrange them from the voting public. Therefore, the resource transfers from the Centre and the States should facilitate to meet the requirements of the GPs.

According to the First State Finance Commission Recommendations, local bodies receive three kinds of revenues i.e., (i) Assigned revenues, (ii) Grants-in-Aid, (iii) Revenue sharing. Under assigned revenues the important sources are profession tax, surcharge on stamp duty and land/local cess. Under grants-in-Aid two kinds of sources are important namely, (a) untied per capita grant (varies for each tier-Rs. Four for the gram panchayats, rupees eight for the Mandal panchayats and rupees four for zilla parishads) and (b) Capital grants, which are meant for rural water supply, minor irrigation, rural roads, school buildings, Mandal Parishad office buildings rural sanitation etc. capital grants are meant for creation of infrastructure as well as for the maintenance of existing infrastructure. Under revenue sharing, assignment of taxes levied by government to local bodies is not recommended.

Revenue sharing between the state government and local bodies was preferred. The First State Finance Commission recommended a sum of Rs. 229.15 crores towards civic and developmental functions be devolved to gram panchayats has not been accepted by the State Government[8].

CONCLUSION

The present scenario of AP is not satisfactory regarding functions of PRIs and it requires dedicated personnel to implement the rural development programmes and it is required to bring all the 29 subjects under the control of PRIs. To make local bodies vibrant and dynamic fiscal and functional decentralization are imperative. At present PRIs in the State are receiving grants under various centrally sponsored schemes. The present form of per capita grants is not much helpful. Both Zilla Parishads and Mandal Parishads are restricted by the tied grants they receive from State and Centre. Therefore, untied grants need to be provided to plan and prioritise their own specific needs.

In Andhra Pradesh most of the schemes that local governments tend to implement are that of the State government. Further substantial proportion of the local governments' resources is spent to meet the wage bills of employees. In order to meet the requirements of the local governments division of the schemes between State and District and division of State budget into State Wide and District wide is required.

The State government should release grants-in-aid to the district planning bodies to enable them to utilise funds even after the close of the financial year. All amounts devolved by the State and Union Finance Commissions to local governments should be passed on to them subject to only such conditions as the Commission may have prescribed.

NOTES AND REFERENCES

1. Kanchana Ratnam, S. (1989), *"Strategies for Rural Development and Planning of Performance"*, Dominant Publishers and Distributors, New Delhi, 110002, p. 9.

2. Government of Andhra Pradesh (2000), "*Gram Panchayats Account Manual Panchayat Raj & Rural Development Department*", Dr. MCR Human Resource Development Institute of Andhra Pradesh, Hyderabad, p. 2.

3. Gopinath Reddy, M.(2003), " Decentralised Local Bodies: Post 73rd Amendment Scenario", Ed. in *Andhra Pradesh Economic Reforms and Challenges Ahead*, by Ch.Hanumantha Rao and S. Mahendra Dev, CESS, Hyderabad, p. 597.

4. Government of Andhra Pradesh (1999), "People Centered, Growth Oriented Governance", in *Andhra Pradesh Vision 2020*, Hyderabad.

5. Government of India (2001), *Report of the Working Group on Decentralised Planning and Panchayati Raj Institutions for the tenth Five year Plan*, Ministry of Rural Development, New Delhi.

6. Government of India (2001), *National Commission to Review of the Working of the Constitution*, A consultation Paper on Review of the Working of the Constitutional Provisions for Decentralisation (Panchayats), Vigyan Bhavan Annexe, New Delhi.

7. Government of Andhra Pradesh (2003), *Second State Finance Commission Report*, Hyderabad.

8. National Institute of Rural Development (1998), *State Finance Commission Recommendations and Action Taken Reports of State Governments*, State Finance Commission Cell, Hyderabad.

25

FISCAL PLIGHT OF URBAN LOCAL BODIES–AN ANALYSIS OF FISCAL IMBALANCE OF BHIMAVARAM MUNICIPALITY

G. Durga Prasad

INTRODUCTION

Fiscal decentralization in respect of local bodies is the catchword nowadays which can help mobilize resources by introducing local solutions and promote equitable growth by bringing the poor into mainstream development. New systems of local and intergovernmental finance are being established as part of the evolution. The trend has been noted particularly since the early 1990s with the passage of 73rd and 74th Constitutional Amendment Acts, 1992 that accelerated the process of decentralization with greater devolution and delegation of powers to local governments and the recognition of Panchayat Raj Institutions (PRIs) land Urban Local Bodies (ULBs) in the book of statute as institutions of self-government. As a result, the Constitution made the State Legislatures to be responsible to transfer functions and resources to the local governments, i.e. PRIs and ULBs. For financial devolution, the State is supposed to constitute state level finance commissions and for functional transfer all the functions listed in the 12th Schedule (Art. 243-W) to the Constitution. In this list of functions, a majority of them are new and costs huge financial resources. In Andhra Pradesh, already 2 State-Level Finance Commissions have submitted their reports including ATCs by the government. All these efforts show that the higher-tier governments have been showing considerable interest in the local affairs. But still the local governments are subjects of the state governments and it is the prerogative of the states to determine the functions and finances of the local governments. An element of autonomy is lacking with respect of local governments in discharging their functions and levying and collecting tax and non-tax sources of revenue.

The actual trouble lies with the local governments is that of mismatch between resources and functions. The problem is compounded with increasing tendency of centralization of finances and decentralization of functional obligations. Property tax is the main stay of the local governments particularly ULBs. With the 74th Amendment Act the functional obligations were enlarged (20 new functions) by including functions like developmental activity of the town, recycling of garbage, pollution control, etc. But the solace here is that the ULBs somehow increased their collection regarding non-tax revenues. Also, the ULBs have been receiving increased revenue from the state-transferred taxes like profession tax, entertainment tax and surcharge on stamp duty. Thus, there are no regrets on the part of the ULBs for the centralization of local taxes by the state of Andhra Pradesh. In the case of Bhimavaram town, the municipality has achieved 100 per cent tax collection particularly in respect of property tax. The other important point is that Central Finance Commissions have earmarked grants to the local governments. But inter-se distribution of grants is left to the States. On the other hand, in majority of the ULBs, the municipalities have failed even to pay salaries to their staff. This implies the salary-bill has been posing as a "Damocles' Sword" for their ultimate bankruptcy. Moreover, the local governments are attracting the wrath of the States by not showing any interest in their development. Thus, the ULBs have become a centre of attention with respect to higher layer governments, academicians and politicians as well.

OBJECTIVES OF THE PAPER

With a view to take up intensive discussion over the status of ULBs in the present scenario, it is proposed to take up a study of ULBs in AP in general and Bhimavaram municipality in particular. For the purpose, the period of study taken up covers from 1993-94 to 2004-05. The paper is divided into 3 Sections. Section 1 covers Revenue and Expenditure position of the Bhimavaram municipality. Section 2 covers a note of Twelfth Finance Commission including the First SFC. In the last section, conclusions are provided.

SECTION - I

Revenue and Expenditure Position

In Andhra Pradesh, there are 11 municipal corporations, 110 municipalities and 1 Nagar Panchayat. The municipal population accounts for 2.5 crores as per 2001 Census. In the entire India, the ULBs numbered 3717 by the end of 2002. Of which, there are 110 municipal corporations, 1434 municipalities and 2173 Nagar Panchayats[1] (V.N. Alok, Nagarlok, Oct.-Dec. 2004, p. 29). In this paper, our concentration is only on municipalities in general and Bhimavaram municipality in particular.

In the State, revenue sources include tax and non-tax revenues and transfers from the State and Centre. Taxes include property tax revenue, advertisement tax and tax on carts and animals. The revenue transfers include: assigned revenues and grants-in-aid. Assigned revenues are profession tax, entertainment tax, and surcharge on stamp duty. Grants-in-aid covers both plan and non-plan grants. Lastly, the municipalities are permitted to take loans from public financial institutions.

Of the own-tax revenue, property tax is the significant source of income to the municipalities in the state. The other taxes like advertisement tax and tax on carts and animals is quite insignificant which can be better withdrawn taking into account their revenue collection and cost of collection. Property tax in the state is levied as per "plinth area basis" which was imposed since 1992-93. With this the collections have improved considerably. On the other hand, the non-tax revenues are collected through water charges, D & O Trades license fees, market fees, quarters rent, slaughter house fee, betterment charges, building license fee, mutation fee, magisterial fines, sale of forms and old news papers, etc.

Assigned revenues are provided by the State to the municipalities after deducting cost of collection to the municipalities. The municipalities in the State have received considerable revenue from the profession tax revenue transfer since 1986-87 when the tax was taken over by the State. Previously the municipalities used to collect only a meager amount from this source. In respect of entertainment tax, the state government levies and collects the tax and the collected revenue will be provided to the municipalities on the basis of population. This is also a lucrative source of revenue to the municipalities in the State. The State is levying surcharge on stamp duty at the rate of 12 per cent on the transactions and of which 5 per cent of the revenue is provided to the local municipal authority.

Grants-in-aid have occupied an important place in the finances of municipalities in the state. But for the Grants-in-aid, the municipalities could not withstand with the pressure from the municipal administration. These grants include plan and non-plan grants. Plan grants are given by the State and Centre to take up developmental activity. Some of the important grants in this category are Environmental Improvement of Urban Slums, Low Cost Sanitation, Integrated Development of Small and Medium Towns, National Slum Development Programme and SJSRY. Non-plan grants are statutorily devolved to the municipalities. These include compensatory grants, road grant, and percapita grant. The compensation grants are provided to compensate the loss of revenue to the municipality as a result of taking over of certain local tax by the State. These include MV tax, toll and octroi, etc.

Loan-financing has been playing a crucial role in the finances of municipalities in the state. The loans are raised from public financial institutions such as HUDCO, LIC, World Bank, DFID, etc. Recently, municipalities are entering into the capital market for raising loans. In this respect, municipal bond banking is to be noted.

On the other hand, municipal expenditure has an important bearing on the fiscal health of the municipalities. The expenditure is divided into revenue expenditure and capital expenditure. In the state, revenue expenditure is far exceeding capital expenditure leaving very little to the developmental activity. One of the major heads of municipal expenditure is expenditure on municipal administration which includes salary-bill. The other important heads of expenditure include public health, education, water supply and drainage, town planning, and communications including roads.

The following table 1 explains about the municipal revenue position in the State.

Table 1
Position of Municipal Revenues in the State

(% in Total Revenues)

Year	*Own Revenues (%)*			*External Revenues (%)*				*Total*
	Taxes	*Non-Taxes*	*Total*	*Assigned Revenues*	*Non-Plan Grant*	*Plan Grant*	*Loans*	
1993-94	31.01	23.74	54.75	25.19	3.83	16.24	—	45.25
1994-95	29.33	25.55	54.88	28.02	3.18	13.91	—	45.12
1995-96	29.29	27.75	57.05	27.27	0.91	14.77	9.00	42.95
1996-97	28.35	28.33	56.68	30.88	2.55	9.89	—	43.32
1997-98	24.86	32.17	57.02	29.51	2.31	11.16	—	42.98
1998-99	18.48	23.45	41.93	24.64	2.79	29.83	0.80	58.07
1999-00	16.31	25.32	41.63	24.57	1.41	31.75	0.64	58.37
2000-01	24.38	31.21	55.60	25.50	2.59	16.24	0.07	44.40
2001-02	20.75	23.89	44.64	25.57	9.68	18.75	1.36	55.36

Source: V. Gnaneshwr, Municipal Finances in AP.

From the above table, internal resources decreased steadily from 54.75 per cent in 1993-94 to 44.64 per cent in 2001-02 in Andhra Pradesh. On the other hand, external resources increased from 45.25 per cent to 55.36 per cent during the same period under study. Within the own-sources of revenue, the fiscal importance of non-tax revenues has been gradually increased compared to the tax revenues, which comprises mainly of property tax. On the external source side, assigned revenues had shown superiority and stability in respect of its share in the total revenues. While plan grants had shown fluctuations, the loans are not of much significance in the total revenues of the municipalities in the state.

Table 2 provides an account of growth of revenues during the period 1993-94 to 2001-02.

Table 2
Growth Rates of Various Sources of Revenue in the State

Year	*Own-Sources of Revenue*			*Transfers*	*Total Revenue*
	Taxes	*Non-Taxes*	*Total*		
1993-94	198.03	178.61	189.11	186.17	187.77
1994-95	180.85	185.33	183.00	179.18	181.26
1995-96	206.60	230.55	217.60	195.16	207.36
1996-97	217.33	255.87	235.03	213.97	225.42
1997-98	237.17	361.49	294.25	264.13	280.50
1998-99	249.77	373.27	306.48	505.57	397.34
1999-00	249.17	455.74	344.02	574.43	449.18
2000-01	362.30	546.34	446.86	425.06	436.88
2001-02	354.92	481.33	412.97	609.94	502.86

Source: V.Gnaneshwr, Municipal Finances in AP.

From the Table, it can be observed that total revenues increased by 5-fold during the period 1993-94 to 2001-02. The external sources of revenue i.e. transfers have registered a higher rate of growth since 1998-99. On the other hand, own revenues increased from 189.11 per cent to 412.97 per cent during the period. Of the own revenues, non-tax resources have registered a higher growth compared to the tax revenues. The percapita revenues have increased from Rs. 142.94 in 1990-91 to Rs. 421.13 in 2000-01[2](V.Gnaneshwr, Municipal Finances in AP). Of which, tax revenue increased from Rs. 83.84 to Rs. 210.07.

In Andhra Pradesh, the municipalities are facing the problem of increasing demands for the provision of services over the limited availability of revenue. The problem gets aggravated due to steady increase on account of the establishment costs. Therefore, to meet this increasing demand, the municipalities have depended heavily on grants and loans.

In the State, the municipal expenditure is grouped into salary bill, maintenance, capital, loan repayment, and miscellaneous expenditure. Of these heads, salary bill accounts for 35 per cent of total expenditure of the municipalities in the State during 2001-02. The maintenance expenditure has occupied the second place with 26 per cent in the same period. For the developmental activity, the expenditure constitutes 24 per cent during the period. No amounts were spent on loan repayment. On the miscellaneous expenditure, the expenditure accounts for 15 per cent. According to the standard norms, the expenditure bill shall not cross 10 to15 per cent of total expenditure. The above figure of 35 is nowhere near this. As such, certain municipalities in the State have failed to pay even salaries to their staff let alone the developmental activity in their localities.

Table 3
Per cent Shares of Various Sources of Revenue in the Total Revenues

Year	*Own Sources of Revenue*				*State Financial Transfers*			
	Prop. Tax	*Other Taxes*	*Non-Taxes*	*Prof. Tax*	*Entmt. Tax*	*Surch. on stamp duty*	*Grants in-aid*	*Comp. Grants*
1993-94	21.29	0.34	20.42	6024	10.88	7.12	32.84	0.88
1994-95	20.06	0.30	23.91	6051	10.82	5.62	32.06	0.73
1995-96	18.52	0.43	27.48	2.76	12.40	7.91	30.12	0.38
1996-97	18.00	0.26	32.72	4.92	9.31	9.35	24.82	0.61
1997-98	18.41	0.29	21.91	7.24	9.53	9.49	32.52	0.60
1998-99	14.65	0.23	24.60	4.01	7.59	9.26	39.24	0.42
1999-00	14.88	0.25	24.81	9.01	7.71	7.46	35.29	0.59
2000-01	20.33	0.41	24.54	5.58	3.96	7.89	36.73	0.56
2001-02	20.62	0.84	24.16	—	7.82	10.42	35.64	0.49
2002-03	28096	0.40	17091	—	3.80	9.29	39.30	0.34
2003-04	29.05	0.33	20.53	—	3.72	8.63	37.40	0.28
2004-05	30.16	0.29	27.52	—	3.35	8.37	30.13	0.18
Average	20.50	0.36	23.75	5.78	7.57	8.40	33.84	0.51

Source: Annual Account Statements of Bhimavaram Municipality.

From the above two tables, the State picture is clear. Now let us examine the position of Bhimavaram Municipality with respect to revenue and expenditure. Table 3 gives an account of the fiscal importance of various sources of revenue in the overall finances of the municipality during 1993-94 to 2004-05.

From the above table, it is very clear that own sources of revenue are lagging behind as compared to that of external sources of revenue. For instance, own revenues including both taxes and non-taxes constitute nearly 44 per cent as against 56 per cent of external sources of revenue during the period under study. Also, compared to tax revenues, non-tax revenues have registered a higher percentage share in the total revenues of the municipality. This is a welcoming feature in the light of the inelastic property tax revenue and growing internal resource mobilization other than levying taxes. This will promote the municipal autonomy in the discharge of its functions.

Average Revenue from different Sources

Category	*Rs. Lakhs*
Property tax	204.73
Other Taxes	3.17
Non-Tax Revenue	210.83
Profession Tax	36.01
Entertainment Tax	54.26
Surcharge on StampDuty	74.97
Grants-in-aid	299.87
Compensation Grants	3.56
Total Revenues	887.40

In absolute terms, the revenue from property tax increased from Rs. 82.38 lakhs to Rs. 630.75 lakhs during 1993-94 to 2004-05. This shows nearly an 8-fold increase in the revenue from the tax. This marked increase in the revenue is due to the introduction of plinth area basis in the assessment of property tax and also remarkable increase in the collections. In Bhimavaram municipality, 100 per cent collection efficiency in the tax revenue has been achieved. On the other hand, non-tax revenues increased from Rs. 79.02 lakhs to Rs. 575.50 lakhs during the period under study. The municipality has successfully achieved considerable increase in non-tax revenues. The other lucrative revenue sources are Grants-in-aid, profession tax, entertainment tax and surcharge on stamp duty. There was a phenomenal increase in the revenue from these sources. Taking the total revenues into account, the municipal revenues increased from Rs. 386 lakhs in 1993-94 to Rs. 2091 crores, more than 5-fold increase during the period under study. The average revenues from various sources are given in the following exhibit.

Table 4
Average Annual Growth Rates of Various Sources of Revenue of Bhimavaram Municipality (1993-94 to 2004-05)

Category	*Growth Rate (%)*
Property Tax	20.76
Other Taxes	19.54
Non-Tax Revenue	21.79
Profession Tax	21.94
Entertainment tax	9.70
Surcharge on StampDuty	18.71
Grants-in-Aid	15.95
Compensation Grants	4.99
Total Revenues	16.02

From the above Table 4, the annual growth rates pertaining to property tax varies in between 1.71 per cent to 87.30 per cent during 1993-94 to 2004-05. On an average, its growth rate accounts for 20.76 per cent. The other local revenue source, namely, non-tax revenues also grows at an annual rate of 21.79 per cent during the period. The municipality is successfully mobilizing additional and increasing revenues from non-tax revenues. This has become an important source of revenue to the municipality. On the other hand, state transfers of revenue show increasing trends. For instance, the annual growth rate in respect of grants-in-aid ranges from 1 per cent to 60 per cent during the period under study. On an average it registers 16 per cent rate of growth per annum. Lastly, total revenues register an annual per cent of varying between 2 per cent to 40 per cent during the period under study. Its annual average growth rate accounts for 16.02 per cent.

Table 5 explains about the expenditure pattern of Bhimavaram Municipality during the period under study.

Table 5
Per cent Share of each Component of Expenditure in the Total Expenditure Bhimavaram Municipality

Year	*Revenue Expenditure*	*Capital Expenditure*	*Total Expenditure*
1993-94	82.87	17.13	100
1994-95	80.14	19.86	100
1995-96	86.89	13.11	100
1996-97	85.77	14.23	100
1997-98	83.76	16.24	100
1998-99	81.67	18.33	100
1999-00	79.25	20.75	100
2000-01	87.92	12.08	100
2001-02	80.91	19.09	100
2002-03	75.09	24.91	100
2003-04	74.95	25.05	100
2004-05	64.43	35.57	100
Average	80.30	19.70	100

Source: Annual account Statements of Bhimavaram Municipality.

From the table, it can be observed that revenue expenditure is dominating the capital expenditure in the municipality. A major slice of the cake goes to the maintenance expenditure of the municipality. In this category, expenditure on salaries and administration accounts for nearly 40 per cent. In absolute terms, revenue expenditure increased from Rs. 305.43 lakhs in 1993-94 to Rs. 1350.75 lakhs, more than 4-fold increase. On the other hand, the minor head, namely, capital expenditure rose from Rs. 63.15 lakhs to Rs. 745.60 lakhs in the municipality during the period under study. The average revenue expenditure account for Rs. 651.84 lakhs and capital expenditure constitutes Rs. 198.47 lakhs during the period under study.

On the other hand, on relative terms, revenue expenditure constitutes 80 per cent and capital expenditure accounts for 20 per cent during the period under study in the municipality.

In the municipality capital expenditure is growing at a higher rate compared to the revenue expenditure. This is a welcoming feature of the municipality. This is shown by the following exhibit:

Revenue Expenditure	13.56% p.a
Capital Expenditure	32.15% p.a
Total Expenditure	16.30% p.a

Regarding the position of grants-in-aid in Bhimavaram municipality, these transfers including assigned revenues is a deciding factor in the mobilization of finances by the municipality. This implies that own sources of revenue have been playing a not-so-good role in the finances of Bhimavaram municipality. Also, a major portion of expenditure has been met by grants-in-aid in the town. For instance, nearly one third of the total expenditure has been met by the grants-in-aid. Combining grants-in-aid with assigned revenues and other transfers, nearly 57 per cent of the expenditure has been met as shown by the following Table 6.

Table 6
Proportion of Expenditure met by State Transfers in Bhimavaram Municipality

Year	*% Share*
1993-94	59.91
1994-95	59.16
1995-96	56.20
1996-97	49.67
1997-98	58.41
1998-99	69.66
1999-00	62.08
2000-01	58.40
2001-02	54.29
2002-03	55.46
2003-04	53.45
2004-05	41.93
Average	56.56

Thus, revenue transfers have been playing a crucial role in the finances of Bhimavaram Municipality.

Also, with reference to the provision of quality standard services, the municipality failed to do so, taking into account the standard norms fixed by the Zakaria Committee and NCAER. The municipality hardly meeting its expenditure obligations with the funds collected from both internal and external sources. To provide services on par with standard norms, it is beyond the capacity of the municipality. There is no hope of reaching that level in the near future. Therefore, the gap between revenue sources and expenditure obligations is fast widening leaving the municipalities in a delt-trap.

SECTION - II

A Note on Twelfth Finance Commission

The Twelfth Finance Commission (TFC) has contributed significantly towards healthy fiscal federalism[3] (M.A. OOman, May 14, 2005, p. 2022). In order to secure better horizontal equity and equitable economic growth, local bodies are yet to be put on the public finance map of India. Section 4 (iii) of the terms of reference (TOR) of the TFC stipulates that "the measures needed to augment the consolidated fund of a state to supplement the resources of the local bodies in the state on the basis of the recommendations made by the State Finance Commission". The TFC wanted not to ignore both rural and urban local bodies particularly in matters of any 'restructuring of the public finances' with reference to restoring budgetary balance, equitable growth and so on. There is an organic link between various tiers of government in the Indian fiscal federalism making an addition to Article 280 under the 73rd and 74th amendments. Broadly speaking , federal transfers through Central finance Commission (CFC) have to address two types of imbalances–firstly, vertical imbalance i.e. constitutionally built-in mismatch between division of the expenditure liabilities and revenue-raising powers of the Union and the States; and secondly, horizontal imbalance between States and sub-States jurisdictions with extreme diversities in resource endowments, economic growth and revenue capacities.

The TFC initiates fiscal decentralization which enhances political and fiscal autonomy of rural and urban local bodies. These initiatives must be matched by central equalization funds so that the gap between rich and poor areas may be done away with. On the other hand, while making transfers to these sub-state bodies, the objectives of the federal transfers must be very important. The most important rationale in the local governance is the provision of standard quality of services to the locals. In this context, the horizontal equity in between local bodies is the prime concern of the State Finance Commissions (SFCs). The CFC has also a shared responsibility in this regard. To remove these inequalities, the SFC and CFC have to work in a complementary manner to any real progress has to happen.

The other area touched by the TFC is data-consolidation pertaining to local bodies. There is indeed woeful lack of standard accounting practices and book-keeping among the local governments in the country. The Eleventh Finance Commission (EFC) attempted to publish a set of state-wise data relating to PRIs and ULBs for a period of 8 years from 1990-91 to 1997-98, but the EFC has not made use of this data. For this, the EFC has spent an amount of Rs. 200 crores for the creation of database. The TFC also made efforts for the creation of database regarding local governments. The Commission has collected the data for 5 years. But it is also a futile attempt.

Another area of concern is that though the appointment of the SFCs has been made a constitutional requirement, they have so far not been synchronized with the appointment of the CFC's Report[4] (K.P. Kannan and R. Mohan, EPW, June 5, 2004, p. 2368). It needs to be stipulated that the SFC's Report should be placed within 2 years of its establishment in the state assembly and recommendations should be acted upon within 6 months' of submission. The devolution of grants from the centre to the states in 4th and 5th years of quinquennial period should be conditional on states implementing the SFC recommendations. In Andhra Pradesh, already 2 such SFCs' work has been completed. On the Report of the 1st SFC, the government has already taken ATR. In this the important thing is 'global sharing' of state taxes.

Regarding the transfers recommended for rural and urban local bodies, the EFC has recommended grants amounting to Rs. 10,000 crores (Rs. 8,000 crores for PRIs and Rs. 2000 for ULBs) for the period 2000-05. The inter se distribution in the state of AP has been made as follows:

Basis	• *Weight*	*Proportion*
Proportion of Urban Pop.1991	40%	8.604
Proportion of Urban Area1991	10%	8.087
Distance from Highest PCI+ 0.5 S.D.	20%	8.978
Revenue Effort w.r.t. State	5%	7.538
Revenue Effort w.r.t GSDP	5%	7.319
Index of Decentralization	20%	7.219
Composite Index of State'sShare (%)	%	8.233
Total for the State (Rs. Crores)		Rs. 32.93

Source: EFC Report.

Compared to the EFC, the TFC has recommended a very generous grants-in-aid of Rs. 25,000 crores, with a break up of Rs. 20,000 crores (80%) for PRIs and Rs.5000 crores (20%) for ULBs for the period 2005-10. As against the share of Andhra Pradesh of 8.233 per cent as recommended by the EFC, the TFC a per cent of 7.480 for the ULBs during the period 2005-10. For inter se distribution of grants-in-aid, the TFC followed the criteria adopted by the EFC, namely, population, geographical area, and distance from the highest percapita income with the same weights, but dropped the decentralization index substituting it with the index of deprivation, besides modifying the revenue effort factor. The TFC's index of deprivation with 10% weightage taking into account inter-state disparities on the basis of state-wise data regarding drinking water and sanitation is to be welcomed as helping providing basic minimum amenities and the equalization of civic services. TFC has deviated from the longstanding practice of CFCs and violated its own TOR 7 and followed 2001 census for tax devolution and grants-in-aid.

AP STATE FINANCE COMMISSIONS

Though not synchronized with the establishment of CFC, the government of AP has constituted its first State Finance Commission (SFC) on June 21st, 1994 under the 74th Amendment Act, 1992. The government has to adopt the policy of devolution of funds on the basis of the recommendations of the SFC. The implementation is taken up for a period of 3 years from the date of submission of its report. The SFC submitted its report on 31st May, 1997. The period covered was 3 years from 1997-98 to 1999-2000. The recommendations of the SFC along with the Action Taken Report (ATR) were placed before the State Assembly on 25th November, 1997. Later, the government issued orders accepting some of the recommendations in February, 1999. The State government has also constituted the Second SFC on December 8th, 1998. The report was submitted to the government.

The First SFC examined various financial problems of the rural and urban local bodies in detail and made several recommendations for their up-liftment. Regarding ULBs, its recommendations are : enhancement of the per capita grant; a fixed per cent of compensation under MV tax, transfer of 95 per cent of proceeds of Profession Tax, enhancement of compensation under property tax, Octroi and entertainment taxes; a grant of Rs. 94/- crores for taking up developmental works by the municipalities and global sharing of state revenues–tax and non-tax–to the tune of 39 per cent with the local bodies for both, rural and urban local bodies every year. The SFC made 39 recommendations–financial and non-financial-concerning the ULBs. Of these recommendations, the governments accepted 11 recommendations in principle in February, 1999. Though the government accepted these recommendations, they were not implemented in total. There are marginal adjustments. These are as follows:

1. Revision once in 3 years;
2. 95% of proceeds from Profession tax to be given to municipalities;
3. Enhancement of property tax compensation by 5% and Octroi by 10%;

4. Enhancement of MV tax compensation to Rs. 20 crores initially and later a fixed per centage based on length of roads;
5. Computerization of local administration;
6. Global sharing of State' tax and non-tax revenues to the tune of 39.4% (Rs.160.32 crores per annum to municipalities); accepted norm was 60% on population, 15% area excluding slums, 5% slum area, 20% revenue effort);
7. Rs. 18/- crores p.a. for water supply schemes;
8. Sanction of Rs. 50,000 as and when a gram panchayat converted into a municipality;
9. Sanction of Pension to the non-teaching staff of the municipality;
10. Enhancement in the user charges by the municipality; and
11. No government inference in matters relating to taxation.

In total, annual additional transfers or devolution to the tune of Rs. 65/- crores are provided by the government from 1998-99 onwards based on the recommendations of the First SFC as detailed below:

Developmental Works	Rs. 31 crores
Water Supply	Rs. 18 crores
Pension Grant Enhancement	Rs. 3 crores
Enhancement of property tax, Octroi and profession tax compensations	Rs. 7 crores
Total	Rs. 65.6 crores

The following exhibit shows the actual releases by the government:

Category	1998-99 to 2000-01
Developmental Works	Rs. 97.66 Crores
Water Supply	Rs. 58.00 Crores
Property Tax Compensation	Rs. 8.61 Crores
Total	Rs. 164.00 Crores for the 4-year Period.

SECTION - III

Policy Implications

Due to close proximity to the local citizens, the municipalities are unable to tap enough revenues from their local tax handles particularly property tax. The problem valuation of properties is an age-old problem confronting the municipal officials. The problem has some how been eased out with the implementation of 'plinth area basis' of taxation segregating the properties on the basis of building material used, area in which the property is located, etc. Even this also is not in a position to maxmise the revenue from the source. There are number of local hurdles which are coming in the way of objective assessment of the properties. Recently, instead of revising the assessments for every 3 years, the government of AP has passed legislation empowering the municipalities to enhance property tax rate by 10 per cent every year. Property tax is normally base-inelastic and hence, it is better to convert into a rate-elastic tax. In respect of Bhimavaram, the municipality has successfully achieved 100 per cent mark in the tax collections. It is a welcoming feature. Like Hyderabad Municipal Corporation, self-assessment of properties just like income tax assessments is a better measure of securing enough revenue from the property tax. This self-assessment has become a grand success in Bangalore.

There is a possibility of collecting a good amount of revenue from advertisements in the town as the town is abuzz with huge advertisements. By suitable tax mechanism of assessing advertisements should be taken up. It should be insisted that all the advertisements should be compulsorily carry the license number. Here come the cable operators. The other local tax, namely, tax on vehicles and carts should be better abolished because the cost of collecting the revenue is exceeding that of actual collections in the town.

Regarding the state transfers to the municipality, apart from the plan grants, the municipality is not given the non-plan grants on a regular basis. This will disturb the budgeting process of the municipality. Of the grants-in-aid, the municipality is getting a per capita grant of Rs. 8 under the recommendations of the First SFC. Also, there is a need to raise the compensation grants to the municipality as these amounts wcie fixed a long time back. The First SFC has done a good thing of recommending a hike in the MV tax compensation. The State government has readily accepted the recommendation by releasing Rs. 20 crores for the period 1998-99 to 2000-01.

In respect of irreducible number of local functions, the municipalities must be given the right to enter into the capital market for mobilizing finances to meet increasing number of functions. This is particularly so with reference to the enhancement of municipal functions by 20 by the 74th Constitutional Amendment Act, 1992. Under this policy, many municipalities have taken up garbage recycling plants so that the question of dumping the garbage does not arise. The municipality under study must also take certain steps to start such a plant in the town, as the municipality is finding it difficult to dump the garbage. To make the town clean and neat, the municipality introduced green-box and red-box garbage collecting bins for each household in the town.

'Development from below' is the slogan once used by our first Prime Minister, Pandit Jawaharlal Nehru. There is a relation between this slogan and the municipal development. The municipalities have been increasingly depending on the state for aid to meet their irreducible number of municipal functions. The state is providing funds, besides the central funds. The EFC and TFC are also making available the funds directly to the municipalities. As a result of these things, the municipalities are subject to severe controls and in fact they have become spending departments of the State governments. In order to promote local autonomy for which they were constituted more than a Century back, mobilization of internal resources is a must. In this context, non-tax revenues come into mind There is an increasing scope for maximizing revenues from this lucrative source. Leaving alone the rigidities associated with property tax, non-tax revenues are an important source of income these days. The municipality is required to invent many new targets of tax sources such as cable operators, mobile operators, kalyan mandaps, etc. to earn huge amount of resources. These days of globalization, etc., the municipality can tap enough revenue from non-tax sources. This is a double-edged knife–one is getting increased revenues and the other is reducing the burden of taxes on the locals. The other important source of revenue from non-taxes is that of 'development impact fee' to be levied on incremental value of the properties developed. Also, the municipality under the 74th amendment is supposed to protect the environment. In this context, it can levy a pollution tax. In Bhimavaram, it is of limited use as there are little number of industries around.

The EFC and CFC have earmarked certain funds to the municipalities for the building up of database for their ultimate development. In this context, the municipality must completely computerize its administration and data. It is better to open a web-page for its world–wide information. This will pave the way for a real research into the subject and thereby all round development can be initiated.

These days of privatization, municipality must invent ways and means of privatizing certain services like water supply distribution, sewerage, garbage, road surfacing, etc. This means that some of its services can be contracted out for their efficient delivery.

Also, the municipality should ensure community participation in all its activities, so that the municipality can make the people to understand its real attitude. In this context, APUSP is the best example. In this programme, the civic amenities to be taken may be judged in a people-participatory mechanism.

Last but not the least, the State's attitude towards the all round health of the municipality should be changed. Now, the state has been showing a sense of apathy towards improving the financial health of the municipality. It does not like the municipality to get their real share of power. Even then, it provides an eye-wash to the decisions taken at the higher level, i.e. Centre. Thus, the state is coming in the way of complete amelioration of municipalities in particular and local bodies in general. To change this attitude and also to provide enough financial powers and all that, the Centre should immediately amend the constitution only to provide a "Local List" along side the Union List and State List. This paves the way for their real empowerment.

CONCLUSION

The municipal finance is an abstract subject for which a concrete solution is often considered as a mounting task. Bhimavaram municipality is considered to be a middle income municipality in the light of its mobilization of resources both from its internal and external sources. The municipality is increasingly depending on external sources like assigned revenues and grants-in-aid. There is an increasing chance of mobilizing non-tax revenues in the municipality. Most of its expenditure is on the salary bill, leave alone the developmental activity. Somehow, it is managing both ends meet. To relieve some of its increasing functions, the municipality can think of privatizing some of its services. Also, the must be allowed to go into the capital market for mobilizing funds. In this context, municipal bond banking must be taken up to meet its increased financial requirements. Therefore, to protect its real autonomy, the municipality must look within but not without.

REFERENCES

K.P. Kannan, and R. Mohan (2004), "Twelfth Finance Commission–View from Kerala", EPW, June, 5, p. 2361.

V.N. Alok (2004), "Assessment of State Finance Commissions in Improving the Fiscal Health of Urban Local Bodies", Nagarlok, October-December, p. 28.

EPW (2005), "Twelfth Finance Commission, A Symposium", July 30-August 5.

C. Rangarajan (2004), "Issues before Twelfth Finance Commission,", EPW, June 26, p. 2707.

M.Govinda Rao (2002), "State Finances in India, Issues and Challenges", EPW, August 3-9, p. 3261.

V. Gnaneswar (2005), Municipal Finances in Andhra Pradesh, Nagarlok, June-August.

26

TRENDS IN EXPENDITURE AND INCOME PATTERNS IN ANDHRA PRADESH

N.B. Reddy & D. Pulla Rao

INTRODUCTION

The survival of all representative democracies depend much upon their quality expenditure to provide public goods and services to meet the majority's choice. Since Independence most of the Federal States in India are involved in the reconstruction and developmental activities under the guidance of the Planning Commission of India. But, in later periods, there has been a shift from 'mass benefit approach' to 'individual benefit approach', mainly because of emergence of various regional parties, leading to increasing state expenditure. To meet these expenditures, every state must depend upon central finances apart from generating its own tax revenues. The 12th Finance Commission has recommended that the total transfer to the states be limited to 38 per cent, which is not sufficient.

There are three ways in which the transfer of resources takes place from Centre to States. They are: (1) Statutory Transfers through Finance Commission (2) Plan Transfers by Planning Commission under a set of clearly laid out rules and (3) Discretionary Transfers for Centrally Sponsored Schemes and for different non-plan proposals by various Union Ministries, especially the Ministry of Finance.

Since the Fourth Five Year Plan period Discretionary Transfers have been on the decline due to absence of one single party rule both at Centre and state, which is a bygone era. The

Planning Commission is in Competition has a complementary role with the Finance Commission in this respect. Against these, a financial relation between the Centre and State Governments, an attempt is made here to study the case of Andhra Pradesh State. Since its formation in 1956 it has-been under the rule of two major parties, either Congress or Telugu Desam.

OBJECTIVES

The following are the objectives of the Study:

1. To analyse the growth of fiscal and revenue deficits over the period 1984-2004.
2. To analyse the flows of capital and revenue expenditure, and
3. To examine the patterns of revenue and capital receipts.

METHODOLOGY

To examine the Andhra Pradesh State's finances, a 20-year period 1984-85 to 2003-2004-was considered. From the successive budgets, of the Government of Andhra Pradesh, data relating to Expenditure and Receipts on Agriculture, Irrigation and Police were collected. Since A.P. Economy is much dependent upon Agriculture, the Capital and Revenue Expenditure, Receipts of Agriculture was considered. Moreover, the expenditure on Police was collected to elicit the State's expenditure of law and order problems. For technical analysis compound growth rates were calculated wherever necessary. The data were analysed in two ways i.e. for the total selected period 1984-1985 to 2003-04 and 1990-91 to 2003-2004. During this period a regional party ruled A. P. State.

AP FINANCES

In India, states do not have any constitutional obligations to bring down the deficits within a given time interval. The budget deficit adjustments may be possible either by increasing its revenues or reduction in its revenue expenditure or both. But, the existing committed expenditure incurred by the State and to meet the expenditure in providing social goods and services which have a prime importance due to market failure lead to financial crisis of any State Government. Moreover, the Indian Constitution has entrusted the states with functions, both expensive and expansive, such as agriculture, Irrigation, Roads and Buildings, Medical and Health, Law and Order etc, together with some other revenue powers. This tendency has been continued since the 1935 Act.

FISCAL AND REVENUE DEFICITS

The revenue and expenditure policies of the successive Governments in the State up to 1982-83 were surplus on Revenue Account and since then Fiscal and Revenue deficits followed. The change in Government in the State after 1984-85 paid more attention to social sector and it did not make any provisions to minimise the fiscal and revenue deficits. It is revealed from Table 1 that during 1984-85 and 2003-04, the compound growth rate of Gross Fiscal Deficit was 15.90 per cent and this was prominent during 1990-1991 and 2003-2004 with a registered rise of 16.69 per cent. The Revenue Deficit for the same periods was found to be 23.82 and 25.28 per cent.

Table 1
Compound Growth Rates of Allocations In A.P. Budget From 1984-85 to 2003-04

Years	*Gross Fiscal*	*Revenue Deficit*	*Primary Deficit*	*Revenue Receipts*	*Capital Receipts*	*Revenue Expenditure*	*Capital Expenditure*
1984-1985 to 2003-2004	15.90	23.82	9.17	13.02	16.20	13.69	14.21
1990-1991 to 2003-2004	16.69	25.28	8.41	12.67	16.87	13.55	14.75

Source: R.B.I. State Finances, 'A study of Budgets', 2003-2004 and other relevant Years.

REVENUE AND CAPITAL EXPENDITURE

The growth of Revenue Expenditure was recorded at 13.69 per cent during 1984-85 and 2003-04 and it declined between 1990-91 and 2003-2004. On the other hand, the Capital Expenditure during the above period was recorded at 14.21 per cent and

14.75 per cent. The Revenue Receipts for the period (1984-85 to 2003-04) registered a compound growth rate of 13.02 per cent and slowly declined during 1990-91 and 2003-04. The Capital Receipts registered a growth rate of 16.20 per cent and was increased to 16.87 per cent by the terminal period.

STATE'S OWN AND SHARED REVENUES

After 1970s, the ruling regional parties in different states showed much concern other social sector to strengthen their political position. As a result, the allocation of resources was on the basis of 'individual benefit approach' instead of 'mass benefit approach'. This tendency was also started in the State since 1984-85 onwards. As a result, the State's committed expenditure has increased. The State's finances are reviewed (Table 2). The main sources of finances for the State are (1) Own Tax Revenues (2) Own Non Tax Revenues (3) Share in Central Taxes (4) Grants in aid from the Centre, and (5) Loans. It is revealed from the data that during the period 1984-85 and 2003-04 the compound growth rate of Own Tax Revenues was at 13.48 per cent and this was 14.33 per cent for the period 1990-91 and 2003-2004. The Non Tax Revenues grew of 12.15 per cent and 9.38 per cent respectively. Grants in aid from the Centre during 1984-85 and 2003-2004 registered a growth rate of 13.45 per cent and it was 12.18 per cent during 1990–1991 and 2003-2004. Loans from the Centre during 1984-85 and 2003-2004 registered at growth rate of 13.11 and it was 11.30 during 1990-91 and 2003-2004. The foregoing analysis reveals that except Own Tax Revenues the other revenue and loan resources declined during the period 1990-91 AND 2003-2004, which lead to severe shortage of revenues to the State.

INVESTMENTS AND REVENUES FROM IRRIGATION, AGRICULTURE AND POLICE

It was felt necessary to review the expenditure on Agriculture and Irrigation, since there two sectors are the backbone of the A.P. Economy. Recent literature on Agricultural productivity and production recorded a stagnation and formers suicides due to crop failures. It further prompted to analyse State's, efforts on Agricultural development. The increasing naxalite activities and law and order problem in the State, again, prompted to analyse the State's expenditure on police. Data relating to these aspects are presented in Table 3.

Table 2
Compound Growth Rates of Allocations in A.P. Budget From 1984-85 to 2003-04

Years	*Own tax Revenue*	*Own Non-tax Revenue*	*Share in Central Taxes*	*Grants from the Centre*	*Loans from the Centre*	*Interest pay-ments*
1984-1985 and 2003-2004	13.48	12.15	11.78	13.45	13.11	19.50
1990-1991 and and 2003 -2004	14.33	11.06	9.38	12.18	11.30	19.05

Source: R.B.I. State Finances, 'A study of Budgets', 2003-2004 and other relevant Years.

Table 3
Compuund Growth Rates of Expenditure 1990-91 to 2003-2004 in Andhra Pradesh

Sector	*Capital Expenditure (%)*	*Revenue Expenditure (%)*
Agriculture		
A. Crop Husbandry	- 4. 64	8.39
B. Agriculture research and education		10.92
Irrigation		
A. Major and medium	11.08	- 1.04
B. Minor irrigation		-5.45
Police		12.10

Source: R.B.I. State Finances, 'A study of Budgets', 2003-2004 and other relevant Years.

The Capital Expenditure on crop husbandry during 1990-91 and 2003-2004 showed a negative growth rate of 4.64 per cent and the interest on Agricultural Research and Extension Education were found to be nil. The compound growth rates for the same period for these sub-sectors are 8.39 and 10.92 per cent respectively. The compound growth rate of Capital Investment on major and medium irrigation schemes was 11.08

per cent for the period 1990-91 to 2003-04. The Revenue Expenditure on irrigation schemes, all major, medium and minor, recorded negative growth rates of 1.04 per cent and 5.45 per cent. On police the growth rate of revenue expenditure recorded at 12.10 per cent.

REVENUE RECEIPTS FROM AGRICULTURE AND IRRIGATION

The growth of Direct Revenue from Agriculture and Irrigation were presented in Table 4. The compound growth rate of revenues from Crop Husbandry and Land Revenue during 1990-91 and 2003-2004 are 14.27 and 6.07 per cent respectively. There was a negative growth of Receipts from Major, Medium and Minor Irrigation for the above period. It was further revealed from Land Revenue, data that there was no stability in Land Revenue collection and it fluctuated between 17.82 and 39.60 per cent during 1984-2005 and 2003 - 2004.

Table 4
Compound Growth Rates of Revenue Receipts From Agriculture, Irrigation 1990-91 to 2003-2004

Sl.No.	*Item*	*Growth Rate %*
1.	Crop Husbandry	14.27
2.	Land Revenue	6.07
3.	Major and Medium Irrigation	-18.40
4.	Minor Irrigation	-10.63

Source: R.B.I. State Finances, 'A study of Budgets', 2003-2004 and other relevant Years.

The State's Public Debt was also analysed. The compound growth rate of interest payment during 1984-85 and 2003-2004 was 19.50 per cent was and this 19.05 per cent during 1990-91 and 2003-04. In absolute terms, the State's debt in 1983-85 was reported as Rs.2, 533 crores and this has increased to Rs.58, 770 crores by 2003-2004. Thus, a phenomenal growth of Public Debt in the State could be observed since 1984-85 and it reflects in filling Fiscal Deficit of the State.

SUMMARY AND CONCLUSIONS

The foregoing analysis reveals that State's share in Central Taxes and Grants-in-Aid have declined. The burden of Public Debt has increased. In absolute terms for the year 2003-2004 the State's Public Debt was about Rs. 58,770 Crores. Though Agriculture and Irrigation are the backbone of the State's economy, the investments on these sectors have been neglected. Revenue collection from Irrigation sector showed a negative growth rate. On the other hand, the compound growth rate of Fiscal and Revenue Deficits have been more alarming. In these circumstances, the ruling party should follow strict financial discipline, mainly in reducing the Revenue Deficit. Investment on Agriculture, Irrigation, Education, Health and the like should not be neglected. Expenditure on social sector should reach the real target groups. These expenditures should be positive and result – oriented in the long run. To minimize the expenditure on police, in the name of law and order, to provide protection to politicians and elected representatives, the high commands of different political parties and the National Election Commission and various State Election Commissions should hereafter nominate and enroll only those who are popular, well–educated and are endowed with good conduct and character. The social programmes like Housing, Land redistribution, etc., must be cautiously implemented as land is scarce and limited in supply and it is nowadays becoming prohibitively costly even for acquisition. In this respect strict population control measures must be followed. Otherwise it will be a perennial problem to any ruling party for providing subsidies and to provide Housing. Health and Education facilities to the masses. Thus, in future the Andhra Pradesh State Government must improve its expenditure pattern on quality lines. Vote bank and/or populist programmes should not be encouraged hereafter. This expenditure policy of any state government should reflect in controlling growth of population, increase in per capita incomes of weaker sections and increase the Foreign Direct Investment in the State.

REFERENCES

RBI State Finances 'A study of Budgets' 2003-2004 and other relevant years.

Fiscal Reforms and Finances of Government of Andhra Pradesh by R.Sudarsana Rao, Working Paper 33, 2005, Published by National Institute of Public Finance and Policy, New Delhi.

Government of India Economic Surveys–1990-1991 to 2004-05.

Andhra Pradesh Statistical Abstract–1983-84 to 2004-2005.

27

FISCAL MANAGEMENT IN ANDHRA PRADESH–AN ANALYSIS

D. Atchyutam

SECTION I : INTRODUCTION

The state of Andhra Pradesh is formed by joining three different regions namely Costal Andhra, Telangana and Rayalaseema. Both intra and inter regional variations relating to cultural, social, economic and institutional aspects do exist as we found glaring disparities between South and North Costal Andhra districts as well as between South and North Telangana districts. Andhra Pradesh with a geographical area of 274.40 lakh hectares and with population of 7.57 crores (as per 2001census) is the fifth largest state in the country (both in area and population). The density of population in the state was 275 persons per square kilometer and thus less than the All India density of 324 persons per square kilometer. As per 2001 census, the literacy rate of the state is 61 per cent with male and female literacy rates at 71 per cent and 51 per cent respectively. The GDP of the state at constant prices (1993-94) for the year 2004-05 stood at Rs.1,04,884 crores while per capita income (at constant prices) stood at Rs 11,722.Economic development is concerned more or less the state Andhra Pradesh is following the national trends as the share of agricultural sector diminished, while that of service sector increased with industry's share remaining constant.

In the case of agricultural output in 2000-01, the second biggest producer of cotton 17 per cent cashew nut 19 per cent and the third biggest producer of rice, sunflower, onion, tobacco.

Andhra pradesh is endowed with varied agro-climate conditions for a variety of horticulture crops like fruits, take, spices timber crops and plantation crops. An area of about 13.35 lakh hectares is production, the state is the biggest producer of groundnut in the country with 33 per cent of India's under various horticulture crops with an estimated production of 70.42 lakh metric tones. Andhra Pradesh is recognized as the best potential state and pioneer in oil palm cultivation that accounts for about 60 per cent of the country's area under oil palm and first in area and production. In Andhra Pradesh still nearly 60 per cent of the employment is originating from the agricultural sector. Further the state ranks second in inland fisheries, first in costal aquaculture and seventh in marine fish production in the country. It is a potential income generation sector with 21.5 lakh persons employed in different activities. The state contributes about Rs. 1300 crores of marine product exports sharing more than 30 per cent of value of exports from the country.

The state has the largest number of state level public enterprises in the country having 128 in number with the largest investment of about Rs. 488 billions. The state has a balanced mix of large, medium and small industries producing a wide variety of products. According to annual survey of industries by CSO. The state contributes about 5.7 per cent of the manufacturing value added of industries in the country. According to vision 2020 document of Andhra Pradesh, the industrial sector will account for 21 per cent of its economy and will need to provide 43 per cent of new jobs in the state.

SECTION II - MACRO ECONOMIC PERFORMANCE OF ANDHRA PRADESH

The Gross State Domestic Product (GSDP) of Andhra Pradesh is found to increase at an annual growth rate of 5.5 per cent during the 1980's (1980-81 to 1990-91 i.e., pre reform period) and this rate is seem to be just marginally higher(0.13 per cent point) than that compared to All India growth rate of 5.37 per cent. However, during the period 1993-94 to 2000-05 (post reform period) the growth rate of GSDP of Andhra Pradesh recorded 5.43 per cent, while that of all India growth registered 5.79 per cent. Thus growth rate of GSDP of Andhra Pradesh during second period (1993-94 to 2004-05 i.e., post reform period) witnessed a decline by 0.07 per cent point compared to first period and 0.36 per cent point compared to All India growth rate. Analysis of per capita GSDP of Andhra Pradesh implies an annual growth rate of 3.33 per cent and 4.25 per cent respectively for two periods against All India growth rates of 3.24 per cent and 4.09 per cent respectively for the said periods. Thus the state per capita income seems to be improved during the second period compared to first period by 0.92 per cent while during the same time, All India per capita income observed to be improved by 0.85 per cent. Thus in terms of per capita income, Andhra Pradesh is observed to be improved by 0.85 per cent. Thus in terms of per capita income, Andhra Pradesh is observed to improve not only during the second period but also compared to All India. in terms of Performance of Andhra Pradesh during 1980's in comparison with other states in terms of growth rates of GSDP implies fourth rank to Andhra Pradesh next only to Rajasthan, Haryana and Maharastra. However, the rank has come down to nine during the second period. Performance of Andhra Pradesh in terms of growth rate of per capita GSDP reveals Fifth and Ninth ranks respectively during the two periods. Thus both in terms of growth rate of GSDP and per capita GSDP the performance of the state experienced a deceleration in its rank compared to the performance of other states.

Analyses of sectoral growth rates of GSDP (at constant prices) of Andhra Pradesh during the first period implies 2.21, 7.36 and 7.69 per cent respectively for agriculture, industry and services. During the second plan period (1993-94 to 2001-02) the respective growth rates of Andhra Pradesh are registered as 2.47, 6.20 and 6.48 per cent respectively for the three sectors. At the same time sectoral growth rates of GDP(at constant prices) for All India during the first period were recorded as 3.12, 6.6 and 6.48 per cent respectively for agriculture, industry and service sector and for the second period (1993-94 to 2001-

02) those rates were registered as 2.73, 6.25 and 8.13 per cent respectively for the three sectors. Thus it is clear that during the first period though the agricultural growth rate was low compared to All India, yet the growth rates of industry and services are seen to be higher than that of All India growth rates. However, it is interesting to note that during the second period the growth rates in respect of all three sectors of Andhra Pradesh were below those of All India growth rates. Comparisons of sectorial growth rates among states also reveal that Andhra Pradesh's rank has come down from fifth to ninth in respect of industry and that of services also come down from second to twelfth.

Further, growth rate of GSDP of Andhra Pradesh for manufacturing sector is noticed to decline from 8.39 per cent to 6.2 per cent during the two periods, while the All India GDP for manufacturing sector during the two periods increased from 6.95 per cent to 6.47 per cent. Similarly during the two periods, for Andhra Pradesh the growth rate of trade, hotels and restaurants drastically declined from 8.66 per cent 5.51 per cent, while the same growth rate for All India increased from 5.89 per cent to 8.11 per cent. Further, the growth rate of GSDP of Andhra Pradesh for public services also marginally declined from 7.68 per cent to 7.4 per cent while that of All India improved from 7.4 per cent to 8.1 per cent. However, only in respect of transport and communications a significant increase in the growth rate of Andhra Pradesh from 5.16 per cent to 7.86 per cent was noticed, while a reserve trend i.e., a drastic decline from 7.08 per cent to 5.40 per cent was experienced by All India transport and communications sector.

In fact Andhra Pradesh initiated economic reforms along with the Indian economy and become popular as reforming state in all respects compared to other states of the nation. However, it is rather interesting to note that despite rigorous exercise of economic reforms and the macro economic performance is not satisfactory and on the other hand there was deterioration in the growth rates.

SECTION III-FISCAL PERFORMANCE OF ANDHRA PRADESH

In order to analyse the fiscal performance of the state Andhra Pradesh it is essential to examine the trends in revenue and expenditure.

Table 1 It is clear that revenue receipts of Andhra Pradesh increased from Rs. 488.73 crores in 1983-84 to Rs. 1090.24 crores in 1988-89 it shoes the compound growth rate of 16 per cent. The analysis of revenue expenditure reveals that it has increased from Rs. 1310.61 crores in 1989-90 to Rs. 3135.49 crores in 1994-95 that is the compound growth rate is recorded 18.92 per cent. The non-development expenditure increased, the growth rate of 58.5 per cent in 1995-96 to 70.3 per cent in 2003-04. Further, not only the non development expenditure was growing at higher compared to development expenditure, but at the same time the growth in development expenditure is declined a little. This sort of expenditure pattern is not at all useful and at the same time poses difficulties to the economy.

Table 1
Growth rates of Revenue Receipts, Expenditure

	1983-84 to 1988-89	*1989-90 to 1994-95*	*1995-96 to 2001- 02*	*1995-96 to 2003- 04*
Revenue Receipts	16.24	14.72	27.98	20.32
Revenue Expenditure	15.27	14.92	14.21	13.70
Dep. Expenditure	15.02	13.32	12.05	11.53
Non. Dev. Expenditure	16.00	18.92	18.31	17.62

Source: Calculated based on data drawn from Andhra Pradesh Statistical Abstracts

Table 2 presents revenue receipts and expenditure of Andhra Pradesh percentage of GSDP over the period and it is clear that except in 1980-81, revenue receipts fall short of revenue expenditure in all cross section years . Only in early 1980's revenue receipts are observed to be higher than that of expenditure. The reason is obliviously due to decline in the state own receipts as percentage of GSDP, besides decline in state own taxes and even steady decline in state own non-taxes. At the same grants and other transfers from center to the state are also observed to decline. Due to all these reasons the revenue deficit of the state is increased from 1980's on wards and particularly deteriorted from 1990's onwards and consequently the state has been in debt trap.

Table 2
Revenue Receipts and Expenditure of Andhra Pradesh
(Per centages)

	1980-81	*1985-86*	*1990-91*	*1995-96*	*2000-01*	*2004-05*
State Own Taxes	7.11	9.42	7.94	5.16	7.53	8.76
State Own Non-Taxes	2.72	2.56	2.33	2.01	1.96	2.15
State Own Receipts	9.83	11.98	10.27	7.17	9.49	10.85
Transfers from Center	5.61	6.18	5.77	5.20	4.40	5.23
Total Revenue Receipts	15.44	18.17	16.04	12.37	13.9	16.07
Revenue Expenditure	14.17	18.21	16.51	13.29	16.46	16.81
Capital Expenditure	3.03	2.48	1.39	3.03	1.94	2.95
Total Expenditure	17.20	20.69	17.90	16.32	19 11	19.76

Source: Calculated based on data drawn from Andhra Pradesh Abstract.

The Andhra Pradesh Government's policy of expenditure during the 1960's and 1970's was such as to develop the infrastructure relating to irrigation, power, transport etc. According these sectors used to drawn more than 60 per cent of plan expenditure. The seventh plan document is also stressed the need for the more allocation to social sector development and accordingly let us examine the expenditure pattern of Andhra Pradesh.

Table 3 Presents information about expenditure on education, health and family welfare, water supply and sanitation as percentage of GSDP over the period. It is clear that expenditure on education as percentage of GSDP declined since mid 1980'S and particularly declined to below 3 per cent of GSDP. Similarly expenditure on health and family welfare as percentage GSDP declined from 1990-91 and there after never touched even 1 per cent of GSDP. Further expenditure on water supply and sanitation as percentage of GSDP also observed to decline since mid eightites. Thus social sector expenditure of the state over the period is also not satisfactory as these overheads are important and reflects the quality of life. However, most of the government expenditure is incurring to meet the wages and salaries of employees and interest payments.

Table 3
Expenditure on Social Sector Overhead as percentage of GSDP

	1980-81	1985-86	1990-91	1995-96	2000-01	2004-05
Education	2.82	3.53	3.05	2.16	2.69	2.77
Health & Family Welfare	1.10	1.24	0.99	0.76	0.92	0.82
Water Supply & Sanitation	0.40	0.54	0.31	0.31	0.30	0.10

Source: Calculated based on data drawn from Andhra Pradesh Statistical Abstracts

Table 4 presents information about debt. It is clear that the debt burden of the state since its formation in 1956 to 1990 was only Rs. 5867 crores, while it has reached Rs. 29114 crores by 1999-00. Thus with in a period of 10 years the debt was increased by about 5 times.

Further it is clear that the share of central loans the total debt is drastically reduced from about 64 per cent to 39 per cent while the share of provedent Fund increased from about 10 per cent to 22 per cent during the study period. However, the share of debt raised by the state from the capital market is seemed to be increased from 22 per cent to 27 per cent only. At the same time the share of other borrowings of the state observed to be around 2.5 per cent during the period 1989 to 1996 increased, the share increased to 5 per cent during 1996 to 1999 and ultimately reached 11 per cent by 2003-04. Thus, though the share of central loans observed to decline at it is observed a major source of state debt. Thus, the debt burden and debt servicing is observed to increase year after year and hence the state government initiated fiscal reforms to tone up the fiscal discipline.

Apart from the above analysis, it was already mentioned that a major portion of the budget is going in favor of salaries, interest payments and subsidies. In view of all these the Andhra Pradesh government wants to tone up the fiscal discipline through implementing some fiscal reforms like to increase the irrigation rates, to promote the self-help groups through DWCRA schemes, etc.

Table 4
Debt-Burden of Andhra Pradesh

Year	*Loans from Centre*	*Loans from Market*	*Provident Fund*	*Others*	*Total*
1989-90	3774 (64.3)	1357 (23.1)	594 (10.2)	142 (2.4)	5867
1990-91	4368 (64.0)	1596 (23.4)	690 (10.1)	161 (2.4)	6815
1991-92	5056 (63.3)	1935 (24.2)	819 (10.3)	182 (2.2)	7992
1992-93	5852 (64.3)	2273 (24.5)	957 (10.3)	204 (2.2)	9286 (100)
1993-94	7094 (64.1)	2609 (23.6)	1109 (10.0)	253 (2.3)	11065 (100)
1994-95	8342 (64.1)	3046 (23.4)	1334 (10.3)	283 (2.2)	3005 (100)
1995-96	9675 (63.8)	3916 (23.2)	1600 (10.6)	373 (2.4)	15614 (100)
1996-97	10484 (60.9)	4045 (23.5)	1843 (10.7)	848 (5.2)	17220 (100)
1997-98	12059 (60.4)	4694 (23.5)	2185 (10.9)	1033 (5.2)	19971 (100)
1998-99	13941 (58.3)	6038 (25.3)	2517 (10.5)	1408 (5.9)	23904 (100)
1999-00	15415 (52.9)	7239 (24.9)	4152 (14.3)	2308 (7.9)	29114 (100)
2000-01	16510 (46.3)	9138 (25.6)	6365 (17.9)	3639 (10.2)	35652 (100)
2001-02	19033 (44.8)	11039 (26.0)	7830 (18.4)	4590 (10.8)	42492 (100)
2002-03	20080 (40.2)	13887 (27.8)	10090 (20.2)	5887 (11.8)	49944 (100)
2003-04	22301 (39.0)	15566 (27.3)	12918 (22.6)	6356 (11.1)	57141 (100)

Source: Memorandum submitted to Twelfth Finance Commission.

The annual budget of Andhra Pradesh 2006-07 was presented by the Finance Minister on 20th Feb. 2006 and deficit is accounted to the tune of Rs. 996 crores. Further, it is pertinent to note that two-thirds of budget share has taken away by non plan expenditure. As per the budget provisions, an allocation of Rs. 10,000 crores for irrigation, which is a record allocation and was so far not allocated by any state Government in the country. The budget has given topmost priority for the cause of farmers as irrigation, agriculture and power account for a lion's share (61 per cent) of Rs. 19,551.9 crores in budget outlay.

Thus the state is progressing in the reform path and one has to wait for some time to assess the impact of such reforms. However, with the change of the government in the state during

2004, the priorities are changed and some of the decisions may reverse be and new decisions were taken. Some of these are free power supply to the farmers, Jalayagnam Programme, Indiramma Programme (house sites for weaker sections) etc. The welcome feature is, the present Government is planning to take up all these programmes ambitiously and one has to wait for successful completion of those programmes which will do at least some good for the cause of common man.

REFERENCES

Mahendra Dev, A. and Ravi, C. (2003), "Macro Economic Scene: Performance and Policies", Economic and Political Weekly, Vol. 38, No. 12 & 13, March, pp. 1143-1157.

J. Siva Ram (2003), "Economic Development of Andhra Pradesh: An Over View Southrn Economist, Vol. 42, No. 14, November pp. 13-14.

Economic Survey (2000-01), Government of Andhra Pradesh, Hyderabad.

Ibid. p. 3.

Vision 2020 Draft Document, Government of Andhra Pradesh . Hyderabad, p. 231.

28

DEBT MANAGEMENT SCENARIO IN ANDHRA PRADESH

Surya Rao Kappagantula

The purpose of the paper is to examine the debt–management scenario in Andhra Pradesh in the light of Twelfth Finance Commission's Recommendations. In fact AP initiated economic reforms along with the Indian economy and became popular as reforming state in all respects compared to other states of the nation. However, it is rather interesting to note that despite rigorous exercise of economic reforms and radical decisions, the debt burden is seen to increase substantially over the period. Public debt of Andhra Pradesh since its formation in 1956 to 1991 was only Rs. 6815 crores, while it has reached Rs. 66203 crores by 2004-05. Thus with in a period of 15 years particularly during the reform period the debt burden was increased by about 10 times. Further, public debt of state increased at an average annual growth rate of 17.71 per cent during the period 1990-91 to 2004-05. Against this backdrop, an attempt is made to examine (1) The sources of revenue receipts and trends in revenue receipts (2) The components of expenditure and trends in expenditure (3) The trends in debt and its impact on economic development.

AP ECONOMY

Andhra Pradesh with a geographical area of 274.40 lakh hectares and with a population of 7.57 crores (as per 2001 census) is the fifth largest state in the country (both in area and population). The density of population in the state was 275 persons per square kilometer and thus less than the All India density of 324 persons per square kilometer. As per 2001 census, the literacy rate of the state is 61 per cent with male and female literacy rates at 71 per cent and 51 per cent respectively. The GDP of the state at constant prices (1993-94) for the year 2004-05 stood at Rs. 1,04,884 crores while per capita income (at constant prices) stood at Rs. 11,722. Economic development is concerned more or less the state AP is following the national trends as the share of agriculture sector diminished, while that of service sector increased with industry's share reaming constant. On the agricultural front, the state is the biggest producer of groundnut in the country with 33 per cent of India's output in 2000-01, the second biggest producer of cotton (17 per cent) and cashew nut (19 per cent) and the third biggest producer of rice, sunflower onion, tobacco. AP is endowed with varied agro-climate conditions for a variety of horticulture crops like fruits, vegetables, spices, tuber crops and plantation crops. An area of about 13.35 lakh hectares is under various horticulture crops with an estimated production of 70.42 lakh metric tones. AP is recognized as the best potential state and pioneer in oil palm cultivation that accounts for about 60 per cent of the country's area under oil palm and first in area and production[1]. In AP still nearly 60 per cent of the employment is originating from the agricultural sector. Further, the state ranks second in inland fisheries, first in costal aquaculture and seventh in marine fish production in the country. It is a potential income generation sector with 21.5 lakh persons employed in different activities. The state contributes about Rs. 1300 crores of marine product exports sharing more than 30 per cent of value of exports from the country[2].

The state has the largest number of state level public enterprises in the country having 128 in number with the largest investment of about Rs. 488 billions. The state has a balanced mix of large, medium and small industries producing a wide variety of products. According to annual survey of industries by CSO, the state contributes about 5.7 per cent of the manufacturing value added of industries in the country.

MACRO ECONOMIC VARIABLES–AP

The Gross State Domestic Product (GSDP) of AP (at constant prices) is found to increase at an annual growth rate of 5.43 per cent during the period 1993-94 to 2004-05, while growth rate of GDP of all India during the same period registered 5.79 per cent. Thus growth rate of GSDP of AP witnessed a decline by 0.36 per cent point compared to All India growth rate. Analysis of per capita GSDP of AP implies an annual growth rate of 4.25 per cent against All India per capita GDP growth rate of 4.09 per cent for the said period. Thus in terms of per capita income, AP is observed to experience higher growth rate compared to All India. However, performance of AP during 1993-94 to 2004-05 in comparison with other states in terms of growth rates of GSDP and per capita GSDP implies Ninth rank to AP. Thus both in terms of growth rate of GSDP and per capita GSDP the performance of the state experienced a deceleration in its rank compared to the performance of other states. Analysis of sectoral growth rates of GSDP (at constant prices) of AP during the period 1993-94 to 2004-05 implies 2.47, 6.20 and 6.48 per cent respectively for agriculture, industry and services. At the same time sectoral growth rates of GDP (at constant prices) for All India during the period were recorded as 2.73, 6.25 and 8.13 per cent respectively for the three sectors. However, it is interesting to note that during the period the growth rates in respect of all three sectors of AP were below those of All India growth rates. Comparisons of sectoral growth rates among states also reveal that AP's rank has come down from fifth to ninth in respect of industry and that of services also crawl down from second to twelfth. Further, growth rate of GSDP of AP for manufacturing sector noticed to be 6.2 per cent during the period, while the All India GDP for manufacturing sector during the period registered 6.47 per cent. Similarly, for AP the growth rate of trade, hotels and restaurants observed to be 5.15 per cent, while the same growth rate for All India increased noticed to be 8.11 per cent. Further, the growth rate of GSDP of AP for public services found to be 7.4 per cent while that of All India seen to be 8.1 per cent. However, only in respect of transport and communications AP experienced significant growth rate of 7.86 per cent compared to All India growth rate of 5.40 per cent by transport and communicates sector.

ANALYSIS OF REVENUE AND EXPENDITURE

In order to analyse public debt, it is essential to examine the trends in revenue and expenditure. Table 1 presents information about growth rates of revenue receipts, revenue expenditure etc. Revenue receipts of the state AP increased from Rs. 1466.29 crores in 1981-82 to Rs. 5347.18 crores by 1990-91 and thus registered an annual compound growth rate of 13.81 per cent. Further, the revenue receipts, which were at Rs. 8250.45 crores by 1993-94 increased to Rs. 31995 crores by 2004-05 and thus accounted for an annual compound growth rate 11.95 per cent. Thus the growth of revenue receipts observed to be declined during second period compared to first period.

Table 1
Growth rates of Revenue Receipts, Expenditure

	1981-82 to 1990-91	*1993-94 to 2004-05*	*Decrease in growth rate between the two periods*
Revenue Receipts	13.81	11.95	1.86
Revenue Expenditure	14.78	12.64	2.14
Dev. Expenditure	14.36	11.56	2.8
Non-Dev. Expenditure	15.56	15.22	0.34

Source: Calculated based on data drawn from Andhra Pradesh Statistical Abstracts.

Analysis of revenue expenditure reveals that it has increased from Rs. 1386.29 crores in 1981-82 to Rs. 5504.78 crores by 1993-94 and thus implied an annual compound growth rate of 14.78 per cent. Further, the revenue expenditure reached Rs. 33455 crores by 2004-05 from Rs. 8018.17 crores in 1993-94 and hence recorded an annual compound growth rate of 12.64 per cent. The analysis clearly indicates that between the two periods the growth in revenue receipts declined by 1.86 per cent, while the growth in revenue expenditure too declined by 2.14 per cent indicating a possibility of revenue deficits in future also. Further, not only the non–development expenditure is growing at a higher rate compared to development expenditure but at the same time growth in development expenditure between two periods declined by 2.80 per cent, while that of non-development expenditure declined by only 0.58 per cent. This sort of expenditure pattern is not at all desirable and at the same time poses difficulties to the economy.

Table 2
Total Revenue and Sources of Revenue – AP

(Rs. Crores)

Year	*State Own Tax Revenue*	*State Own Non-Tax Revenue*	*Transfers from Center*	*Total Revenue*
1990-91	2647 (49.50)	777 (14.53)	1923 (35.97)	5347 (100)
1991-92	3055 (48.63)	981 (15.62)	2246 (35.75)	6282 (100)
1992-93	3448 (49.60)	965 (13.88)	2540 (36.52)	6953 (100)
1993-94	3833 (46.46)	1351 (16.38)	3066 (37.16)	8250 (100)
1994-95	4144 (48.28)	1355 (15.79)	3085 (35.93)	8584 (100)
1995-96	4121 (36.30)	1605 (14.14)	5626 (49.56)	11352 (100)
1996-97	4883 (39.04)	1625 (12.99)	5999 (47.96)	12507 (100)
1997-98	7113 (44.96)	1788 (11.30)	6921 (43.74)	15822 (100)
1998-99	7961 (47.89)	1847 (11.11)	6817 (41.00)	16625 (100)
1999-00	9008 (45.06)	2442 (12.21)	8543 (42.73)	19993 (100)
2000-01	10551 (45.57)	2743 (11.85)	9857 (42.58)	23151 (100)
2001-02	11551 (43.25)	2918 (10.93)	12239 (45.82)	26708 (100)
2002-03	12616 (44.72)	3529 (12.51)	12064 (42.77)	28209 (100)
2003-04	13806 (41.17)	3605 (10.75)	16124 (48.08)	33535 (100)
2004-05	17311 (44.74)	4280 (11.06)	17098 (44.20)	38689 (100)

Source: Calculated based on data drawn from Andhra Pradesh Statistical Abstracts.

Note: Figures in brackets are per centage in total.

Table 2 presents information about Revenue Receipts and sources of revenue. The analysis indicates that state own taxes are important sources of revenue as the share of taxes is fairly between 45 to 50 per cent for 10 out 15 years considered. Only during 1995-97 the share is between 36 to 39 per cent. However the share of taxes in the total revenue is found to decline from

50 per cent to 45 per cent. The share of state own non–tax revenue is observed to decline from about 16 per cent to 11 per cent while that of transfers from center is found to increase from about 36 per cent to about 44 per cent. Thus transfers from center also observed to be important sources of state revenue. In order to examine the importance of various sources of revenue, multiple regression model is attempted by regressing Total Revenue (TR) on Sales Tax (ST), State Excise Duties (SED), Motor Vehicle Tax (MVT), Electricity Duty (ED), Land Revenue (LR), Stamps and Registration (SR), Tax Share Transfers from Center (TST) and Grants in–Aid (GA). Thus the estimated model is obtained as follows:

$$TR = \underset{(1.1439)}{217.61} + \underset{(3.3063)^{*}}{0.8488\,ST} + \underset{(3.7202)^{*}}{1.2080\,SED} + \underset{(1.3923)^{**}}{2.3477\,MVT} + \underset{(0.8159)}{1.3808\,ED}$$

$$+ \underset{(1.6354)^{**}}{5.7225\,LR} + \underset{(3.5523)^{*}}{3.549\,SR}$$

$$+ \underset{(7.037)^{*}}{0.9548\,TST} + \underset{(8.5975)^{*}}{1.0561\,GA} \quad R^2 = .99 \quad DW - \text{Statistic} = 1.9856 \quad F - \text{Value} = 7018.708$$

* - Coefficients are significant at 5%

** - Coefficients are significant at 20%

Thus from the estimated equation it is clear that the coefficients of all variables turns out to be positive which is desired on a priori knowledge. Further, as the value of adjusted R^2 found to be .99 it implies that the variables considered in the model account for 99 per cent of variation in Total Revenue receipts. Based on the estimated coefficients the important sources of revenue are Land Revenue, Stamps and Registration, Motor Vehicle Tax, State Excise Duties and Grants in – Aid, Tax Devolution and Sales Tax respectively. The analysis implies that one per cent change in LR will bring about 5.7 per cent in total revenue. However, the coefficient is statistically significant at 20 per cent. Similarly, one per cent change in SR, MVT, SED, GA, TST and ST will bring about 3.5, 2.3, 3.7, 1.1, 0.95 and 0.85 per cent change respectively in the total revenue. All these coefficients, except MVT are statistically significant at 5 per cent while MVT is statistically significant at 20 per cent. Howevei, the coefficient of ED is found to be statistically insignificant. Further, as the impact of tax share transfers from center is only to the extent of 0.95 on the total revenue, it implies that tax share as per the recommendations of the earlier commissions is not commensurate with the state revenue.

Table 3 presents revenue receipts and expenditure of AP as per centage of GSDP over the period and it is clear that revenue receipts fall short of revenue expenditure in all the cross section years. The reason is obliviously due to decline in the state own receipts as per centage of GSDP, besides decline in state own taxes and even steady decline in state own non-taxes. At the same grants and other transfers from center to the state are also observed to decline. Due to all these reasons the revenue deficit of the state is increased from 1980's onwards and particularly deteriorated from 1990's onwards and consequently the state has been in debt trap. Before analyzing the debt trap, let us examine the expenditure pattern of the Government relating to social sector overheads.

Table 3

Revenue Receipts and Expenditure as Per centage of GSDP

	1990-91	*1995-96*	*2000-01*	*2004-05*
State Own Taxes	7.94	5.16	7.53	8.70
State Own Non- Taxes	2.33	2.01	1.96	2.15
State Own Receipts	10.27	7.17	9.49	10.85
Transfers from Center	5.77	5.20	4.40	5.23
Total Revenue Receipts	16.04	12.37	13.9	16.07
Revenue Expenditure	16.51	13.29	16.46	16.81
Capital Expenditure	1.39	3.03	1.94	2.95
Total Expenditure	17.90	16.32	19.11	19.76

Source: Calculated based on data drawn from Andhra Pradesh Statistical Abstracts.

The expenditure policy of the state during 1960's and 1970's was such as to develop the infrastructure relating to irrigation, power, transport etc. and hence these sectors used to draw more than 60 per cent of plan expenditure. However, with the emergence of Telugu Desam party into power in 1983, there was a shift in the policy of Government expenditure and accordingly popular welfare schemes such as 'Two Rupees Kilo Rice' were promoted. Table 3 presents information about expenditure on social sector development. It is clear that over the period the allocations for social sector development declined and is not satisfactory as these overheads are important and reflects the quality of life. However, most of the government expenditure is incurring to meet the wages and salaries of employees and interest payments.

Table 4
Expenditure on Social Sector Overheads as Per centage of GSDP

	1990-91	*1995-96*	*2000-01*	*2004-05*
Education	3.05	2.16	2.69	2.77
Health and Family welfare	0.99	0.76	0.92	0.82
Water supply & sanitation	0.31	0.31	0.30	0.10

Source: Calculated based on data drawn from Andhra Pradesh Statistical Abstracts.

Table 4 presents information about debt–burden of the state. Public debt of the state Outstanding) since its formation in 1956 to 1991 was only Rs. 6815 crores, while it was increased to Rs. 66203 crores by 2004-05. Thus with in a period of 15 years the debt was increased by about 10 times. Further, it is clear that public debt increased at an average annual growth rate of 16.41 per cent during the period 1990-91 to 2004-05. Public debt as per centage of GSDP was below 20 up to 1996-97 but has reached a maximum of 33.26 by 2004-05 indicating the growing magnitude of debt burden. With the increase in public debt the debt servicing i.e., interest payments are increasing year after year and noticed to increase at an average annual growth rate of about 20 per cent during the period 1990-2005. Interest payments as per centage of revenue receipts, which was at 10.47 in 1990-91 steadily increased year after year and ultimately reached 26.66 per cent by 2002-03 and thus more than doubled during the period 1990-2005. It is generally argued that debt is an indicator of development and hence an attempt is made to

Table 4
Debt–Burden of Andhra Pradesh

(in Rs. Crores)

Year	*Public Debt Out Standing*	*Annual Debt*	*Annual Growth Rate*	*Debt as % GSDP*	*Interest Payments*	*Annual Growth Rate*	*IP as % RR*
1990-91	6815	1069	18.9		589	25.05	11.01
1991-92	7992	1177	10.1		695	17.99	11.02
1992-93	9286	1294	9.9	21.02	830	19.42	11.75
1993-94	11065	1779	37.5	19.12	1025	23.49	12.42
1994-95	13005	1940	9.1	18.87	1256	22.54	14.33
1995-96	15164	2159	11.3	18.99	1529	21.74	15.48
1996-97	17220	2056	-4.1	19.10	1839	20.27	16.43
1997-98	19971	2751	33.8	20.85	2153	17.07	15.56
1998-99	23904	3933	42.9	20.79	2644	22.81	18.54
1999-00	29114	5210	32.5	23.25	3101	17.28	18.45
2000-01	37025	7911	51.8	26.42	4354	40.41	22.36
2001-02	44784	7759	-1.9	29.58	5158	18.47	23.61
2002-03	53524	8740	12.6	32.98	6131	18.86	26.66
2003-04	58770	5246	-59.9	32.50	6856	11.83	25.52
2004-05	66203	7433	41.7	33.26	7228	5.43	22.59
		AAG	16.41		AAG	19.84	

Source: Calculated based on data drawn from Andhra Pradesh Statistical Abstracts.

examine the impact of debt on GSDP. The estimated regression equation is obtained as follows:

$$\text{GSDP} = \underset{(3.33)^*}{41630.31} + \underset{(6.6255)^*}{16.31}\ \text{Debt} \quad R^2 = 0.7674$$

Thus the equation implies that a one per cent change in Debt will bring about 16.31 per cent change in GSDP and thus it seems debt has a positive impact on economic development of the state. However, a major part of the budget is going in favour of salaries, interest payments and subsidies. In view of all these bottlenecks in fiscal sector, the AP government wants to tone up the fiscal discipline through implementing fiscal reforms and accordingly initiated certain measures. The measures that are initiated as part of reforms, during 1995-00 were listed in a white paper released by the Government in 2001.

1996-97

Prohibition was partially rolled back to mobilise more revenue.

Subsidy price on rice increased from Rs. 2 to Rs. 3.50.

Un economic state public sector unit namely Alwyn was privatised.

Ban on recruitment implemented and unnecessary expenditure curtailed.

1997-98

Decided to increase the irrigation rates by five times.

Committee appointed for restructuring of public enterprises.

Steps initiated to promote watershed management.

To promote the self–help groups through DWCRA schemes.

1998-99

People's participation extended to manage schools, hospitals and nutrition programmes.Indian Institute of Information Technology (IIIT), Indian School of Business (ISB), Hi-Tech etc., were taken up with investment from Indian and foreign business houses.

1999-2000

The concept of User charges was introduced in several departments including hospitals. APSRTC bus fare rates enhanced to cover hike in diesel price. Thus the state is progressing in the reform path and one has to wait for some time to assess the impact of such reforms. However, with the change in the Government in the state during 2004, the priorities are changed and some of the decisions may reverse and new decisions were taken. For instance, as an election promise, the new Government has taken the decision to implement free power to farmers and to households using only one bulb, which costs the state finances to a large extent. Similarly the Government also with drew the user charges from hospital (Government) users. However, the welcome feature is the present Government planning to take up irrigation projects ambitiously to the tune of more than Rs. 40000 crores. If irrigation projects were really completed at least to some extent if not fully, definitely it helps in promoting agriculture sector besides providing drinking water facility to some more people.

NOTES & REFERENCES

1. Economic Survey (2000-01), Government of Andhra Pradesh, Hyderabad.
2. Ibid., p. 3.
3. Vision 2020 Draft Document, Government of Andhra Pradesh, Hyderabad, p. 231.
4. Mahendra, Dev A. and Ravi C. (2003), "Macro Economic Scene: Performance and Policies", Economic and Political Weekly, Vol. 38, No. 12 & 13, March, pp. 1143-1157.

29

FISCAL RESPONSIBILITY AND BUDGET DISCIPLINE IN ANDHRA PRADESH –THE CHALLENGES AHEAD

B. Lilly Grace Eunice & P. Krishna Babu

The finances of the Central and State Governments have been out of balance for more than 20 years. Fiscal situation has run into rough weather due to rapid increase in revenue expenditure without corresponding increase in receipts, extraordinary rise in establishment costs, escalation of debt and its service costs, lower recovery efficiency and rise in non-plan expenditure. The serious deterioration of State finances led policy makers to plan and implement remedial measures.

In order to lay down fiscal management principles for the guidance of government the Central government has enacted a Fiscal Responsibility and Budget Management Act in 2003 (FRBM Act), which came into force on 26th August 2003, and rules there under were notified on 2nd July 2004. EFC suggested State governments to take immediate relief measures such as the debt swap scheme and the Fiscal Reform Facility. In this context many States have drawn up their Medium Term Reform Programmes with specific monitorable targets Andhra Pradesh being one among them to adopt this programme. It may be noticed that these changes are likely to contribute to more effective and transparent fiscal management.

Referring to the issue of budgetary imbalance, the Eleventh Finance Commission (EFC) had observed that revenue deficit have become 'malefic fixtures' in the Central and State budgets and that a restructuring of public finances was called for to steer up public finances away from the "Self – perpetuating spiral of debt and deficit". Therefore, under clause5 of the TOR, the Twelfth Finance Commission (TFC) has been asked to "review the state of finances of the Union and States and suggest a plan by which the Governments collectively and severally, may bring about a restructuring of the public finances restoring budgetary balance, achieving macroeconomic stability and debt reduction along with equitable growth"[1].

According to the Recommendations of the Twelfth Finance Commission, each State to enact a fiscal responsibility legislation providing for elimination of revenue deficit by 2008-09 and reducing fiscal deficit to 3 per cent of State Domestic Product. The benefit of debt consolidation is conditional on a state's enacting a fiscal responsibility law with some basic features. Few eminent writers criticized that the conditionalities prescribed for availing the benefit of write–off would spell the death of fiscal federalism in India by pointing out the bulk of the transfers proposed by the Finance Commissions are unconditional[2]. Accordingly the government of Andhra Pradesh enacted FRBM Act in June 2005 and thus made provisions for fiscal correction. While taking the appropriate measures for increasing revenue and/or for reducing the expenditure, care should be taken to enlist public support. Macro-management of the state's economy cannot succeed unless adequate fiscal correction takes place.

OBJECTIVE

The present paper made an attempt to examine the steps taken by the Government of Andhra Pradesh to ensure Budget discipline and fiscal reforms in accordance with the FRBM Act enacted by Government of India and examine its impact on the finances of the Government of Andhra Pradesh.

METHODOLOGY

The analysis is largely based on information and findings of the earlier studies on the subject relating to the State. The data are obtained from the Reserve Bank of India Bulletins, Budget Documents of Government of Andhra Pradesh and CMIE

Reports. Statistical tools such as ratios, percentages, graphs, etc. have been used. The study has been divided into two sections. Section – I deals with the Ordinance made by Government of Andhra Pradesh regarding the Fiscal Responsibility Act and Section –II deals with the Fiscal Performance of the State in recent past as per the provisions of the FRBM Act.

SECTION - I

Programme of Fiscal Restructuring in Andhra Pradesh

In the light of the Recommendations of the Twelfth Finance Commission, the Government of Andhra Pradesh has enacted a Fiscal Responsibility and Budget Management Act (FRBM Act), by the Governor on the 3rd June 2005, under Article 348 (3) of the Constitution of India and laid down its principles.

Responsibility in the management of public finances, including integrity in budget formulation, the State Government shall in each financial year lay before the House/Houses of the Legislature, the following statements of fiscal policy along with the budget, namely:

(a) The Macroeconomic Framework Statement;

(b) The Medium Term Fiscal policy Statement; and

(c) The Fiscal Policy Strategy Statement.

(a) The Macroeconomic Framework Statement, in such form as may be prescribed, shall contain an overview of the State economy, an analysis of growth and sectoral composition of GSDP, an assessment related to State Government finances and future prospects.

(b) The Medium Term Fiscal Policy Statement shall set forth in such form as may be prescribed the fiscal management objectives of the State Government and three year rolling targets for the prescribed fiscal indicators with clear enunciation of the underlying assumptions. The provisions contained in sub-section (1), the Medium Term Fiscal Policy Statement shall include the various assumptions behind the fiscal indicators and an assessment of sustainability relating to:

(i) The balance between revenue receipts and revenue expenditure;

(ii) The use of capital receipts including borrowings for generating productive assets;

(iii) The estimated yearly pension liabilities worked out on actuarial basis for the next ten years;

(c) The Fiscal Policy Strategy Statement shall be in such form as may be prescribed and shall contain.

The fiscal policies of the State Government for the ensuing year relating to taxation, expenditure, borrowings and other liabilities (including borrowings by Public Sector Undertakings and Special Purpose Vehicle and other equivalent instruments where liability for repayment is on the State Government), lending, investments, other contingent liabilities, user charges on public goods/utilities and description of other activities, such as guarantees and activities of Public Sector Undertakings which have potential budgetary implications;

1. The State Government may prescribe such targets as may be deemed necessary for giving effect to the fiscal management objectives.

   (a) Reduce revenue deficit by an amount equivalent to at least 0.30 percentage point of GSDP in each financial year, beginning from the 1st day of April 2005, so as to eliminate it by 31st March 2009 and generate revenue surplus thereafter;

   (b) Reduce fiscal deficit by an amount equivalent to at least 0.20 percentage point of GSDP in each financial year beginning from the 1st day of April 2005, so as to bring it down to not more than 3 per cent by the year ending March 2010.

   (c) Ensure within a period of five years, beginning from the initial financial year on the 1st day of April 2005, and ending on the 31st day of March 2010, that the outstanding total liabilities do not exceed 35 per cent of the estimated GSDP for the year;

(d) Limit the amount of annual incremental risk weighted guarantees to 90 per cent of the TRR in the year preceding the current year;

Provided that revenue deficit and fiscal deficit may exceed the limits specified under this section due to ground or grounds of unforeseen demands on the finances of the State Government arising out of internal disturbance or natural calamity or such other exceptional grounds as the State Government may specify.

Whenever there is either shortfall in revenue or excess of expenditure over the intra-year targets mentioned in the Fiscal Policy Strategy Statement or the rules made under this Ordinance, the State Government shall take appropriate measures for increasing revenue and/or for reducing the expenditure, including curtailment of the sums authorized to be paid and applied from out of the Consolidated Fund of the State:

Provided that nothing in this sub-section shall apply to the expenditure charged on the Consolidated Fund of the State under clause (3) of Article 202 of the Constitution or any other expenditure, which is required to be incurred under any agreement or contract, which cannot be postponed or curtailed[3].

SECTION - II

This Section deals with the fiscal performance of the State of Andhra Pradesh in accordance with the fiscal reforms envisaged in the FRBM Act.

The most important aim is restructuring of public expenditure in such a way to increase the developmental impact of expenditure and simultaneously reducing the unproductive revenue expenditure through a policy of reprioritisation of the expenditure items. In other words, by reducing the establishment costs, rationalization of subsidies, revamping the welfare schemes, reforming the State Level Public Enterprises (SLPEs) and simultaneously increasing expenditure on infrastructure, both physical and social, as well as expenditure on operation and maintenance of public assets.

The proportion of revenue expenditure in GSDP during 1980-81 to 2003-04 is presented in Chart 1. It may be seen from the chart that the revenue expenditure, which was 16.51 per cent of GSDP in 1990-91, shows a declining trend since 1995-96 onwards indicating a level of compression of public expenditure due to the fiscal reforms but again shows an increasing trend from 2000-01 onwards. In comparison with the ratios revenue expenditure shows much increase than the capital expenditure.

Chart 1
Public Expenditure of Andhra Pradesh

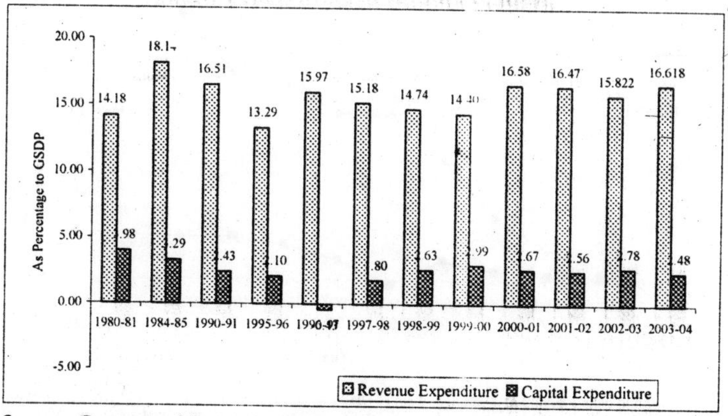

Source: Computed from the Reserve Bank of India Bulletins and Annual Fiscal framework, GOAP, 2003-04.

The revenue expenditure as a proportion of total expenditure has increased from 78 per cent in 1980-81 to 83 per cent in 1999-2000 and further to 87 per cent in 2003-04. This reveals the undue growth of revenue expenditure relegating the growth of capital expenditure in the State. Chart 2 shows the growth of public expenditure in Andhra Pradesh.

Medium Term Fiscal Framework

The government of Andhra Pradesh launched a Medium Term Fiscal Framework (MTFF) through its Strategy Paper on Fiscal Reforms published in February 2001 to plan fiscal policies. The main objectives of MTFF are 1) to enforce that public expenditures are stable and sustainable and not prone to fiscal crisis, 2) to improve the efficiency of allocation decisions and also to protect high priority public expenditures such as social

Chart 2
Growth of Public Expenditure in Andhra Pradesh

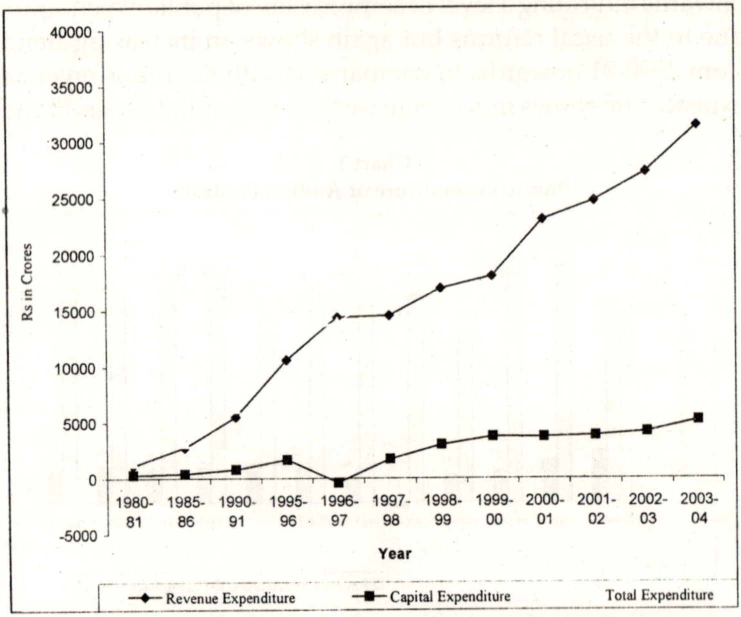

Source: Computed from the Reserve Bank of India Bulletins and Annual Fiscal framework, GOAP, 2003-04.

expenditure, expenditure on operation and maintenance and infrastructure investments. The MTFF aims for establishing overall affordability of government expenditure within reasonable revenue forecasts simultaneously envisaging a broad path for protecting the priority expenditures. It also proposes to identify important fiscal policies necessary to reverse the growing debt problem. The important features of MTFF are (i) Resource mobilization (ii) Expenditure compression and (iii) Fiscal sustainability.

With the proposed resource mobilization efforts along with the restructuring and reprioritisation of expenditure in addition, the State is also covered by the Fiscal Reforms facility of the Government of India as recommended by the Eleventh Finance Commission. The government has undertaken the Medium Term Fiscal Reform Program (MTFRP). The MTFRP envisages a fiscal correction programme more explicitly covering tax reforms, reforms in user charges, expenditure compression, power sector reforms, public sector restructuring and budgetary reforms. Under the MTFRP States, which implement monitorible fiscal reforms, are entitled for funds from the Incentive Fund of Rs. 10607 crores during the period 2000-05.

Formulated under a fiscal restructuring plan, the debt-GDP ratio which stood then at 81 per cent will come down to 75 per cent (eventually to 56 per cent) and the ratio of interest payment to revenue receipts will also go down to such a level that would make financing the government viable. With the assumed revenue growth, centre's interest payment to revenue receipts will come down to 28 per cent from 45 per cent at present and of the states to 15 per cent from the present 25 per cent. All this will require some modest effort in the raising of revenues and current expenditure compression, making room for larger capital spending[4].

Andhra Pradesh is one of the twenty-two States until 30th September 2003 to adopt this programme. The release of funds from the Incentive Fund is based on a single monitorible fiscal objective. According to MTFRP each State is expected to reduce a minimum of 5 percentage points in the revenue deficit as a proportion of their total revenue receipts each year till 2004-05 over the base year (1999-2000). States having revenue surpluses can show an annual improvement of 3 percentage points in the Balance from Current Revenue (BCR) as a percentage of their non-plan revenue receipts to be eligible for funds from the Incentive Fund. The Government of Andhra Pradesh has been implementing most of the reforms under the MTFRP. An attempt is made to make a comparison of important fiscal indicators of State finances between the base year 1999-2000 and the subsequent years of 2000-04. It may be observed from the Table-1 that the State own Revenues and own tax Revenues as a proportion of Total Revenue Receipts show slight increase in 2000-01 over the base year but declined in the following year. However, it shows considerable increase in the year 2002-03. The revised estimates of 2003-04 and the average 2000 to 2004 also show a decline in the percentage of ratios compared to the base year 1999-2000. The Non-Plan Revenue Expenditure as a ratio of Total Revenue Receipts shows a decline in almost all the years over the base year except in 2000-01 implying the positive impact of the reforms in compressing this kind of expenditure. A steady increase may be noticed in the Interest Payments and Public Debt as a percentage of Total Revenue Receipts in all the years as well as the average over and above the base year percentage explaining the growing burden of debt and debt servicing[5].

The Revenue Deficit as percentage of Total Revenue Receipts as a single monitorable indicator as suggested by the Eleventh Finance Commission may be seen in Table 1. It is evident from the Table that instead of a decline in the percentage, the percentage increased by 11.12 in 2000-01 over the base year indicating further deterioration in the fiscal management. However, the percentage shows a decline by 5.28 percentage points in 2001-02 indicating an improvement over the year 2000-01 which continued more or less the same in 2002-03 also. The improvement in the reduction of percentage may be observed in 2003-04 (revenue estimates) over 2000-01 situation, but deterioration in the fiscal indicator is discernible as the percentage in almost all the years and the four-year average are much more than the base year percentage suggesting the need for severe reform initiatives.

Table 1
Some Fiscal Indicators Including Single Monitorable Indicator of Andhra Pradesh

Year	*1999-00*	*2000-01*	*2001-02*	*2002-03*	*2003-04 r.e.*	*Average 2000-04*
SOR/TRR	68.14	68.27	66.36	70.20	66.57	67.85
OTR/TRR	53.61	54.18	53.00	54.85	51.58	53.40
RD/TRR	-7.34	-18.46	-13.18	-13.28	-10.60	-13.88
IP/TRR	18.45	19.48	20.98	26.65	25.24	23.09
NPRE/TRR	91.78	96.70	90.89	90.29	84.49	90.59
Debt/TRR	173.25	183.06	194.52	207.09	195.08	201.35

Source: Budget Documents, GOAP, Hyderabad.

Note: SOR = State Revenue, OTR = Own Tax Revenue, RD = Revenue Deficit, IP = Interest Payments, NPRE = Non-Plan Revenue Expenditure, TRR = Total Revenue Receipts.

The single monitorible indicator, revenue deficit/Revenue receipts, may be simple to apply but may not provide for an objective assessment of fiscal consolidation. This is mainly because of the size of the indicator in the base year. To elaborate, a State with a large percentage of deficit in the base year finds it easy to comply with this measure. For a State with smaller size percentage may feel it difficult to reduce the percentage by 5 points every year. However, this measure helps in explaining broadly the fiscal improvement or deterioration in the State compared to the base year. Not withstanding the limitations of this measure what is evident from the analysis of the fiscal indicators is that the deficits, debt and debt servicing has been on the increase during the period following the base year.

Archana Dholakia argues that the Fiscal Self Reliance and Improvement Index adopted by the TFC and also EFC does not provide an adequate measure of the relative efficiency of the states in the matter of fiscal management. The reason behind this is that they constructed Fiscal Self Reliance and Improvement Index (FSRII) to judge the relative fiscal efficiency of the States is based on only one indicator, viz, the ratio of revenue deficit to revenue receipts of the state. As a result, the measure is narrowly based, unstable and biased against the better fiscal performers.

Fiscal Policy Strategy Statement

As per the rules laid down in the FRBM Act with regard to the fiscal policy Strategy Statement the Government of Andhra Pradesh have adopted certain measures in order to maintain fiscal balance or deficits on its budgets.

The fiscal health of a government is revealed by the fiscal balance or deficits on its budgets. The twin deficits–Gross Deficit (GFD) and Revenue Deficit (RD)–are very important in view of their effects on the economy. While there exists difference of opinion regarding the right size of fiscal deficit among economists, there is unanimity with regard to its adverse impact. It is opined that the adverse impact of large fiscal deficit includes increasing interest payments, fall in the growth rate of developmental expenditure and the consequent impact on the growth rate[6]. Similarly revenue deficits have again two types of economic implications. Firstly, a revenue balance is considered as a non-debt source of finance of capital assets and instead the revenue deficits become a source of indebtedness. Secondly, revenue deficits lead to vicious circle as the borrowing made to bridge the deficit entails an interest cost in the future necessity further borrowing leading irretrievably into a debt trap[7].

In Andhra Pradesh also the twin deficits have been increasing. The gross fiscal deficit and revenue deficit as a proportion in GSDP covering the period 1980-81 to 2003-04 are presented in Chart 3. The gross fiscal deficit, which was only 2.72 per cent in 1980-81 increased to 4.54 per cent and 4.90 per cent in 1984-85 and 1986-87 respectively, declined in the subsequent years. But it is pertinent to note that the fiscal deficit has been more than 3 per cent since 1995-96. In fact it was as high as 4.96 per cent in 1998-99. This may be due to the increased allocations on social and community services, pay revision of government staff without commensurate reduction in the non-development expenditure in the post-reform period, given the level of revenue receipts. The gross fiscal deficit was as high as 4.63 per cent in 2002-03.

With regard to revenue deficits, the State used to maintain revenue surpluses in 1980-81, 1981-82 and 1982-83 and since then it has been reeling under revenue deficits throughout the period, except a year or two. In fact the revenue deficit was as

Chart 3
Deficits as Percentage to GSDP

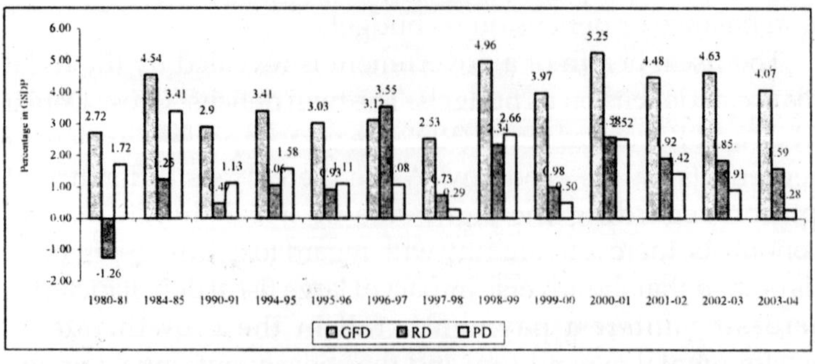

high as 3.55 per cent in 1996-97 mainly because of a sharp decline in the current revenues with increased expenditure commitments. Even after the reforms, still the fiscal and revenue deficits are as high as 4.07 per cent and 1.59 per cent in 2003-04 (Revenue Estimates) respectively. However, substantial reduction is discernible in the primary deficit, which stands testimony of the governments efforts in reducing non-interest expenditure during the reform period. The primary deficit, which was as much as 2.7 per cent in 1998-99, has come down to 0.9 per cent in 2002-03. While the projected target of the primary deficit for the year is 0.5 per cent, the revised estimate is only 0.3 per cent in 2003-04.

CONCLUSION

The serious deterioration of the state finances at the Central level led the policy makers to plan and implement remedial measures. With reference to the TOR (5) the TFC has been asked to "review the State of finances of the Union and States and suggest a plan by which the Governments collectively and severally, may bring about a restructuring of the public finances restoring budgetary balance, achieving macroeconomic stability and debt reduction along with equitable growth". Therefore, Government of India enacted Fiscal Responsibility and Budget Management Act (FRBM Act) in 2003.

Finances of the Government of Andhra Pradesh, since 1995-96 onwards, indicating a level of compression of public expenditure due to the fiscal reforms but again it shows an increasing trend from 2000-01 onwards. In comparison with the ratios of total expenditure revenue expenditure shows much increase than the capital expenditure. After launching the FRBM Programme in 2001 it is striving for the restructuring of public finances and could reduce the revenue expenditure as per cent of GSDP from 16.58 in 2000-01 to 15.82 per cent in 2002-03.

Twelfth Finance Commission conditions the benefit of debt consolidation, on a States' enacting a fiscal responsibility Law with some basic features. Hence the government of Andhra Pradesh enacted FRBM Act in June 2005 and thus made provisions for fiscal correction.

Although the Eleventh and Twelfth Finance Commissions fully recognized the importance of different fiscal parameters, like the composition of government expenditure, sources and pattern of government finances, the magnitude of debt, subsidies and interest burden, they have suggested revenue deficit/total revenue receipts as the only measure of fiscal discipline. While constructing the Fiscal Self Reliance and Improvement Index the TFC has taken into consideration RD/TRR as a measure, which is narrowly based, unstable and biased against the better fiscal performers. So it is suggested to measure the fiscal performance by considering the Composite Index of fiscal performance is much stable and just towards better performers and also useful for state level policy making[8].

NOTES

1. Government of India (2004), *Report of the Twelfth Finance Commission (2005-10)*, New Delhi.
2. Amaresh Bagchi (2005), "Symposium on Report of Twelfth Finance Commission Introduction and Overview", *Economic and Political Weekly*, July 30th, p. 3389.
3. Government of Andhra Pradesh (2005): *The Andhra Pradesh Gazette, Part IV–B*, Hyderabad, June 4th.
4. Amaresh Bagchi (2005): *Op.Cit.*, p. 3390.
5. Sudarsana Rao R. (2005), "Fiscal Reforms and Finances of Andhra Pradesh", *NIPFP Working Paper, No. 33*, June 2005.
6. Rangarajan C. (2004), "Issues Before Twelfth Finance Commission", *Economic and Political Weekly*, June 26th.
7. Government of Andhra Pradesh (1996), *"State Finances, The Factual Position"*, June 1996.
8. Archana Dholakia (2005), "Measuring Fiscal Performance of States an Alternative Approach" *Economic and Political Weekly*, July 30th, p. 3421.

INDEX

A

B

C

D

E

F

H

I

N

O

P

R

S

U

W

Z